OUT OF THE
CORNER

OUT OF THE CORNER

A Memoir

JENNIFER GREY

BALLANTINE BOOKS
NEW YORK

Published in the United States by Ballantine Books,
an imprint of Random House, a division of
Penguin Random House LLC, New York.

BALLANTINE and the HOUSE colophon are registered
trademarks of Penguin Random House LLC.

Photograph credits appear on page 337.

Library of Congress Cataloging-in-Publication Data
Names: Grey, Jennifer, 1960- author.
Title: Out of the corner: a memoir / Jennifer Grey.
Description: First edition. | New York: Ballantine Books,
[2022] | Identifiers: LCCN 2021054442 (print) | LCCN
2021054443 (ebook) | ISBN 9780593356708 (hardcover) |
ISBN 9780593356715 (ebook)
Subjects: LCSH: Grey, Jennifer, 1960- | Motion picture actors
and actresses—United States—Biography. | Surgery, Plastic—
Patients—United States—Biography.
Classification: LCC PN2287.G68727 A3 2022 (print) |
LCC PN2287.G68727 (ebook) | DDC 791.4302/8092 [B]—
dc23/eng/20220127
LC record available at https://lccn.loc.gov/2021054442
LC ebook record available at https://lccn.loc.gov/2021054443

Printed in the United States of America on acid-free paper

randomhousebooks.com

9 8 7 6 5 4 3 2 1

First Edition

Book design by Susan Turner

For Stella, may you have an enduring understanding that your story is more up to you than you realize and is always evolving. And in moments of darkness, be still, breathe, be gentle with your tender heart. Look for breadcrumbs; you will always be led out of the woods.

CONTENTS

OUT OF THE
CORNER

PROLOGUE

Whenever I found myself stuck in one of life's big dips, I could count on my ever-loving mother's familiar refrain, "In case of emergency, break nose." And while she didn't exactly say those words, the message was implied. So when I was still waitressing at twenty-five, unable to land the kind of parts I was auditioning for, she suggested, and not for the first time, that perhaps I should ask our family's longtime dermatologist, Arnie Klein, for the names of the top nose-job docs in Hollywood. Arnie was *the man,* the crypt keeper of every star's secret. I left his office with the numbers of three doctors handwritten on the back of his business card.

I went to the first consultation with my mother, always eager to offer her support. I had those butterflies from the promise of a silver bullet, the possibility that I could somehow look like a better version of myself, the version I saw in my head. But along with that nervous excitement was a soul-sickening dread.

We were ushered into the doctor's lair by a waxen-faced, eerily pretty woman who spoke to me in the kind of hushed tones usually reserved for requesting sexual favors. The consultation would take place in what looked like a sumptuously designed living room, or a private bungalow in the Beverly Hills Hotel. Everything about the plush experience was curated to make you feel like the luckiest person in the world.

The surgeon, his starched white doctor's coat buttoned up to his Hermès tie, made an entrance and wasted no time zeroing in on his plan of action. It would be "necessary" to "break the nose, reset it, shave down the bump, then define and minimize the nostrils."

"What's wrong with my nostrils?"

"People can see right into your nose." He drove home his point with the corroborating evidence of his trusty vanity-sized three-sided mirror.

I guess I could see what he meant.

"But I kinda like my bump, ya know?" I looked to him to agree with me. How could he not? If someone *likes* something about themself, isn't it somehow unethical for a plastic surgeon to disagree? "So, I was wondering . . . is there any way you could just 'fine-tune' it so I could be a little easier to cast, maybe a bit more photogenic? But you know, still look like me?"

He smiled ever so slightly. "Trust me. You won't like the bump when it's in a different context."

I didn't know what he meant by "a different context," but I guessed he meant my bump wouldn't work in the new landscape he was envisioning for my face. I felt myself fighting back tears. He stood up, a busy man on a tight schedule. "Well, that's what I would do. I think you'd be very happy." My two-hundred-dollar consultation was over.

The second doctor was more of the same.

Both times, I left shaken, and completely dismissed the way of the knife as preposterous and unsavory. While it was seemingly very effective for some people, it was *not* going to be my way. I tucked that business card into a small pocket in the back of my Filofax for the next few years.

———

I had always felt my nose needed protection, like a kid sister who regularly got bullied on the schoolyard. I was my nose's keeper. It had survived my teens, when the other girls were modifying their profiles in time for their bat mitzvahs. I had been resolute, determined that it was my *job* to love myself as I was. By the time I was twenty-nine, I was a little long in the tooth to be still grappling with this inane issue. Plus, it was unfathomable, actually looking for trouble, to have a change of nose *after* becoming famous.

Oh, and, yeah, I had become really fucking famous.

After *Dirty Dancing,* I was America's sweetheart, which you would think would be the key to unlocking all my hopes and dreams. Well, that's what I had anticipated, too. But it didn't go down that way. For one thing, there didn't seem to be a surplus of parts for actresses who looked like me. My so-called "problem" wasn't really a problem for me, but since it seemed to be a problem for other people, and it didn't appear to be going away anytime soon, by default, it became my problem. It was as plain as the nose on my face.

So a few years after I'd met those first two doctors, I finally said uncle and did the thing I'd been resisting for a good part of my life. I went to see the third doctor. The granddaddy of nose jobs. He was a pioneer, seminal in his field, wrote the book on rhinoplasty. I mean, he literally *wrote* the definitive two-volume textbook, the bible used by every surgeon doing nose jobs. This guy was all nose all the time. Unlike other plastic surgeons, he didn't mess with boob jobs or face-lifts. He was known for reconstructive surgery, after people had been in disfiguring accidents or as a last resort after multiple failed nose jobs. He was not a demolition man but more of a builder, and based on that, I liked him already.

His office was noticeably lacking in decor. It wasn't jazzy, it was like a real medical doctor's office, more dentist than spa, a departure from those other plastic surgeons' offices in Beverly Hills. Everything about the place was no-frills. His office staff didn't look like call girls;

they looked like real nurses, and the good doctor looked like a nondescript father figure. I was unfamiliar with this kind of man. He had no personal style. His affect, very dry and supremely confident. He was a real *doctor* doctor. When I walked in the room, he didn't see an actress. All I was to him was a nose. A nose that demanded his attention.

Not a huge fan of having my nose stared at, but that's what these guys do. For these hammers, every nose is a nail. They watch it move. They want to see it in action. Then they get out their nasal speculum to check under the hood and examine your septum. Of course, mine was extremely deviated. So I had that going for me, a legitimizing medical condition.

Right out of the gate I wanted to be clear about what I had come for. I didn't want to waste anyone's time. "I actually really like how I look. I know I'm not the prettiest girl, but I'm pretty enough for my purposes, and what I would want *you* to do is just fine-tune my nose, not change it. Leave the bump. Leave my look intact but make it so that I can smile and not have my nose smush down flat.

"You see, Doctor," I went on, with a bit of a wink, "I was in a little movie called *Dirty Dancing*," because it seemed that he really didn't know who I was. It's not that I was expecting a parade or anything, but there was a distinct lack of energy compared to what I had become accustomed to, and only recently, mind you. This was my new reality. My fame still had the dealer plates.

"Oh yeah, I saw that movie," he said. "I remember thinking, 'I wonder why that girl didn't do her nose?'"

Oof! But overall, for me this surgeon's cluelessness was a good thing. It gave him gravitas. Doctors in Hollywood tend to fawn over famous people, which has always made me feel a tad squirrely. Like, you save lives for a living, have some self-respect.

"Well, trust me. I'm pretty well established as I look today."

But he really didn't seem to be hearing anything I was saying. He was transfixed by assessing the challenge ahead.

Once he'd basically gathered all the information he needed, he moved over to sit on the front edge of his desk. "Look at this." He leaned in toward me. "The problem here is, you have no tip at all." His blunt, very clean thumb pushed up against where the tip of my nose would have been, had I been born with one. "We would have to build you a tip, which would act as a tent pole to hold up the end of your nose. Also, your septum is so severely deviated I'm surprised you can breathe at all. We'll have to completely reconstruct the interior of your nose, but you'll be amazed, because right now you're only breathing at twenty percent capacity."

I felt dizzy as I tried to make sense of how I had gotten this far in life with no tip whatsoever, breathing through airways narrow as cocktail stirrers. I had no tip! Why had nobody else said that to me? That was the issue. Most people who have their noses done have a lot of material to work with, but I had a deficit. Most people are looking to minimize what they have; theirs are your garden-variety, business-as-usual nose jobs. But building *up* the nose? Sold! To the oxygen-deprived chick with no tip.

It was clear this was the next right indicated action. I said to the good doctor, "I actually have a very particular preference. I have a thing about tiny noses, a real, I'm sorry to say, disdain for nose jobs. The only reason I'm even in your office is because I need to broaden my range so I can get work. So that I can, hopefully, someday be cast as something . . . other than a Jew."

He stood and said, "Okay, so next time I see you, bring in photos of noses that you like."

Did I dare even dream that it might be possible to have a nose I could forget about? "So, is that something you think you can do?" I asked.

He looked at me like, "Obviously I can. I wrote the book. I could build you a tip with my eyes closed."

I knew I was an outlier, because there is an unspoken cultural agreement about what is considered beautiful, and a plastic surgeon is expected to facilitate this groupthink. With noses, like boobs, there is this very specific idea of what they are "supposed to" look like at their best. There's an agreed-upon symmetry. A formula, a balancing act of facial features, in which noses never steal the spotlight. Most people go to a plastic surgeon to reap the benefits of such an approach, and fulfilling that popular expectation is the plastic surgeon's bread and butter.

I could tell by the almost quizzical look on his face that I had made a rare request. I was asking him, imploring him, to color outside the lines, because I was almost thirty and had spent much of my adult life trying to love and accept myself as I was. And I was actually making strides. So going under the knife felt dangerously close to an admission of defeat. To capitulate after so many years of resolve felt like a loss of sorts, but I was willing to split the difference.

And he did it. He did exactly as I wished. He expertly sculpted a tip with repurposed bits and bobs of my septum. Ultimately, my nose was actually bigger, which was fine by me. I was beyond grateful.

This man changed my life. He answered my prayers. I loved him. (I've always had a soft spot for a savior. Selfishly, I find that unmitigated, unrelenting suffering is not my jam, and I love nothing more than for somebody else to swoop on in and solve my problems.) Oh, I had done *such* a good job finding a surgeon. I had done the impossible: I had gotten the job done with my integrity intact, and my soul seemingly unscathed. I hadn't cut off my nose to spite my face. It was like a magic trick, and no one was the wiser. I was so relieved. I couldn't believe I'd actually pulled it off. I had long been on a mission, which was now accomplished. I had been relentlessly specific, unflinching.

I don't think I was ever as scared as I was going in for that surgery, but my doctor so successfully made good on his promise in giving me exactly what I had asked for that my trust was complete. I had never trusted a doctor more. He was my hero. My nose still reigned supreme, taking up a bit more real estate than it had previously. If it erred on the side of bigger, it was better than the alternative.

———

After this brilliant surgeon had his way with my nose, I finally made real money for the very first time in my life. I started working non-stop, also for the first time in my life. It seemed that all I had ever been missing was the tip of my nose. Who knew?

I'd signed with Creative Artists Agency and immediately started booking TV movie gigs, and then I was cast as the female lead in *Wind,* a big-budget movie directed by Carroll Ballard, the visionary behind *The Black Stallion,* and produced by Francis Ford Coppola. It was like a dream. And if that wasn't enough, I was playing the first woman ever to sail in the America's Cup, something no woman had yet done in real life. I wore cable-knit sweaters; the wind whipped my sun-bleached curls. Let me just say, she was not Jewish. We shot on a giant racing sailboat—in Australia, Rhode Island, and Hawaii. After shooting for six months out at sea, naturally, I was tan. Very, very tan.

One day, John Toll, the brilliant cinematographer, came up to me and said, "So I've been meaning to ask you about something. I'm noticing, there is this little white—I don't know, it looks like a bump, on the end of your nose."

He stared at the tip of my nose, a little too close for comfort, and then moved in even closer, as if studying a rare butterfly he was trying to name. "What *is* that?" As soon as he said it, I knew what he was talking about. I'd been telling myself that it was probably nothing anyone but me would ever notice. There was this tiny corner of cartilage close to the surface protruding from the tip of my nose.

The doctor had informed me my nose would, "just look better and better as the swelling subsided, but it would take about a year to see the final result." As predicted, around the year anniversary of my new proboscis, this thing appeared. This minuscule irregularity, looking like a tiny bit of white knuckle making itself known, poking against and contrasting with my tanned skin.

I had this sinking feeling; a dread came over me. I thought I had closed the book on this chapter. Was it possible that it was not over?

At the end of six months, production on *Wind* went on hiatus. The filmmaker was going to edit the footage they had, then we would reconvene to shoot whatever additional scenes might be necessary.

I came back from location feeling great. I loved this job. I loved my new life. And I had made enough money to buy my first home. A charming Spanish 1920s bungalow in Benedict Canyon. I even had the money to buy myself a Mercedes. I was thirty.

I called my trusty doctor to report my concern over this new development. He sounded unfazed and reassured me, "Sure, that's no problem. Happens all the time. Just come on in and let me have a look."

I was so stoked. I couldn't wait to see his face when I told him about all the great stuff that had been happening over the past year, eager to share my success because I genuinely felt I couldn't have done it without him. I wanted to take a victory lap with him. We were a great team.

When I saw him, I made sure he knew how grateful I was. He had been a key player in changing the landscape of my life, altering my destiny. He took a beat to bask in my exuberant appreciation, and beamed while surveying the finished product, which had settled in, as promised.

He initially seemed pleased with his work, but it took him no time to home in on the real purpose for my visit.

"Oh yeah. This is nothing to worry about. As I told you, once the swelling goes down sometimes a little bit of the graft might need to be smoothed out. It's *very* small, but we can see it because your skin is particularly thin there. We just need to go in and shave down that little bit."

"What do you mean 'go in'?"

"Just a follow-up, to fine-tune the original."

I was trying to wrap my head around what "going in" might entail. He said, "The tip is really quite bulky."

"Oh no. No, no. I love it."

"I know, I know. You *like* a prominent nose. But your other features are so delicate. If I refined it a little, it would be more in balance with the rest of your face—"

I cut him off as quickly as I could without being rude. "Oh, I can't do that. I just did this big movie where I'm the female lead. I can't look any different."

"Fine. If that's what you want. But we do have to take care of *that*. You can't just leave it there."

"The movie is not actually finished. They still are going to be shooting some additional footage, not exactly sure when, but *soon*, and I can't show up even the tiniest bit swollen."

"Then let's get you in right away. I can do it for you outpatient at our surgery center in Beverly Hills."

This was a new wrinkle. I'd assumed this tiny bit of cartilage was something so minor he could take care of it in the office. Like a mole removal. "I thought you could just maybe—inject it or something?"

He could see my trepidation about going under the knife again, but tried to assuage my fears by explaining, "I have to put you under because I have to go *into* your nose. Schedule it with my nurse and we'll take care of it this week. I'm not going to charge you. Great to see you doing so well."

———

A day or two later, I went to the private surgery center on Brighton Way in Beverly Hills with my mother, ever my copilot in these matters. I was wheeled into the frosty, brightly lit OR in my adorable regulation hospital gown and little paper shower cap. Having survived and triumphed after betting the farm the year before, I couldn't have felt more at ease and trusting of this gifted doctor.

He came over to the gurney in his scrubs and greeted me warmly, like we were old pals, his hand on my shoulder. "Good morning, sunshine. How you doing? Are you ready?"

I looked into his kind, paternal eyes. "Absolutely. Feeling good. Just shivering because it's frrreezing in here!"

"Let's get her a nice warm blanket. So, what kind of music do you like?" He was looking down at me, unsubtly focused on one feature in particular.

"This is your house, Doc. Play whatever you like."

"Just to be sure, before we send you off to dreamland, you're happy with your nose, right? As it is?"

"Uh. Yeah. I told you. It's great. Couldn't be happier."

"Okay then. Well, you have a good sleep now."

The anesthesiologist started the drip, and I remember loving the feeling of "eight" in the countdown from ten. Wanting to languish in that cocoon forever, suspended in a blissful opiate high, like nothing bad could ever happen to me.

Coming to, post-op in the recovery room, I was lolling in the hazy twilight, that newly out-of-anesthesia yummy feeling where all is right with the world. The doctor came over to me. "It went very well." His confidence made me feel confident. I was so grateful that it was finally done. I would never have to think about my nose again.

"Just don't be alarmed when we take the bandages off. Initially, it might look a bit high because of how I taped it, but don't worry, it'll drop. I'll see you in a week."

I remember thinking, "He's so nice. I looove him. Wait! What's he talking about? What's 'high' and why is it 'dropping'? Aww, he's the best."

My mom had been in the waiting room, and when I was lucid enough, she and the nice nurse helped me put my clothes back on. I don't remember whether I walked out or was pushed in a wheelchair, but I distinctly remember there was this smoked-mirror paneling in the elevator. And I noticed, in the mottled unflattering light, some discoloration around the perimeter of my bandage. I said, "What's that? Oh my god, Mom. Look."

"Honey, relax. He was working in there; bleeding is completely normal. I had black eyes after my nose job. Everyone does."

"Well, I didn't last time."

A week later, my friend Pamela took me to my doctor's appointment to get my bandage removed. First, the cast comes off. There's this sensation of intense suction pulling on your nose, which might as well be attached to your brain, being brain adjacent. A nose in this state is the very definition of tender—the shock of the sudden exposure is like removing the protective shell off a turtle's back.

The next order of business is the internal unpacking of the nose. The dried blood has cemented a bounty of bandages to those delicate mucous membranes lining the narrow tunnels of your nose. In my memory, there were also these very thin straws placed up the center of the packing, so you could breathe, but just barely.

As the nurse is tugging at the stiffened gauze, it's like a clown car of bloody paper products. You can't believe how much they've shoved up there. How in the world did they get seven miles of mesh up my nose? She's like a magician pulling at the never-ending scarf, unearthing untold lengths. I couldn't decide if this sensation was one of the best or one of the worst feelings I'd ever experienced. But I had been here before, a year ago. I just never expected to be here again.

When the nurse had finished cleaning me up, she cheerfully handed me a mirror. "Looks great. The doctor will be with you shortly."

I almost didn't know what I was looking at. I couldn't make sense of what I was seeing. As my adrenaline was cresting, I was sliding down a slo-mo well of calm. I knew something bad had happened. I just didn't know what it was.

Pamela was there, sitting on the extra chair intended for the patient's plus-one, a few feet away. Was she seeing what I was seeing? What was it I was looking at? Something odd. Distorted. The way the nose was oriented on my face was all wrong. Twin unfamiliar holes staring back at me. Are those my nostrils? This nose looked truncated or dwarfed. Something about the proportion was off. The placement. I wasn't expecting this. I'd had invested so much in it not being what it was now. It was like I was on mushrooms, having a bad hallucinogenic trip.

In the distance I could faintly make out Pamela's sweet voice trying to reassure me. "It's okay. Your doctor will be here any minute. Just wait." She was trying to do what a good friend does, which was to stay calm.

The doctor came in. He couldn't have been more upbeat. Cheerfully soaping up his hands in the sink, happy to see me. Jolly. He sat down on the rolling stool and wheeled over until our knees were almost touching. His gaze trained on my nose, carefully checking out his work. So painful I couldn't help but wince with every touch.

I blurted out, "It looks really different. I don't get it."

"Well, I told you it's going to drop. You're still really swollen. It's only been a week."

"But wait, I don't get it. What happened? Why do I look so . . . different?"

He coolly studied my face, puzzling it out. "You know. You really *do*. I don't think I've ever seen such a dramatic change in anyone before."

This isn't happening. I can only hope to God this is just me freaking the fuck out, being exceedingly neurotic, panicking, overreacting. Maybe it *is* just that swollen and will go back to the way it was before.

"It looks good. It really fits your face," he said, admiring the anatomy of my nose from every angle. He asked the nurse to hand him a roll of Scotch tape and he proceeded to demonstrate my home-work assignment. He wanted me to place a piece of tape across the end of my nose from cheek to cheek. This primitive technique was supposed to "train" the tip to drop and encourage a sexy little indenta-tion just north of the graft. The doctor told me to tape my nose like this every night, "or just whenever you think of it when you're home alone. You'll see. It's very, very swollen still. Just give it a couple of weeks."

This dream was getting exponentially weirder. And knowing me, I was probably crying, or trying very hard not to, because it really hurt my nose to cry.

A few weeks later, I was invited to attend an event at the Director's Guild honoring the director and actress Lee Grant. As I walked the gauntlet of paparazzi, for the first time since *Dirty Dancing* opened, the photographers looked right through me, their cameras hanging slack down by their sides, their necks craning to grab a shot of the next star coming in. I walked the endless length of the red carpet, all the way into the theater, without anyone so much as looking at me.

Once I'd settled into my seat, I spotted Michael Douglas in the row in front of me, so I leaned forward over his shoulder to say hello. I'd recently bonded with him on a ten-hour plane ride home from London, where we'd sat side by side talking, our faces so close we could feel each other's breath.

"Hey, Michael."

He turned around to see who was cooing in his ear and stared back at me blankly.

"It's Jennifer. Jennifer Grey?"

In the days and weeks that followed, I'd walk into Kings Road Cafe on Beverly Boulevard, a place I'd been going to for years, and the waiters looked at me like a stranger. I would see the same panicky look on the faces of old friends, even an old boyfriend or two, family friends, everyone. The look that says, "Who the fuck are you, and why are you talking to me like you know me?" I felt like Emily in the third act of *Our Town*, or George Bailey in *It's a Wonderful Life*.

The first time I saw my father after this latest development, I went to his rental house in West Hollywood for dinner. He hadn't seen me because he'd been out of town, but I'd been talking to him on the phone about how freaked out I was. I was looking forward to him reassuring me that it wasn't so bad. What I really was hoping to hear, of course, was that I looked beautiful. As I walked in the door, I tried to read his face, but it gave nothing away. He volunteered nothing about my appearance. After ten minutes of predinner small talk, I finally got up the nerve to ask him point blank, "So, what do you think?" He said, "I think it would probably be best if you just didn't go out in public for a while."

In the world's eyes, I was no longer me. I had unwittingly joined the Witness Protection Program. And if that wasn't bad enough, soon I would be due up at Francis Ford Coppola's Napa Valley estate to shoot additional scenes for *Wind*.

Pacing the length of my beautiful green kitchen in Benedict Canyon, I made the dreaded call to my director, Carroll Ballard, to warn him of the recent development. "Listen, we got a problem. I had a minor procedure that has had some unexpected complications, and it might be fine by the time I get there. I just wanted you to know what's up. I cannot tell you how sorry I am. I'm super freaked out but I'm hoping it's all gonna be fine."

I arrived in Napa a few weeks later, wearing a "funny nose and glasses" to greet everyone. After the big reveal, I said, "I know. This is weird, right? I don't know how this happened. I really don't. But I am so unbelievably sorry. Just tell me what I can do. How can I fix this?"

They ended up having to shoot me through mirrors, from a distance, scrambling to make it work. But it didn't work. When the movie came out, in the press, Carroll Ballard declared my botched nose job the reason for the movie's commercial and critical failure.

I knew how much shit people were talking behind my back, about how I represented everything silly and vain and tragic in show business. I felt so much shame about finding myself in this surreal position. People just assumed I never liked how I looked, or that my "dysmorphia" was in full bloom, or that I had become addicted to the knife. To the outside world, this imagined compulsion to eradicate my defining facial feature became a cautionary tale, a punch line.

It seemed that I had committed an unforgivable crime: willfully stripping away the only thing that made me special.

For years after my nose's surgical "fine-tuning," I will remain in this purgatory, unrecognized and unseen. I no longer look like myself. I am unable to get work. Strangers come up to me in grocery stores and conspiratorially whisper in my ear, "I still think you look pretty. I know everyone else doesn't, but I don't know what they're talking about." Holding a stalk of celery or a carton of milk, I look back into their eyes, unsure how to respond. "I mean, of course I liked you better back then," they add. "But you still look nice."

I am as I was at the beginning, not a whole person but a nose. There is no rest of me worth knowing. Overnight, I lose my identity and my career. Eventually, this will be one of the single best things that ever happens to me. But I don't know that yet. I found myself at the entrance of the cave I most feared to enter.

"Oh, Jennifer Grey, like the actress," says the woman checking me in at the airline counter one afternoon.

"Well, actually it *is* me," I tell her with a small smile.

"No, it's not," she says, like I'm trying to get away with something.

"Well, actually, it is me," I tell her.

"No, it's not," she says.

"Yes, it is. That's me," I lob back. "See my driver's license?"

She studies my ID, puts it down, and glares accusingly at me over the counter. "I've seen *Dirty Dancing* a dozen times," she says. Her words cut like a knife. "I know Jennifer Grey. And you are not her."

PART ONE

1

Life Is a Cabaret

When you're born into a family you really have nothing to com-
pare it to. There is no opinion, no preference, no judgment,
no awareness of anything even existing outside of your reality. There
is just the instantaneous and immutable devotion to these beings,
your source for everything you need to survive, and an acute myopia rendering whatever is beyond this complete triangle, if indeed there exists anything at all, blurry and moot. Which is fine

because, if you're lucky, everything you need is right here. And it was for me.

I made an early entrance, a month before I was due, while my dad, the actor Joel Grey, was out of town, doing his nightclub act in the Catskills. My mother's water broke while she was at a party in West Hollywood, and two of her actor pals drove her downtown to Cedars of Lebanon Hospital, where I was delivered via an emergency C-section.

When the doctor called my dad to tell him of my surprise arrival, it was six in the morning on the East Coast. The operator said, "I've got a person-to-person call for Mr. Joel Grey from Dr. Maury Lazarus," and my dad, who picked up the phone in his sleep, promptly hung up. The doctor called back and yelled over the operator, "Tell him his daughter is born so he better accept the call!"

My dad had been acting professionally since he was a little kid, but in his late twenties, around the time I was a year old, he was hitting his stride, and his career was cookin'. He landed his first Broadway show, replacing the lead in the Neil Simon comedy *Come Blow Your Horn*. It was Simon's first play, and a huge hit. So our family picked up and moved from the modest cottage in the Hollywood Hills where they'd set up house, to two floors of a brownstone on East 30th Street in New York City.

My mom, Jo Wilder, was a performer, too. Every baby's their mother's biggest fan, and I was no different, but my mom actually looked like a movie star. Visual timelines of my parents' careers lined the walls of wherever we were living. Framed, black-and-white production stills of my mom as Peter Pan, with a pixie cut, flying in midair in green tights. As Gypsy Rose Lee in *Gypsy*, a femme fatale mid-striptease, her spaghetti straps suggestively hanging off her bare shoulders. As Polly Peachum, donning a man's bowler in *Threepenny Opera*. With her cropped bangs, heavy brows, and winged eyeliner, she looked more than a little like Audrey Hepburn. Everything about her in these photographs exuded theatricality, her mouth impossibly wide, in full song. She looked like she was born to be on the stage.

I loved it when my mom would sing me the lullaby "Little Lamb" from *Gypsy* and tell me about how the real-life lamb would sometimes pee while she held it in her lap on stage, and she'd have to pretend it hadn't. She sang around the house all the time.

She wasn't a kid when she had me. She was closer to thirty than twenty, and had been at it, knocking around the business for some time, ready for her ship to come in when she met my dad. He was very keen to get married and start their family right away. She didn't know what the hurry was, but got swept up in his vision for them.

My parents had lost a baby before me, and my mother had struggled to carry me to term. So when I was four and a half, my parents decided to adopt a baby boy. The three of us flew out to Los Angeles, and we left a few days later a family of four, bringing back with us to New York my newborn brother, James Rico. (Not the most Jewish of middle names, but my parents were fans of the painter Rico Lebrun.) Jimmy was one of those gorgeous babies right out of the gate. Blond, big blue eyes, white-white skin, and in addition to our genetic differences, my brother felt energetically almost like a different species from the three of us, but a breathtakingly beautiful one. He looked like an angel.

My parents referred to our gang as the four J's: Jo, Joel, Jenny, and Jimmy. Being a close family was of paramount importance to them. There was a lot of love there.

My dad and I were tight. When I was little, I would wear his old crew neck undershirts, worn so thin and ridiculously soft the cotton was almost diaphanous. I remember the perfect stack of his white tees, folded with origami-like precision in his antique armoire, weighted down by a heavy round bar of Roger & Gallet soap, wrapped in its signature crinkled silk paper and seal. Opening the cabinet door filled my nose with the most intoxicating combination of lemon, bergamot, rosemary, orange, neroli, rose, and carnation. I'd sleep in his T-shirts as nighties, comforted by that warm scent, probably the closest approximation to what happens when a baby smells her mother's breast milk. Does that sound weird? Well, so be it. I was never breastfed, but I felt utterly peaceful and held, enveloped in that sensorial refuge.

My dad was the one I woke up in the middle of the night when I was scared that I was about to be sick. He'd immediately get up and follow me silently into the bathroom to keep me company. He'd place the bath mat on the cold tile floor in front of the toilet for me to bravely kneel on as he lifted the seat. We'd sit in silence. He'd softly repeat, his eyes at half-mast, "You're gonna feel much better once you get this out." I hated that feeling so much, terrified of what was coming, my tiny body wracked with overpowering waves of spasms and retching. But with him at my side, his quiet presence, the cool washcloth he placed on my forehead or the nape of my neck, I could stay the course through this gastrointestinal storm. Afterward he'd have me splash my face with cool water, brush my teeth, and he'd tuck me back into bed.

I felt special, if not guilty, that I got what seemed to me the best of my dad. But within the family, my mother, brother, and I were a team, the spokes that sprung from the hub of the wheel that was my dad and his career. He was a rising star on Broadway, and when he was doing a show, we ate dinner at 5:30. Because theater folk are night owls, Jimmy and I were on our own on weekend mornings, expected to "quietly amuse ourselves," watching cartoons and helping ourselves to bowls of cereal, so our parents could sleep in until eleven.

For me, there was no place cooler on earth than hanging out backstage with my dad on Saturday matinees, following his every move as his diminutive shadow. Watching him apply his Kabuki-esque makeup for the role he originated as the Master of Ceremonies in the stage version of *Cabaret* filled me with this deep knowing of how lucky I was to be right where I was. The years 1966 to 1968— when I was six till I was eight—were my *Cabaret* years. My dad performed eight shows a week, and though he wasn't around most evenings, I was thrilled when I got him all to myself on a Saturday afternoon. I would sit quietly in his dressing room, fully cognizant of the special honor and privilege it was to bear witness to this sacred preshow ritual and transformation.

It felt like a delicious mix of fizzy and calm, but mostly of reverence. The makeup mirror was an altar, my dad's face, like the center of a sunflower, both making the art and being the art simultaneously. One step removed, I'd watch every brushstroke in rapt attention, gazing at my father's reflection from behind him, the image framed by the tiny globes of vanity mirror lights. I surveyed the scene like a detective, making mental notes of the accoutrements in evidence. The cough drops and good-luck totems, photos of my mother, brother, father, and me in Lucite DAX frames. Taped to the outer edges of the mirror were opening-night telegrams from friends, along with pencil and crayon stick-figure drawings my brother and I regularly made for him to wish him luck.

From inside his dressing room, I could feel the kinetic energy of the company percolating just outside his open door, the raucous laughing, singing, vocal warm-ups with booming scales echoing through the stairwell. Flirtatiousness was the native tongue of this sexy company, his spirited, fun-filled "work family" spontaneously popping their heads in, paying respect. My dad only momentarily averted his gaze from his painstaking task to proudly announce my presence through the mirrored reflection.

The only person other than me granted an all-access pass into my dad's sanctuary was his dresser. The relationship between actor and dresser is an intimate one. In addition to dressing the actor from head to toe like a small child, the dresser is responsible for maintaining, mending, and laundering the costumes, as well as coordinating post-show visitors. Their job is to facilitate and smooth over everything the artist shouldn't have to be bothered with, intuiting every mood and unspoken request, whether it be cheerleader or dead silence. The really good ones anticipate every need before the performer is even aware of it.

Quiet as an apparition, their complexion pale and waxy from lack of fresh air and sunlight, a dresser is like a ghost who has no needs other than to serve. A special breed, usually attired in all black to be invisible when moving in the shadows of backstage, they sport sensible shoes and an apron—the equivalent of a tool belt for costumes, stocked with solutions for any potential emergency: tape, tissues, safety pins, miniature flashlight for quick changes in the pitch dark. Dressers are Broadway's selfless, unsung heroes.

As far back as I can remember, my dad always had a personal dresser, more than happy to cater to his every wish, calibrating the timing of the kettle and requisite mug of tea and honey, setting out his costumes in pristine order, their assistance at the ready with calm assuredness. I recognized the value and importance of the role they played: the seemingly relaxed yet precise way they earned their keep, not unlike a fantasy wife, a good mother, or a great nanny.

In my dad's dressing room, everything on his makeup table had been preset, laid out on a white terry cloth towel with the precision of a surgeon's tray. I knew by heart the step-by-step application of the Master of Ceremonies' makeup: the fleshy pink pancake stick in "Juvenile Pink," first crudely drawn on like war paint, then smoothed until every pore was spackled over, in the unnatural hue of a Barbie doll. He glued on the double layer of cheap, false eyelashes, like the cartoonish lids of a marionette. (When he was first creating the look for the character, my mom had brought out her makeup kit from her summer stock days, and he'd found some of her old heavy strip lashes, thick with ancient mascara.) His index finger smeared his lids an unnatural blue, and on his cheeks, the exaggerated crimson rouge of an antique doll on acid. Next, he would sharpen, in two quick twists of wood shavings curled onto the towel, the darkest maroon lip pencil for outlining the razor-sharp points of heartless lips and click into place a fake gold cap on a tooth. Last, he slicked down his springy curls of brown hair, like mine, with gobs of translucent gel, Dippity-do, until his hair resembled the shiny patent leather of my dress-up shoes.

Every one of his features was reinvented from scratch. This self-drawn mask blotted out any trace of my dad as I knew him, but I found nothing about the Emcee's character menacing; it was just my dad's "work look." He was an artist, and this was his creation, his beautiful monster. I was endlessly fascinated by the ritual, his expertise, and supreme confidence. His systematic transformation into this nefarious character reminded me of the haunted faces in Egon Schiele's drawings that hung on our apartment walls.

This time together was beyond magical, especially because there was nothing I wanted more than to someday be a part of this creatively rich and stimulating world, a world so familiar to me I could practically taste it. The only one in my family invited into his inner sanctum, privy to such a delicate and personal process, I knew the drill, knew to be quiet, polite, to contain my excitement amid the mounting tension. The stage manager's voice would break in over the scratchy loudspeaker, announcing the countdown to show time: "Half hour. This is your half-hour call." Eventually progressing to "Five minutes. Ladies and gentlemen, this is your five-minute call."

My butterflies would suddenly take flight against my better judgment with this news. Of course, I knew I wasn't the one about to go on stage, but this reasoning was lost on my chemicals, unable to make the subtle distinction.

Until the stage manager called half hour, it had been just us, cozy and quiet in his familiar dressing room, and on a dime, the energy shifted into something else. It was kind of scary—or was it exciting? It felt somehow dangerous, but I couldn't put words to it. Was it the high stakes of live theater, where anything could happen or go wrong once he left the safe refuge of his private chamber? I would get this queasy feeling in the pit of my being every time my dad went on stage. There was this dread. I needed somehow to protect him, to keep him safe, less exposed to the elements out of his control and mine once he stepped onto the stage.

I would watch him go into a zone, an energy that felt bigger than I was able to comprehend or maybe even manage. The performance was the whole point. The why of everything else leading up to it. A shift into another dimension along with a deadly seriousness. Something I would eventually come to understand for myself, this hyper focus fueled by elements of adrenaline and risk. A high-wire act.

When it was "that time," I'd follow him out of the dressing room.

He'd take my hand and lead me through the theater's dark maze of hanging ropes and huge moving flats of painted scenery, mindful of every step I took, because, as he made sure to impress upon me, "the theater is a dangerous place."

The scantily clad Kit Kat Girls warmed up their powerful legs like giant nutcrackers, doing their grand battements in the bowels of the Broadhurst Theatre. These idols of mine, their powdery faces in dramatic showgirl makeup, smelling strongly of hairspray, pressing scratchy sequins and satin against me as they fawned over me, Joel's little girl, Jenny. Kissing and hugging me gingerly, careful not to smudge their freshly applied greasepaint.

The visceral pressure mounted as we drew closer to the entrance of the stage. I could hear and feel the thrum of the audience's rowdy anticipation, muffled by the heavy velvet curtain. It was a serious thing, this transition from skipping down the sidewalk with fun dad, to focused dad, gathering energy like a storm timing landfall.

On either side of the proscenium are the "wings," where the performers enter and exit the stage, just outside the audience's view. From that vantage point, I carefully peek out at the audience. Around me, the cast assembles, in increasingly tight quarters, for the opening number, smiling down at me, winking, revving their engines, the tension growing like an arrow pulled back, ready to let fly.

My destination, the place of honor, was this safe spot in the wings, planted in front of the stage manager, so close I could feel the vibration of his murmured lighting cues against my thin frame, my shoulder blades sensitive as antennae.

The overture began, the now iconic Kander and Ebb score, played by an orchestra so close the musicians in the pit would nod or wave hi to me. My stomach felt funny, turning over from the nearness to such strong energy.

I stood stock-still, watching the show from my perch, my eye trained on my dad's every move. When he'd have a costume change,

I'd scurry back with him to his dressing room, or behind the set for a lightning-fast quick-change, as he and his dresser had it timed down to the second, the Velcroed costume breaking away with a tug, like a magic act.

I had the closest proximity imaginable to these performances—dark, playful, curious, and electrifying. For me, it was a peak experience every time. Thrilled to be so near the real action as well as sharing this special thing with my dad.

I had my favorite musical numbers. I loved the one where my dad waltzed with an oversized lady gorilla in a tutu, declaring his abiding love for her, in spite of how society scorned them. And the kick-line number, where the Kit Kat Girls, including my dear old dad in full drag, performed an unwholesome version of the Rockettes. They all wore matching gold lamé headbands adorned with bejeweled black velvet cats' faces, their whiskers a spray of stiff fishing line. In spangly leotards, they high-kicked in their black-seamed stockings and garter belts in perfect unison, my dad kicking his heels equally high. Passing for one of the girls in his fetching auburn wig, undetected by the audience until he suddenly bellowed in his most macho guttural German, "*SECHS! SIEBEN! ACHT!*" And whipped off his wig, exposing a shock of underarm hair. I never tired of being in on the prank, watching with utter glee as my dad pulled off his brilliant charade, tricking everyone with his perfect facsimile of a sexy showgirl.

My earliest ideas about feminine beauty, power, and sexuality were inextricably linked to *Cabaret*, whether on Broadway, or later, in the Fosse film. The Kit Kat Girls, with their tarty, brazen sauciness, hypnotizing the audience and me with their grinding hips. Spreading their limber, gartered thighs open at impossibly wide angles like a funhouse doorway, luring us into their delicious den of naughty. My dad's character's lascivious energy was normalized for me, enjoyed purely as entertainment.

After the curtain call, the company—sweaty and triumphant as if the war was over and they had miraculously survived—filed back to their dressing rooms. Once in front of his makeup mirror, his dresser got him out of his costume and my dad peeled off his undershirt, now stuck to his skin, soaked with sweat. I'd turn away or he'd step into his tiny bathroom to change out of his dance belt. Once he was in his jeans, usually still half-zipped with his belt unbuckled, he'd sit at his makeup table and smear his painted face with fingerfuls of thick, white Albolene cream out of a giant jar, liberally massaging it all over his face and neck. At the ready, his dresser would hand him a steamy hot towel to remove the now-charcoal-colored muck, and seconds later my dad's face reemerged on the other side of the washcloth, so thoroughly refreshed and pink, so clean. He was back. Handsome, cool, and so much fun. He was nothing like other people's boring dads.

We'd leave the theater, bidding our goodbyes to the burly union guy in charge of who goes in and out of the stage door, with a feeling of renewed vigor. A crowd of clamoring, eager, shining faces waited for the cast members to emerge from the stage door to autograph their outstretched programs. I glued myself to my dad as he signed and signed and signed. Then he took my hand, and we made a break for it. I don't know who was prouder to be with who as we braved the daylight we had almost missed entirely and made our way, me skip-ping to keep up, down the familiar gritty street lined with the giant blown-up production photos from all the other shows.

I felt safe and happy as we either went home for an early dinner with Mom and Jimmy, or out to one of the Broadway restaurants like Frankie & Johnnie's or Joe Allen's, where all the show folk congre-gated, where my dad knew everyone, everyone knew him, where there was always a good table and a warm welcome waiting. He was beloved and he loved us.

It doesn't get much better than that, or at least it didn't for me.

I have heartachingly happy and mouthwatering memories of my mom and dad's late-night snack ritual, too. My mom would be in one of her simple yet elegant long cotton Dior nightgowns and white bal-let slippers with an open robe that fluttered behind her as she walked down the hall.

My dad would come home from the theater, the back of his hair a little greasy from the Albolene. He'd be tired yet wired—as it's hard to come down after all that energy created and expended on stage—and hungry, because you can't eat much before a performance. My mom would unpack every tasty morsel from the fridge. They'd smear the good, smelly triple-crème cheeses from Zabar's on crackers. They'd cut the hard salami, bite by bite, with a sharp paring knife on a small cutting board, slice a pear, pick at leftover cold chicken, or heat up some weisswurst with spicy mustard. My dad would grab a cold Heineken, my mom would finish off the remnants of the bottle of white wine from the fridge, or if in the mood, they'd pour tumblers from frosty bottles of vodka or aquavit stowed in the freezer. Sometimes there would be little ramekins of chocolate pudding, or red Jell-O covered with taut plastic wrap, to conclude the savory kitchen picnic.

When I'd hear them in the kitchen, I'd either force myself awake or pretend I'd been sleeping and would come in, rubbing my eyes, hoping they wouldn't send me back to bed. They'd smile and tease me, "Uh . . . look who's up . . ." I'd try not to smile if I was busted faking my sleepiness. I loved crashing their adult late-night snacks party.

This spark in the middle of the dark, quiet apartment was a welcome reprieve from being banished to my bed. It was a joyous treat, made only more of an event when punctuated by my dad's uncanny ability to make my mom laugh. When my mom got going, laughing hard, it would quickly progress into her involuntary silent scream, with tears streaming down her face. And if he really got her good, she'd beg for mercy, crying-laughing, and with everything she had, try not to pee herself. I don't remember what he'd said or done to put her over the edge, but it looked to me like a highlight of what fun married life could be.

As a kid, I sat at my dad's size-six Gucci loafers, listened to the cast albums of his Broadway shows, his solo LP recordings where he covered pop songs, including the one I knew he sang for me, Donovan's "Jennifer Juniper."

His sun was how we set our clocks. It determined how our constellations would move. He was pretty much in charge of where we lived, and his career was in charge of him. Opportunity, or its distant cousins, hope and possibility, were persuasive forces, part and parcel of the life of an actor. If we needed to move in the middle of a school year to California in 1969 because it was "important for his career to be in Hollywood," there was no question it was what we needed to do.

At that time, New York City's Upper West Side was still a gorgeous ethnic and economic blend of people living within the same city block. Walking down 87th Street from my doorman building on Central Park West to the corner bodega on Columbus Avenue, past my Puerto Rican neighbors hanging out on their front stoops on a sultry summer night, the block throbbing with the beat of bongos, made my heart quicken. The crackle of sexual tension combined with urban grit reminded me of *West Side Story,* one of my favorite musicals. But the dramatic lifestyle change from New York to California was also thrilling.

The laid-back vibe in Malibu came with an everyday freedom I'd never known. I love, and have always loved, the ocean, so it was like a dream to be living right there on the beach. I could feel the rhythmic crashing of the waves making contact with the sand as I lay in bed at night, filling my nose with the briny sea air. Life in Malibu felt like camp, minus the homesickness. An endless summer that played on a loop of chill.

We were living in Malibu in 1973 when my dad was nominated for an Academy Award for his role in the film version of *Cabaret.* It was the same year *The Godfather* came out, and the two movies dominated the Oscar nominations as well as the wins. In my dad's category for Best Supporting Actor, the competition was unprecedented and insane: Al Pacino, Robert Duvall, and James Caan had all been nominated for their roles in *The Godfather*.

The big day finally arrived, and early that afternoon my parents were busy preparing to leave for the awards show. In our parents' upstairs bedroom, overlooking the sparkling ocean, the refection of the afternoon sun was so bright you had to squint. Jimmy and I were bouncing off the walls, bursting with pride and excitement for our dad, tracking our parents' every move as they finished getting ready, darting around like sandpipers in the uncharacteristically messy room. My dad—in his tux, big bow tie, and full head of '70s curls, replete with substantial sideburns—was ready to go, growing impatient with my mother's chronic lag time. My mother looked spectacular, though harried, in a drop-dead sexy Halston gown the color of peach champagne. Jimmy and I, right on their heels, trailed them down the narrow staircase to send them off in their waiting limo, when my dad suddenly made a U-turn back up the stairs into their bathroom. As he dashed back down past me, I saw him slip a tiny pill under the flap of his tux pocket. "What was that?" I asked. And he said, "Just good to have, in case I get nervous." (Hmm. Note to self: If nervous, take pill.) After they zoomed away in a cloud of dust down Old Malibu Road, Jimmy and I had hours to kill until, me in my nightie and Jimmy in his PJs, sat on our parents' unmade bed to watch the live show on their small television set. Jittery and buzzing with excitement, I worried about whether or not my dad would win. I was only twelve and Jimmy, eight, and while I didn't really understand what any of it meant, it felt like a really big deal.

Very soon after the lavish spectacle began, Diana Ross and James Coburn were introducing the category of Best Supporting Actor, and there he was. My dad's face on the screen, so young and full of hope, looking expectantly ahead. One after another, the other nominees' faces appeared, the most brilliant actors of probably any generation, in possibly the most thrilling roles of their careers, basically the cast of The Godfather—plus Eddie Albert for The Heartbreak Kid.

Time seemed to slow to a crawl as the world hung in the balance. James Coburn began that envelope-opening cadence we've all come to recognize as the verbal drumroll that precedes the ultimate validation for an actor. "And the Oscar goes to . . ." Then Diana Ross opened the envelope, her face lighting up as if she had been goosed, flashing her famous megawatt smile, looking personally gratified to be able to announce, "Joel Grey for *Cabaret!*"

Suddenly my dad's shining face filled the whole television screen as he turned to kiss my beautiful mother. She wrapped her toned arms around him, brimming with pride and joy as he sprinted up to the podium, breathless and emotional. His voice cracking as he pumped the air with the gold statue, gazing up at it in disbelief, "Don't let anyone ever tell you this isn't an incredible feeling!" Jimmy and I were screaming, jumping up and down on the bed, so proud and happy for our dad.

I had always known that I was born lucky and that I was to feel grateful. I had the best parents and my parents had the best life. I was raised to believe that art and politics and social justice mattered. Eating healthy foods and eating dinner together mattered. Being a close family mattered. I'd been spared the incomprehensible suffering and deprivation of the less fortunate I'd only heard of or read about. We had enough and we would, more than likely, always have enough.

I knew that many of my friends' parents and my parents' friends had far more money than we did—from the chintz-covered walls of Hal Prince's family's townhouse on the Upper East Side, to the pristine expanse of the Garners' snow-white carpet in Brentwood, to the funky gigantic bedroom with the ocean view in the Hagmans' Malibu house—but we didn't *need* more than we had.

At my parents' dinner parties, the guests would be Barbara Walters, Jim Dine, Beverly Sills, David Halberstam, and E. L. Doctorow. Mayor Lindsay came to dinner, and I developed a crush on him and named my hamster Lindsay. My mother worked for Gloria Steinem at *Ms.* magazine. We lived in some extraordinary places, among extraordinary, accomplished humans.

When we were little, Jimmy and I attended the best private

schools in the city. I went to the Fleming School, aka the École Française, and as a result my French accent is *parfait*. We had to take piano lessons, without either of us exhibiting any affinity or particular talent for it, and I took ballet class starting when I was five years old.

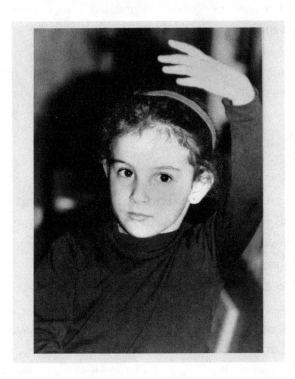

It became apparent later that saving for the future couldn't hold a candle to my parents' desire for living the good life. Even as a young child, I knew to be grateful for the beautiful life we had, going regularly to the theater and to the ballet, where I was mesmerized by the dancing geysers of Lincoln Center's fountains, receiving the falling mist on my face like a blessing.

When I was nine and Jimmy was five, our parents wanted to share with us something they hadn't had as kids, our family's first European vacation. The four of us arrived in Paris at dawn, totally discombobulated, legs rubbery from jet lag, and checked into L'Hotel, a historic jewel-box hotel on the Left Bank. Very chic, very French, with the most minimal square footage, like we were suddenly shrunk to fit into a Victorian dollhouse. Jimmy and I shared a teensy room of our own, with our parents in the room next door. I distinctly remember feeling more than a tad confused, looking around for where we were supposed to put our clothes and where to stow our bulky suitcases. There was barely enough room in the brocade-and-velvet-appointed chamber to pass our little bodies between the desk and the bed.

While elegant beyond words, this hotel was not kid friendly, and for good reason. My mother explained that it was most likely conceived with a certain clientele in mind, someone bringing not much more than a toothbrush, lingerie, and a pair of high heels. She probably didn't use those exact words, but that was what I saw in my mind's eye as she intimated that these rooms were intended to be a kind of high-end destination where wealthy men could bring their mistresses for a lickety-split rendezvous.

It wasn't unusual for me to be privy to this kind of information as a child. It was always put to me, as the highest compliment, that I was "very mature for my age," "wise beyond my years." This precocity was touted as one of my best qualities. It became my calling card, which I took great pride in. Being treated like an adult, let in on the illicit goings-on behind the scenes at L'Hotel served as an amuse-bouche, whetting my appetite for this future thrill, the grown-up, lush, secret world, romantic, feral, and full of mystery.

When we checked into the hotel, we were starving, but since it was only 6 A.M., we anxiously waited for the hotel restaurant to begin its breakfast service. The restaurant was one of the most exotic, if inhumane, renditions of paradise imaginable. There were colorful parrots housed in wire cages, and a monkey in an ornate, tortoiseshell bamboo cage hanging from a wall. Perhaps there was no live caged monkey glaring down at us while we ate? Maybe we were all hallucinating at that point? I wish that we had been, but I'm afraid we were not.

That first night in Paris, my parents went out to dinner while Jimmy and I were instructed to stay at the hotel and order room service. We tried watching French TV, understanding nothing, in spite of my French schooling, and ordered cheeseburgers and strawberries, but we didn't touch the berries. The gourmet berries, a pricey delicacy foraged from the woods, looked more like a bowl of tiny pink erasers to two clueless American kids.

Later that night, my dad had the kind of jet lag where your body is suddenly jolted awake but it's pitch-black outside and everyone in the world will still be sleeping for a few more hours. He tiptoed into the room I shared with Jimmy and sat on the edge of my bed, whispering, "Hey. You up?"

Looking into the darkness, I mumbled, "What's going on?"

"Get up. Let's go on an adventure."

As soon as I heard his invitation, I shook off that special kind of confusion that comes with skipping across international time zones and hurriedly dressed in the dark, careful to not wake my sleeping brother.

I felt like the luckiest girl in the world as we padded out into the predawn Paris morning. The ancient city was still sleeping as we aimlessly explored the winding, uneven streets, marveling at the architecture of this strange and glorious place, steeped in history and beauty.

We wandered without a map or a destination. At one point, we smelled something otherworldly, like in the Saturday morning cartoons when Bugs Bunny, a somnambulist under the spell of a wafting aroma, must follow wherever it may lead. We quickened our pace wordlessly, sensing the proximity of the pot of gold we never knew we were making our pilgrimage for.

The warm, buttery scent of croissants baking bloomed in the last traces of the night air, mingling with the new morning, until we found the blessed source of this powerful spell. We cajoled the baker into giving us the first of his golden creations, decadently plump, with a burnished exterior that flaked at the merest touch. We bit into the lighter-than-air miracles, still hot from the oven, the shell exploding to reveal a meltingly tender center.

The streets of this mysterious city seemed to be gradually coming to life, seamlessly shifting ombré from black to gray to that subtlest glow of golden warmth. Our fronts flecked with the telltale papery crumbs of the most delicate pastry known to man, my dad and I headed back to the hotel to wake my mother and brother with the bag of, still warm, remaining treats.

2

Who Jew You Think You Are?

Our family didn't celebrate Christmas. Instead, we lit Hanukkah candles for eight nights. But we did always attend the Christmas party at Hal and Judy Prince's, an annual fete in their Upper East Side townhouse that was chockablock with the likes of Leonard Bernstein, Stephen Sondheim, Kander and Ebb, Carol Channing, Patti LuPone, Adolph Green and Phyllis Newman, Jerry Orbach, and Elaine Stritch. Every living theater legend was there, dressed to the nines, drinking eggnog and toasting with champagne. We'd climb the staircase in our holiday best to the parlor, where the enormous, twinkly Christmas tree and the lush, colorfully papered walls vibrated with the frequency of legends gathering en masse.

Hal Prince produced or directed (and sometimes both) many of the most important musicals of all time—*West Side Story, Fiddler on the Roof, Sweeney Todd, Evita, Company, A Little Night Music, Phantom of the Opera,* and directed my father in the original Broadway production of *Cabaret*. Hal's wife, Judy, a whip-smart, tough cookie and one of my all-time favorite adults, came from Hollywood royalty, as her dad was Saul Chaplin, born Kaplan, the composer and musical director who had won three Oscars for collaborating on the scores and orchestrations of *An American in Paris, Seven Brides for Seven Brothers,* and *West Side Story*.

The holiday party culminated with all the usual suspects, by then pretty well liquored up, gathering round the grand piano, festooned with Christmas decorations and a shit ton of Tiffany silver-framed photos of family and friends in Mallorca or at the Tony Awards, to sing every great show tune ever written, accompanied on the Steinway by Stephen Sondheim.

Yeah.

So even though we were Jews and didn't have our own Christmas tree, we did okay.

I had been born into this extended family of Broadway royalty. My parents' usual crew was not exclusively show folk—there were plenty of world-class writers, painters, and journalists—but overall, their closest circle of friends was the crème de la crème of musical theater. I grew up surrounded by this community of legit geniuses, more legends than mortals. And with them loving me like I was their own because they loved my mom and dad.

On my father's side, I was not only the daughter of Joel Grey, but also the granddaughter of Mickey Katz, both well-known and beloved entertainers. I grew up knowing that when people were first introduced to me, I was automatically treated to a certain degree of warmth right out of the gate, because of how they felt about my dad and/or my grandfather. One widely celebrated for his showmanship as a song and dance man, the other for the unlikely combination of serious musicianship and his hilarious recordings of Jewish humor. Big feelings of gratitude and joy that, generated by my father and my grandfather, spilled over to me. How lucky was I to have landed in this pot of jam?

Mickey had grown up in Cleveland, Ohio, the son of Latvian and Lithuanian transplants, who had both grown up speaking Yiddish. His dad, Max, was a tailor, and as money was tight, Mickey and his siblings entered amateur musical contests in neighborhood theaters, then brought the cash prizes home to their parents. Mickey, it turned out, was such a gifted young musician that by the time he was thirteen he'd begun supporting his family by playing sax and clarinet gigs, and right out of high school he was hired to tour with Phil Spitalny's big band.

At the station waiting for his train to leave town, seventeen-year-old Mickey met Grace (aka "Goldie") Epstein, a tiny, dark-haired beauty with the body of a pinup. She was fourteen, one of five daughters also born to immigrant parents, desperate to escape the chaos of her home life and the brutal rivalry among the sisters. Mickey was smitten from the moment he met her, and three years later, after Grace turned seventeen, they married.

Mickey got gigs where he could as a musician for hire, and was on the road a lot, while Goldie stayed back in Cleveland with their two small boys, Joel and Ron, making a beautiful home, cooking up a storm, and looking like a million bucks. She was the ultimate *bala-busta* (Yiddish for homemaker), with more innate, creative drive than her petite yet voluptuous frame could contain. She was a force of nature in need of an outlet of her own.

She got her fair-haired firstborn started as a child actor at the Cleveland Play House, and the excitement surrounding his apparent natural talent afforded her some glory by proxy. "You're just like me," she would say. "You're your mother's son." She became so consumed with her budding thespian that her younger son, Ron, was by default somewhat neglected (though he went on to become one of America's preeminent inventors). But being Goldie's creation didn't protect my dad from her erratic moods. When she got really angry, she'd push him out of the room with a broom or beat him with her hairbrush. There was one year when she was particularly displeased with him that she withdrew her love and wouldn't touch him. For an entire year. Fortunately for my dad, he had the refuge of the Play House, a second family, where he was treated with kindness and respect. As a little boy, he interpreted the audience's sobbing over his death scene in *On Borrowed Time* as irrefutable evidence that he was worthy of love.

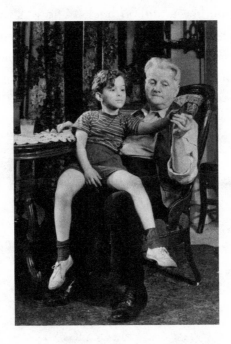

Meanwhile, after touring with Spike Jones and His City Slickers, Mickey found his niche, taking the Spike Jones formula of song parody, adding klezmer and Yiddish. His popularity soared with parodies of pop songs like, "How Much Is That Pickle in the Window?" and "Duvid Crockett." In my grandfather's rendition, "Duvid" was "born in the wilds of Delancey Street, home of gefilte fish and kosher meat." Duvid's frontier was a Jewish world. Mickey's lyrics expressed the experience of immigrant eastern European Jews, helping them feel a part of a truly American song.

In 1946, when my dad was in high school, the Katz family moved from Cleveland to Los Angeles. Mickey's records had become so popular that he put together a variety show called *Borscht Capades* that sold out every week at the Wilshire Ebell Theatre. It was then that Mickey added his teenage son, Joel, to his act, and for two years they did a couple of father-and-son numbers in the show.

In 1951, after seeing them perform together in Florida, Eddie Cantor introduced my dad to the world on NBC's *Colgate Comedy Hour*. That was the end of the *Borscht Capades* for him. He began working the nightclub circuit around the country, making a name for himself, out from the shadow of his famous (and famously Jewish) father.

Almost everyone going into show business in the late forties eschewed their Jewish last name for a stage name, one you could "see up in lights on a marquee." There was a brief period when my dad answered to Joel Kaye, as Danny Kaye was one of his idols, but he finally landed on Joel Grey. As a young actress, my mother also changed her name, from Joan Carrie Brower to Jo Wilder.

Being Jewish was a seminal part of my family's identity, culturally speaking, but I also couldn't help but notice that my parents' generation seemed to think it savvy perhaps not to *lead* with it, and more specifically to downplay it, professionally speaking. Who we were as a people felt more powerfully tethered to show business, worshipful of talent and artistry, than to our Jewishness. Our family crest would have been the comedy-tragedy masks, and from what I could tell "the biz" preferred we not be "*too* Jewish."

In my immediate family, having talent and a career as an entertainer was more the norm than the exception. A life lived in the public eye wasn't considered terribly glamorous, it was almost expected. Most kids going out to lunch with their grandparents probably didn't experience the hero's welcome my grandfather would elicit when we walked into Nate 'n Al's, Barney Greengrass, the Friars Club, or the coffee shop at The Beverly Hills Hotel.

A life in show business was all I ever knew or frankly could conceive of. The most common denominator from whence I came was a desire to be a performer, and preferably a star, because that meant you would actually be able to make a living. Otherwise, you were just some schlub with a hobby or a dashed dream. I didn't see anyone of my parents' crowd having to take a "job" job. They all seemed to be living their best lives, passionately engaged, fulfilling their calling, which looked like the most fun way to live in the world. Creatively alive, making use of all of themselves. Never a dull moment. I didn't know how they did it exactly, but I saw firsthand that it was possible, and I just automatically assumed that I would do the same.

I knew my mom had been a talented performer with a promising career because all kinds of people who'd worked with her or knew her before she married my dad would make a point of telling me so in front of her, and then there would be her melancholy resignation of, "Well, what are ya gonna do?"

Born in Brooklyn, she'd pretty much raised herself, hanging out in Brownsville, the streetwise daughter of a pharmacist. Her father, Izzie, had come over on a ship from Ukraine at only thirteen, with just his younger siblings, to join their father in America, his long wool coat weighed down with the family silver covertly sewn into the lining. My mother had no idea until I participated in the genealogy show *Who Do You Think You Are?* that the reason her dad made the long journey to America without a parent was that his mother had just died during childbirth back in Ukraine. (This would also possibly explain why

Izzie, when he'd come to visit us in Manhattan bearing a small box of cookies tied with red and white string, seemed like the saddest man I'd ever encountered.)

My mother's mother, Clara Mandel (the young girl pictured in the glum family portrait), also born in Ukraine, in 1900, had had her heart set on a life in the arts as a pianist, but *her* mother put the kibosh on her "impractical" ambition, insisting Clara attend pharmacist school, a pretty remarkable endeavor for a woman at that time. During her residency at Brower's Pharmacy, she met Izzie Brower, ten years her senior. She never did become a pharmacist; instead, she married one. They had a son, Mitchell, and then a daughter, my mother, Joan.

Clara's spiritual salve for her compromised life was to play classical music on the Victrola in their Brooklyn apartment—Beethoven, Chopin, Caruso. She and Izzie would sometimes go to the opera in Manhattan, and every Saturday the radio would blast whichever opera was being performed at the Met throughout their apartment as well as in their drugstore.

Brower's Pharmacy was where my mother's neighborhood, made

up of mostly immigrants, congregated, with Izzie acting as the local doctor. In a way, my mom also grew up the child of a local celebrity, her identity formed to some extent through the filter of her association to this revered figure in their community. Not unlike my dad—and, later, like Jimmy and me—she was first known as "so-and-so's kid."

Around the time my mother was seven years old, Clara's health began a downward spiral—she suffered from severe back pain and depression, bedridden, her closet jammed full of back braces. The cause of her chronic pain remained elusive, her coping strategy possibly found in her expertise as a pharmacist with access to prescription drugs.

My mother's older brother, Mitchell, made a break for it as soon as he could. After graduating premed from NYU, he joined the navy to avoid the draft, and after his tour, the GI Bill granted him a scholarship to Yale, quite a coup at the time, as the university had a very limited quota restricting the number of Jews admitted.

My mother worked in her father's pharmacy and became her mother's primary caregiver. She was crowned Miss Tilden at Tilden High, with aspirations of going away to Sarah Lawrence College, but Clara and Izzie were determined that their only remaining child not leave home. After a year or two of community college, she convinced them to allow her to study at the Neighborhood Playhouse in Manhattan with the legendary acting teacher Sandy Meisner. Her parents agreed, on the condition that she live at home with them and take the subway into the city for her classes.

Steve McQueen was one of my mother's classmates at the Playhouse, and he liked her, flirted with her, even invited her for a ride on his motorcycle, which she turned down. (Don't get me started!) One day, Meisner made some snide comment in front of the whole class about my mother chewing gum "like a cow from Brooklyn." It was not unheard of in those days for acting teachers to intentionally and pointedly push their students' buttons to trigger an organic, uncensored emotional reaction. My mother's reaction was to get up and walk out, never to return.

After leaving the Playhouse, she moved in with a bunch of other young actresses, crowded into a funky but very groovy apartment in the Colonnade Row. (Unbeknownst to them, it would become one of the first landmarked structures in the city, and its basement level would later house Indochine, a hot spot I would frequent in the '80s, opposite the Public Theater.) When one of her roommates' mothers came to town, they got tickets for the off-Broadway production of Brecht's *Threepenny Opera* at the Theatre de Lys in Greenwich Village. Deeply inspired by the brilliance of the piece, my mother decided she *had* to be in it. After the performance she walked up onto the stage and asked who she should speak to about getting an audition. Soon after, she auditioned and was cast in the role of "youngest whore." She bleached her hair platinum blond and eventually got to go on as the lead, Polly Peachum. At the time of her audition, she was dating Cliff Robertson, whose career was just taking off, but soon after she was cast she began an ongoing, torrid affair with Carmen Capalbo, the married director of *Threepenny*.

The following year, she was hired to go to California to perform in an "industrial" show for Chevrolet. (Industrials were fully produced musicals for employees and shareholders of car companies and other big corporations, and were a popular way for New York singer-dancers to make some fast cash.) She ended up staying on in LA, shacking up with a few of her actress chums in their West Hollywood apartment, looking for work in television and film. Around that time, she decided it might be a good idea to bob her nose. She did, and got some work on television, including a guest spot in an episode of *How to Marry a Millionaire*.

My mom and dad had met over the years back in New York, through various friends they had in common, but when they were both twenty-six, they ran into each other again at a midcentury furniture auction in Los Angeles. My mother was with a date, but there were sparks between her and my dad, and she wrote her number inside a Du-par's matchbook. "I'm gonna marry her," my dad said to the friend he was with. Dad was ready to settle down and was looking to find "the one." He had been making a living as a performer in nightclubs, and already had pretty stylish digs on both coasts. All he needed was the family.

My mother was charmed, because few people are as charming as my dad when he's in his full-court-press mode. He proposed to her three weeks after their fateful meeting, and very soon after, they were married at a friend's apartment in the Dakota back in New York. My mom wore a dress created by my father's friend, the designer Anne Klein.

Sometime before she met my dad, my mom had attempted suicide. I don't remember at what age she told me this, or what she said exactly, nor can I tell you the context, but I *do* remember the feeling I had. "I went through some tough times, a hard breakup with a boyfriend. I once put my head in the oven. But now I'm fine, so it's nothing you have to worry about." When it was mentioned in that offhand way, so conversational and without fanfare, akin to her just filling me in on some low point of her earlier life, I just took her cue, thinking "Okay . . . Good to know." But it's the kind of thing that once you've heard it, you can't unhear it.

My dad was head over heels in love with my mother, and believed he could make her happy. She had been bred to be a world-class caretaker, so I'm sure that held a certain unconscious appeal for him. But she was also beautiful, talented, and they shared the same taste in music and a love of art, the ballet, and the theater. They looked like a set of salt-and-pepper shakers, even their names were just two letters shy of identical—Jo and Joel. My mom was five four, my dad five five, they'd been born two months apart, and together they would build the kind of close-knit family they both had always craved.

My mom wanted very much to continue to pursue her own career, so when I was six months old, she took me along while she reprised her role of Polly in the West Coast production of *Threepenny,* while my dad was in Italy shooting his first movie with Rock Hudson and Gina Lollobrigida. My dad struggled emotionally, being separated from his wife and baby. Then, when I was three, my mom was hired by Hal Prince, who would cast my dad in *Cabaret* a few years later, to be in the ensemble of a new musical, *She Loves Me,* as well as to understudy Barbara Cook. She brought me with her for the pre-Broadway run out of town. My dad was also on the road, having replaced Anthony Newley in the touring company of *Stop the World—I Want to Get Off.* Stuck on the opposite side of the country from his wife and daughter, my dad felt like he was having a nervous breakdown and would be unable to perform unless we came to join him. His emotional pleas to my mom to come be with him finally won out. She capitulated and told Hal she had to leave the show, that my dad needed her.

The story passed down to me was that my mother gave up her career when she married my father, but I don't think she signed on believing that was the plan. She told me that early in their marriage it became clear that it wasn't practical for there to be more than one actor in the family, and that, according to her, my dad "needed it more."

I could sense an intensity fueling her singing of show tunes and opera around the house, the volume and vibrato reverberating against the tiled bathroom walls as she bathed me, more suitable for a stage than a bath-time melody. Like she'd been cast out prematurely, unfairly ejected from her intended trajectory. I felt her unspoken request for a kind of undivided attention and intuited that I somehow owed her at least that, which put me in a bit of a jam because it really bugged me. The energy was just too much for the intimate venue of a bathtub, but I was the audience by default, unable to move, as she had me by my head, washing my hair with my "No More Tears" baby shampoo.

3

Keep Care of Me

I believe if we're lucky we have many mothers. They can come into our lives at any time, but their influence can particularly permeate and imprint our early years. While my mother will always be my one and only, I was mothered by others as well. Children are so porous. In those early developmental years, our connections with people can significantly contribute to how we will forevermore define ourselves.

Back when I was a toddler, when my dad was starring in his first Broadway show and we'd recently moved to the apartment on East 30th Street, my parents hired an older woman, Effie, a devout Seventh-Day Adventist, to care for me. Effie was kind and extremely serious.

One morning as she and I were leaving for nursery school, I watched as Effie fell, ass over teakettle, in what seemed like slow motion, all the way down the long staircase to our front door. I remember her dress up over her head, exposing a world of confusing undergarments befitting a God-fearing, respectable, older woman. Her heavy, flesh-colored stockings secured by primitive, elastic garters and layers of slips. It was like the inside of a clock that had sprung open. Thankfully she survived the dramatic fall, but when my parents decided to add to our family, it was clear we were going to need a younger nanny.

Soon after Jimmy's arrival, when I was four and a half, we moved uptown to a three-bedroom apartment, with a small maid's room, on Central Park West and 87th Street. And my parents hired Nellie Clark, a beautiful and wise-beyond-her-years eighteen-year-old from Alabama, to come live with us to look after Jimmy and me as well as do light housework. Nellie wore her hair in the same straightened bubble style as the Supremes and had the most gorgeous smile.

She became an integral part of our family, like a big sister to me and one of the most important influences in my life. A boundless resource for unconditional love. Nellie's brand of love was not nearly as exciting as my parents' attention, but there was an ease and consistency to it and a palpable understanding that nothing my brother or I could do would ever affect its steady flow.

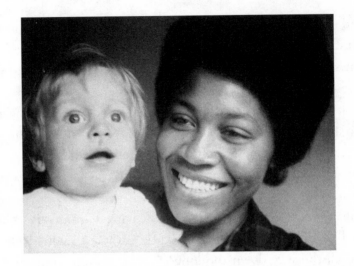

Our parents traveled a lot and I hated it when they went away. I'd become filled with hollow dread, a feeling of impending homesickness, as they packed. I always asked them, "Who will keep care of me?" Their fancy T. Anthony suitcases lying open on the bed, poised to be filled with all the accoutrements required, offered a preview of the exciting life they'd be living without us. I couldn't stand the idea of the coming weeks without them. It was like we lived in a Technicolor world that instantly reverted to black-and-white the moment they left the apartment. Our home felt so different with them gone, like a ghost town.

As soon as they left, Nellie would do a deep clean of our parents' bedroom, the living room, and dining room, pressing their bed linens and puffing up every pillow. We weren't allowed to turn on the lights or the air conditioner, or sit on any of the cushions, and if we did, Nellie would know by the telltale indentation our butts would leave. When Nellie cleaned, everything would be picture-perfect down to the last detail. The rooms she'd made camera ready became off-limits to us, locked away in a state of suspended reality until our parents' return would signal the reopening of those areas. Nellie, Jimmy, and I lived in the kitchen and our bedrooms. There was an eerie quiet, devoid of our parents' usual buzz of activity—phones ringing, deliveries, their busy social calendars differentiating which nights they were going out and which nights were our family dinners. When they went away, there was a sameness to the days, a dreariness that I can feel in the pit of my stomach as I remember the smell of the airless apartment sealed up until they returned. The kitchen and bedrooms Jimmy, Nellie, and I lived in abutted the dingy brick backs of the buildings next door, so we kept our curtains drawn.

When my parents traveled abroad, sometimes for weeks at a time, it felt like an eternity. Our dinners became distinctly kid friendly. Franks and beans, eaten around the kitchen table without much fuss, or my favorite, Nellie's mac and cheese with buttered breadcrumbs. Sometimes Swanson TV dinners, with each nook and cranny of the disposable tin tray organized into Salisbury steak, creamed spinach, corn, and apple cake that would burn the roof of your mouth if you tried to sneak a taste before your main course.

Nellie took her job and our welfare very seriously. House rules were stricter when she was in charge. She expected us to pick up after ourselves, and she had us on a pretty tight schedule. Nellie didn't mess around when it came to bath time. She would wash my face with a washcloth in a way that let me know she meant business, but she also would play Go Fish with us. We'd watch TV together— *Laugh-In, This Is Tom Jones*. Nellie loved her some *Tom Jones*—and we sang along to her collection of Motown 45s she stored in the vertical stack in her round Disk-Go-Case. She'd play all the hits from the Temptations and the Supremes on her tiny portable record player, and she'd teach me the most rudimentary stylings of the cool "vocal choreography" that those groups had introduced to the world.

Nellie taught both Jimmy and me how to ride a bike in Central Park, running alongside us and holding the bike seat till we got our balance. And in the heat of the New York City summer when my parents were away, when it was especially sweltering, Nellie, Jimmy, and I would spread out a soft plaid blanket (that still had my printed name tag, Jenny Grey, sewn on by hand, leftover from camp) and eat our picnic dinner, lying under the lush green trees, listening to the Four Tops' "I'll Be There" on her portable transistor radio until it got dark.

When we moved to Malibu in the early seventies, Nellie stayed in New York, where she'd married and was starting her own family, and we didn't have live-in help. No one had babysitters in Malibu. The neighborhood felt very safe, my first and only experience of living in a small town, the Malibu Colony, a gated community that had been there since the twenties. The kids all hung out on the one street, the main drag that ran the length of the Colony, riding around on bikes rusty from exposure to the salt air. Mine was an old Huffy Sweet & Sassy with pink-taped ape hanger handlebars and a banana seat. I tried to blend in as best I could with the kids in the neighborhood who, to me, were like cute wild animals with their tan bare feet and mops of bedhead beach hair. They nonchalantly popped wheelies off the speed bumps in the Colony or on the trails in the weed-overrun lot next to the Mayfair Market.

Our family floated around to an assortment of funky, furnished rental houses, first on Malibu Road (which we called "the old road")

and later in the Colony, none of which bore any resemblance to the over-the-top displays of wealth that are there now. There were the odd, outlandish bohemian houses like Larry Hagman's, but our family's temporary beach shacks were pretty basic, nothing like our swankier New York apartment. There was a very transient feeling—we never knew how long we would stay in California—but while we were there, we loved it.

It was a sleepy town, but showing the first signs of the development that was to come. A new crop of hangouts had sprung up: Straw Hat Pizza, Swenson's ice cream, Malibu's first movie theater, as well as the new Market Basket, which was pretty big news.

I was trying to establish myself with this cool girl, whose mane of beachy waves swung down her back as she pedaled ahead of me to check out the merch at Market Basket. It was there that a bottle of powder blue nail polish, which would go perfectly with my new, baby blue Ditto high-rise pants from Judy's, caught my eye. We never had cash on us, and polish, especially in that pastel color, was nonessential, but to a preteen following a cool girl around, it became as essential as oxygen. When this nubile mermaid pal of mine blithely instructed me under her breath like a ventriloquist, *"Just put it in your pocket,"* as she blazed the trail ahead of me and out the store, I knew from experience I didn't have what it takes, but I did it anyway.

This beach community was so relaxed and carefree. The adults' regulation uniforms, the leisure wear donned by the hip parents, were custom-made hooded, full-length, terry velour caftans, a close cousin to those robes favored by cults. It was all leisure all the time in those days.

The Hagmans were the cool kids on the block, and my dad and Larry fast became best buds. Their house was like Disneyland for the eccentric and ultragroovy, exemplifying free love and proof that if you had a long-running hit television series like *I Dream of Jeannie,* you, too, could spend the rest of your days instigating parades down the beach and soaking in your Jacuzzi overlooking the Pacific.

Larry's wife, Maj, was the Swedish powerhouse responsible for creating and building their extraordinary funhouse. The front room, right on the ocean, had a custom-made giant bed, and next to that bedroom was my first introduction to a Jacuzzi. This wasn't your run-of-the-mill spa; this was Maj's crown jewel. She'd poured gunite, which ultimately looked and felt like smooth, dark stone, and each family member had lain down in the setting process, so there was a perfect mold for each of their bodies, with jets wherever warranted.

This wasn't a private area, mind you. The tub was the hub of their home, the sweet spot where everyone gathered.

Larry was like a big, loving, funny Peter Pan in a grown-up's body, doing tai chi on the edge of his deck, his muscular naked thighs flexing in slow motion from under his short, white gi. He occasionally took "silent days," where, while still mixing it up socially, he would only gesture in his own makeshift sign language.

I wanted badly to be like these cool California aliens; I liked this tribe of exciting people. I became pals with the Hagmans' daughter, Heidi, who was a year older than I was, and Jimmy was the same age as their son, Preston. Maj was the boss, master builder, and cook. Their house was teeming with food and drink, the sweet stink of pot, and an endless parade of visitors and friends.

Of course, there was a lot of nudity, joints passed, wine and champagne flowing, and bubbles regularly blown from tiny plastic wands. It was extremely exotic and fun, except for the naked part. And the pot part. And the anxiety that came from the high likelihood of inadvertently seeing some man's private parts. And then the inevitable shame about feeling uncomfortable, for being uptight and prudish. It was clear that these very free, very Swedish, outrageously playful and costumed, for no special occasion, adults and their wild child kids were on the right side of cool.

Larry had a giant mustard-colored workhorse step van, customized so there were only the two front bucket seats. The rest was an open floor plan, with a macramé rope hammock that swung wildly under the bubble skylight. There was an oversized upholstered couch with throw pillows in the rear that spanned the width of the van, and the walls were covered in soft brown carpet. We'd all pile in there, singing along at the tops of our lungs to Nilsson's "Lime in the Coconut" or Elton John's "B-b-b-b-ennie's and the Jets," blasting through the state-of-the-art sound system. I remember one particular outing with everyone dressed up in medieval garb, squealing as we careened through Malibu Canyon on the way to the Renaissance Fair in Calabasas.

When I was ten or eleven, still pretty new to the scene, only recently admitted into the Hagmans' crazy lair, I was invited into their Jacuzzi. My dad and Larry had just gotten out but were nearby, and I remember wanting nothing more than to experience that bubbling, steaming communal bath party. Caught in this bind between what I very much wanted and what I definitely did *not* want, I compromised by slipping gingerly into the spa fully clothed in my jeans and shirt. My family had always been pretty free and loose around bodies and nudity, but I was now somehow different, and the timing of my new-found modesty was at cross-purposes with meeting these people who clearly hadn't gotten the memo on personal boundaries.

One evening at the Hagmans', which was lit only by a gazillion candles, people were milling around in sarongs and caftans—maybe I was eleven—and Peter Fonda, one of the regulars there, was intent on proving to me how two people could "actually feel energy passing between them" without physical contact.

Peter, like Larry, had been born into Hollywood royalty. Larry's mom was the legendary musical theater star Mary Martin, and Peter was the son of Henry Fonda and little brother to Jane. Having survived a prickly relationship with his father in his youth, Peter was riding high after the release of *Easy Rider,* a movie he wrote and starred in alongside Jack Nicholson and Dennis Hopper that perfectly captured the counterculture movement of the time.

Obviously, I hadn't seen this biker buddy film, but my new lanky, shaggy-haired friend, who looked like a rock star with bright blue eyes, set about conducting a little *experiment* with me, demonstrating subtle body energy transfer. He instructed me to sit down on the Persian rug facing him with our legs fully extended, the soles of our feet flexed perpendicular to the floor, only a few inches apart, and he told me to close my eyes, which I did, proving to be worthy of this adult attention. I wanted to feel this mysterious energy, and I could *kinda* feel a warm surging sensation on the bottoms of my feet, along with also feeling unsure I should even be having this interaction with a grown man. But I figured since Peter was like family to Larry, who was my dad's best friend, I shouldn't be so uptight. I needed to loosen up and relax.

4

Spin the Bottle

We made the move to California when I was in the middle of sixth grade. I started the year at my French school in New York and finished it at Webster Elementary in Malibu.

My new best friend was a cute, blond, heavily freckled girl from Michigan named Bonnie, who lived down the road in the Colony.

When I slept over at her house on a weekend, her family would be watching TV together in the living room, her dad on his BarcaLounger, her brother and sisters on the large, slippery fake leather couch. Bonnie's mom cooked up thrilling dinners, like Hamburger Helper and Shake 'n Bake, the likes of which I'd never seen before except on commercials. And we were free to gorge ourselves on the exotic trio of "chips, dip, and pop" set up on TV tables for our snacking pleasure. Bonnie's house was like a junk food Comic-Con.

When we'd first met at Webster, as a demonstration of our commitment to be best friends, she and I plotted to wear our new maxi "granny dresses" to school on the same day. It took a lot of nerve to make such a bold fashion statement on the schoolyard, but we were mercifully clueless about how deeply uncool our Tweedledum and Tweedledee eyelet extravaganzas made us look. In seventh grade at Malibu Park Junior High, the gang from Webster, our small community of kids within biking distance of the Colony and Malibu Road, merged with kids from up and down the coast, from Zuma and Point Dume. The result was like a small city of teenagers. And sometime that fall, Bonnie and I got invited to our first boy-girl party at Becca Druckman's house, on Grayfox Street in Point Dume.

Bonnie was super nervous because she'd never kissed a boy. I couldn't understand why she was so freaked out because I was sure I'd been busy kissing boys, loads of boys, for years. When she asked me point-blank *who* I had kissed, I wracked my brain but couldn't come up with a single name or face. I just assumed I had kissed plenty. I don't know if it was because I had been exposed to so much coming from a big city, I just felt more worldly. I don't know if this is weird, but I coulda sworn I'd kissed plenty of people. Probably back when I was living in New York? Perhaps in a past life? For whatever reason, I wasn't worried about winging it.

Bonnie suggested it might be beneficial to practice with each other before the party. She had two older siblings and a younger sister, and she told me her older sister, Lorrie, and her boyfriend would sometimes switch Certs when they kissed, which seemed like a reasonable place to begin. All business, we sat side by side on the perfectly made twin beds with quilted polyester bedspreads, matching dust ruffles and pillow shams, our feet planted on the earth-toned shag carpet. Bonnie and her kid sister, Diane, shared this dimly lit room, which looked like a set right out of *The Brady Bunch* before the crew lit it. Our torsos torqued toward one another as we practiced taking turns with the breath mint.

Having successfully achieved some tongue and lip dexterity, we got our bearings, adjusting to the new perspective of exploring another's mouth. We took turns being the one who initiated the mint transfer, and soon we felt ready to take our kissing skills into the real game.

By dusk, Becca's house was throbbing with the heady infusion of these thirteen-year-olds, now in party mode, a wildly mixed bag of growth spurts and hormonal development, from pancakes to D-cups. (When I whispered, "Oh my god, she's so D," in the snack line, it meant "she's so *developed*," said with more than a touch of disgust. I was so jealous. My snide commentary was my only consolation for being left in the hormonal dust. Another thing we said to make ourselves feel better was, "Oh, he's just using her.")

The boys, their shaggy mops of sun-bleached hair having been wrestled into some kind of awkward side part, were decked out in their finest surfer-dude cool, oversized striped Hang-Ten shirts, baggy cords, and Wallabees. The girls, in skimpy tank tops, their asses lovingly shrink-wrapped in their high-waisted gabardine pants, reeked of Love's Fresh Lemon. There were no parents anywhere in sight.

Bonnie and I, glued to each other, overheard mumblings about some kids disappearing into closets together to play Seven Minutes in Heaven, which sounded fucking terrifying. I mean, what exactly was happening in that closet for *seven minutes*? Bonnie and I were just barely recovering from the shock and novelty of exploring the interior of an unfamiliar mouth.

After milling around in the haze of the sweet smoke of everybody else's pot, compulsively reapplying our Bonne Bell cherry-flavored Lip Smackers, it got to be that time. Suddenly everyone was filing into the den, solemnly taking their place in a largish circle on yet another woolly shag carpet in the near dark. And there it was. The bottle, lying there on its side, looking slightly ominous, like it was smirking at me, "Okay, hot stuff. Show me whatcha got."

I could feel my heart beating pretty hard, rattling my flimsy rib cage, nervously rubbing my lips together like a boxer getting hyped in the corner of the ring. When the bottle pointed to a boy I thought was super cute, he decidedly set his eyes on me, and with a subtle nod from him we both walked on our knees (hard to look cool when walking on your knees, by the way) toward the center of the circle with all eyes on us.

I was sure all the other kids had been kissing on the regular, and plenty more, as they all smoked weed and drank. Bonnie and I were the outliers at that time; we did not partake. The worst we had done was sneak out to sit in her older sister's navy Mustang convertible with white interior, and smoke the ash-covered, accordioned cigarette butts out of the full ashtray. We'd pretend to be cool girls, driving, smoking butts, even though the car was parked directly across from their house and we were basically smoking the amber-stained cotton of the filter.

I was still new to most of these kids. I needed to look like I knew my shit. Sean Penn was in our class, however he was not at this party, but if you picture Spicoli from *Fast Times at Ridgemont High,* you'll know exactly what every single boy sitting cross-legged on that rug looked like. I became keenly aware of and appreciated the way their T-shirts hung loosely on their thin but strong tan frames. These distinctly boy things created an instant buzz that came over me when their pants rode lower, and their oversized shirts rode up, revealing the telltale new crop of body hair. I had seen a flash of what was lurking beneath when they pulled their shirts up to wipe the sweat off their faces on the playground after a particularly vicious match of tetherball.

My first kneeling partner was Mark Buck. He was a surfer and had sun-bleached, stringy, shoulder-length hair with a side part, one eye partially hidden behind its flaxen sweep. He might've been wearing a puka shell necklace, and if he had, it would've suited me fine. He wore one of those classic surfer graphic tees I would kill for today, his smooth brown arms emerging from the roomy opening of his short sleeves.

Mark smiled at me, his white teeth shining with the glint of silver, as his face moved toward mine. We each had our own respective mouthfuls of upper and lower braces, the old-school kind that tasted heavily of metal, and felt like it could, with too sudden a move, be slightly dangerous. When we kissed, there was a sharpness, like an animated tin can just inside a tan, beautiful boy's wide smile. It seemed that from the moment my lips met his, I'd been dropped into a fun house, a tunnel-of-love ride, with no recognizable earthly coordinates. Inside this kissing vortex was a maelstrom of teeth and slippery tongue action, like a muscular sea creature I needed to yield to. All of me that was not my mouth had turned to mist.

I got to kiss a bunch of boys that night. Who knew it would feel so alien from the inside? From the outside, a kiss looked like no big deal. I can think of nothing more awkward than being studied and silently critiqued by your peers as you try to figure out what to do, while sampling a wide variety of styles. There is what is visible to all—the panicky hands hanging limply by their sides having no idea where to go, the hands gingerly placed on shoulders, or the clearly more advanced game, the confident holding of head or face. So many choices. Open eyes vs. closed eyes. Which is better? Cooler? Creepier? Then there is so damn much happening just beyond what anyone can witness. The elusive stylings of lip-to-tongue ratio, the hellish extremes of the pointy tongue jabbing like a jackhammer, or the confusing, gaping abyss of, "Dude, where's your tongue at?"

I felt my stock definitely spike after that little shindig. On Monday morning in the locker-lined outdoor corridors, I could sense a palpable shift in atmospheric pressure. There was this one guy—very popular, very confident, too cool for me—who let it be known that I was "a hot kisser." This new stamp of approval among the too-cool-for-public-school kids in Malibu was a bit of a "Why, Miss Jones!" moment, when the mousy secretary's horn-rimmed glasses fly off and her hair cascades into a bouncy, Breck Girl slo-mo commercial.

Funnily enough, I wasn't surprised. I knew this newfound energy was where I was supposed to be. It had been simmering on a back burner for years. I liked kissing. And apparently, I was good at it. It would still be a long time before I would be able see what this baby could do on the open road. I don't think I kissed a single boy after that party for maybe even a few years. But I knew that I was packing some heat.

5

"Interesting"

My mother taught me everything I know about grooming, both in the classic mommy ways, as well as the more *Gorillas in the Mist* sense of the word. My mother, so very comfortable with her body, taught me precious little about modesty. Nude was the norm, and the night before a vacation, I would find her padding around the apartment, legs bowed like a cowpoke, arms outstretched like the walking dead. Wearing nothing but a shower cap and a thick coat of what looked like cake icing: Sleek, the stinky white hair-removal cream, coating her thighs and underarms, chemically burning away all unwanted hair. I learned that while we as women were born with hair sprouting up in all sorts of places, it had to go. Electrolysis, waxing, depilatory, razor—pick your poison, but it needed to happen.

In her regular postbathing ritual, my mother would furiously slather herself from neck to toe with body lotion, with the rough and hurried style of someone trying to teach herself a lesson, demonstrating

not only record-breaking speediness but also the limberness of a gym-
nast. I'd regularly rear up, shielding my eyes, unable to unsee what I
had just seen. Like when you look too directly at the sun and even
after shutting your eyes, the sun is still there, burned into the inside
of your eyelids.

My mom always wore Chanel No 19 and was religious about her
facial products. She and my dad referred to her beauty rituals as her
"jams and jellies." She had her elaborate Erno Laszlo multistep routine with Sea Mud soap, and in later years, moved on to Janet Sartin
and her white astringent, which transformed my mom nightly into a
Kabuki princess. It was how every night concluded, with her bedtime
ablutions. Mom was also a fan of Elizabeth Arden's Eight Hour
Cream. This amber-colored, heavy-duty emollient sat in her bedside
table drawer in its pale pink plastic jar, for softening rough spots on
elbows, hands, lips, and feet (and when necessary, donning a pair of
white cotton socks after application, also kept in said night table
drawer, to finish the job).

I used to study my mom's hands, her Cartier rolling ring, three
colors of gold, perfectly intertwined to fit together like one. I'd spin
her gold wedding band on her finger, wondering who I would be marrying, in the hopes that I could one day find someone as great as my
dad. I remember being fascinated with the veins on her hands, which
were like tributaries I could make disappear by applying gentle pressure and magically reinflate after removing my tiny finger. My mother's fingernails grew like mine, with their slightly curved nail beds
and very generous moons, and she always wore clear polish. I knew
that I got my curly hair from my dad, and my eyes were a mix of his
brown and her blue eyes, so if you looked closely, mine were a muddy
green.

She was probably the one who fancied sending me to a French
school so I could have a more European education, a broader experience, and as a result I have a perfect French accent. Languages have
always come pretty easily to me, thus I am happy and feel competent
traveling abroad. Good table manners were important to my mom.

Tiffany's Table Manners was required reading. She would say, "If you ever get invited to Buckingham Palace, you should be comfortable dining with the queen." It probably came from her feeling like a girl from Brooklyn who wanted her daughter to be prepared, in case her aspirations for where I might go in the world were realized.

Like her mother, my mom was focused on the latest health fads, believing you are what you eat. She was ahead of her time with health food and wellness practices. She started doing yoga back in the sixties, was the first person I knew to have a Transcendental Meditation practice, and took me along to the kind of exercise classes that Jane Fonda would later make popular.

As I was going through my old box of Polaroids, I found one from one of my costume birthday parties. I was nine, dressed as Camille from the Garbo movie, and would be sure to cough regularly throughout the party, in character as the dying heroine, from under my floppy brimmed hat. My mom bought a crepe pan so she could make and serve my band of costumed pals, all dressed as their favorite characters, cream of chicken crepes. Her ridiculously thoughtful detailed handwritten breakdown of the menu alone made me want to weep. It was clear how much care she put into making my birthday parties special. I can't understand why I have, as far back as I can remember, hated my birthday so much. It's never been about getting older. It's just one of those things I've come to accept as a deep and pervasive feeling of sadness that's hard to explain to the rest of the world, which all seems to look forward to celebrating their special day.

Jo Wilder mastered the art of loungewear. The minute she walked into the apartment from her day of errands, she'd make a beeline for her closet, where she'd promptly relieve herself of her bra, like escaping from some torture device, and slip into a loose caftan and white ballet slippers. Mom passed on to me her love of good bedding (Porthault, *s'il vous plaît*), good hotels (with a capital G), and she has always been one of the first to know about cool things coming into fashion, what books to read, what movies to see, especially foreign films. Her perfect closet lined with shoe trees, good handbags kept in protective felt bags, so tranquil, everything in its designated place. Halston evening gowns preserved, almost lifelike, stuffed with tissue paper in translucent garment bags.

She would take me along on her shopping sprees to Jax on 57th Street, where Our Lady of Chic, former first lady Jacqueline Kennedy, now Jackie O, procured the coolest, classic, casual looks of the sixties. Jax wasn't in the habit of making clothes for kids, but they custom-made matching mother-daughter bikinis for us, in red-and-white gingham. I was mortified when the fitter, amused at the very thought, laughed and asked why I would want a bikini top. It was the sixties, and women were burning their bras, brazenly going braless, nipples were de rigueur, so a kid wearing a bikini top, especially when you were flat as a pancake, was considered unchic and not cool. But I insisted because I wanted nothing more than to feel like I did *very much* have something to cover, which I clearly did *not* in a corporeal sense, I did have the newfound modesty-cum–wishful thinking of a prepubescent girl.

I had been in a state of feverish obsession, longing to one day be granted permission to be the proud owner of my very own training bra. I remember asking my aunt Jean for one because I was getting nowhere with my mom. She insisted I was "too young, and that it just wasn't necessary." My dad thought it was hysterical that it was called a training bra, "What does it do?" He would do a whole comedy routine, miming a circus trainer encouraging young breasts to do tricks, as if they were tiny dogs jumping through hoops. "Up! Over! Oop-lah! Ta-daaa!"

I was slow to develop, and girls my age were transitioning from undershirts, the Carter's ones with the tiny ribbon rosebud directly above where the designated action would someday take place. The training bra came in a small, rectangular, thin cardboard box, a tad bigger than a deck of playing cards. There was a photograph of a modest young girl on the cover. She had a subtle smile, like she had a delicious secret, her eyes downcast as if meditating on the miracle of the very subtle curve to her nubile body. She was the first goddess I prayed to, with fervent aspiration that I, too, would soon be gazing down knowingly at my very own breast buds. This training bra, with soft, stretchy lace panels inset into an honest-to-god bra, replete with the sexy hardware of hooks and eyes, adjustable straps, and things like "Gro-Cup" technology. They not only made you feel more mature, but promised science-based fulfillment. There was so much to take in I felt like a pilot making sure to do my routine instrument cross-check before takeoff.

My first bra was my prized possession. It made me feel so grown-up, like I, too, now had a secret. I would take it in my dance bag, keeping it safely snug in its box. When I got to my ballet class, I'd put it on and diligently, with the greatest care, I'd tease out cotton balls snagged from my mom's bathroom, to create an even, almost translucent pad to slip under the lacey inset. I'd proudly admire the gentle slope in the mirror, my secret safe, in the lineup of beautiful ballerinas at the barre. It actually made me dance better.

———

During the summer of 1973, when I was thirteen, my dad was filming a movie in Connecticut, so we rented a spacious house in New Canaan. It came with a stable, two horses, and a pool. This was like living a dream. I loved riding the horses and grooming them, kissing their plush, velvety noses, deeply inhaling their sweet hay breath.

That summer I had a secret crush on the local pool boy. I never spoke with him, but when I heard his truck pull up into the circular gravel driveway, I'd scurry upstairs to my perch and watch him clean the pool from my bedroom window, hidden behind the sheer curtains. He wore his shoulder-length, straight brown hair parted down the middle, as he worked shirtless in low-slung, sloppy khakis in the humid summer heat. He lazily maneuvered and dipped the net at the end of the long pole. I was mesmerized by his arms' slow, rhythmic strokes and the gentle sounds of his watery toil.

The soundtrack for me that summer was the new Paul Simon album *There Goes Rhymin' Simon*. We listened to it nonstop on the record player in the ecru-toned living room. This home was too vanilla to ever have been one of our own houses, with all its chintz and other signature staples of the Connecticut well-to-do. But more than the pool boy, or the horses, or Paul Simon, the thing that made its most lasting impression on me that summer was something my mother said.

I was lying on the wall-to-wall cream-colored carpeting listening to "Kodachrome," absentmindedly studying the album's liner notes. The living room, in the reflected afternoon light, was dappled pale green from the lush Connecticut summer. The air was humid and thick. And my mother said, "Your *brother* is beautiful. *You* are . . . interesting-looking." I was thirteen years old. I have no recollection of the context, or what prompted her assessment, or if I had even ventured to ask her opinion, but I do remember it knocking the wind out of me. It was like a gong, or an anvil from a cartoon landing on my head. I knew my mom loved me, and if she was just stating an unequivocal fact, which it seemed that she was, I certainly don't think there was ever any conscious malice behind it, but it's almost all I can tell you about that summer.

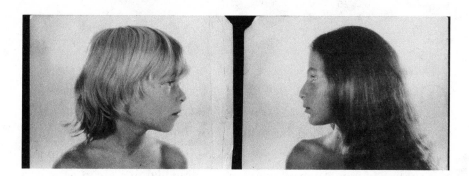

6

August 9, 1974

Coming from a New York City private school to a huge Malibu public school was like not even going to school at all. It was so easy I couldn't enjoy it, like food that tasted like nothing. While I was extremely relieved not to be under the gun, chasing my tail to try to keep up in a demanding bilingual school, suddenly feeling like the "smartest one in the class" (which I'm certain I was not) felt surprisingly icky.

So in eighth grade, I busted another move, switching to the Oakwood School in North Hollywood. I carpooled over the hill with a few kids from Malibu, including Heidi Hagman. The Valley might as well have been another country, at least a forty-five-minute commute each way, but totally worth it. I had landed where I belonged.

Oakwood was, at the time, a super progressive private school, intellectually stimulating, and for the first time, I was in a place where I felt creatively turned on. The students were low-key and super arty. My hippie teachers made learning thrilling.

Almost none of my women teachers wore bras, including my math teacher, Sally Ann, who rode to school on her motorcycle, so her white T-shirt, jeans, motorcycle boots, and long, untamed hair were covered in dust while she was teaching us to factor polynomials. Also memorably braless was our gorgeous poetry teacher, Linda Marin, who sometimes held class outside on blankets on the grass. Oakwood was full of the kids of the iconic seventies filmmakers (the director Bob Rafelson, the composer John Williams, the producer Bert Schneider). The families were well off, but nobody looked fancy, just cool as shit.

The culture and emphasis of the place was on the individual and on the creative—writing, music, dance, filmmaking, photography. Drawing outside the lines is what you were rewarded for. I felt challenged but not overwhelmed. I loved learning from these obviously very smart people whom I really looked up to. All of a sudden, I understood about intellectual stimulation, the kind that happens in an educational setting that aligns with your highest ideals. To do something because you're excited by it. To have peers whose interests are in sync with your own.

It was such a heart-centered school, small, but felt like a large family, where the older kids were big brothers and sisters. There were traditions, rituals, all-school assemblies, and monthly folk dancing at lunchtime in the courtyard, where we got to mingle a bit with the older kids, including the drop-dead sexy seniors—Patrick McDermott in his burgundy BMW coupe, Hart Bochner, another dreamy dude—the two of them walking around the school grounds as if in slow motion, their feathered shags blowing in the wind. I was horny, sure, but not enough to do anything about it beyond swooning over them from afar. And there was this other senior, Steve Doran. I had a crazy bad crush on him, and he knew it.

The only constant in my life, as far back as I can remember, is that I've always been in some state of romantic obsession, with the singleness of focus on an object of desire, a solitary crush, like an anchor. And Steve Doran was that guy for me in eighth grade. He seemed charmed by me, but nothing was ever going to happen. He thought I was "cute." He was part of the filmmaker crowd, with unkempt, dark, shoulder-length hair. Always with a movie camera perched on his shoulder. He looked like a grown-up, had a five o'clock shadow, was scruffy, like an arty filmmaker as opposed to a teenage boy. My first drug of choice was romantic fantasy. It fired me up, focused me, and gave me a safe place to escape to.

In eighth grade, I continued my run of being "the new girl" in yet another school, but finally, I'd landed where I belonged. It was the happiest I'd ever been in any school ever. I loved it. I'd found my people, and just as I found my groove, it was announced we were moving back to New York.

My dad was set to star on Broadway in *Goodtime Charley*.

I don't remember being told we were moving. But I do remember one thing. I was shocked. I remember a lot of tears between me and my friends. It was heartbreaking.

Of course, we didn't have cell phones then, so if you couldn't be with your friends in person, staying connected to your posse meant writing letters, which grows old for a teenager. The rupture was complete; it was a death.

That summer before our move back east, I started keeping a journal. Apparently I had a lot going on and no one to talk to but myself, in the form of my diary. I needed to tell someone who would not judge me, someone who would really understand where I was coming from. Someone like me, but I didn't know anybody like me. My feelings felt too big to be shared. I just felt different. I had watched to see if any of my friends seemed to be going through what I was experiencing between my ears, or between my legs. I knew I crushed harder and had a different level of sexual energy than the other girls reported. I saw the way my friends looked at me when I was just being *myself*.

My parents teased me, irritated by my tunnel vision, my obsessing over whatever boy of the moment I couldn't shut up about. I was extremely emotional, easily upset. My mom would regularly say, "Ohmigod! You're sooo sensitive!" and she didn't mean it as a compliment.

I'd try my best to manage and "control" my feelings, but that was about as practical and fun as juggling cats. I'm pretty sure there were other people who might've felt as I did, but I didn't know them, so I had to download everything onto the page in order to even figure out what I was feeling, to work through and untangle the accumulated clot of cast-off gold chains acquired and ignored for too long in a forgotten chamber of my jewelry box.

As I flip through those early diary entries now, it's like a virtual reunion with some darling girl I knew back in eighth grade. A girl so completely transparent, so dead honest about everything, and clearly seeking some kind of solace, some modicum of understanding of the complexities she was struggling to navigate. And at the bottom of each journal entry that summer was a postscript, a special encoded message, almost like a secret prayer, about Steve Doran. I wrote in my diary about Steve Doran every single night. I had a deep need to express this love and then went to great lengths to hide it. Even today I can't decipher the code.

That summer, our family rented a vacation home for two weeks in Mallorca, Spain, next door to the Princes—Hal, Judy, and their kids, Daisy and Charlie. Their au pair would play card games with us, and showed us how to lighten our hair with lemon juice in the sun. We would lie by the pool and read. We would go on day trips with our parents and their guests to Las Cuevas de Campanet, these caves with trippy icicles, stalactites, and stalagmites. We would take pedal boats out and walk around the port. I mention in my diary about getting my first buzz on after cocktails with my parents. And though I have never been anything but a string bean, I wrote about watching my weight.

We flew home to New York from Spain, and after the eight-hour flight, my parents' limo dropped me off at the domestic terminal at Kennedy Airport where I would be making a connecting flight to LA alone, to get my braces off. Jimmy was going to be dropped off at Nellie's apartment in Queens on the way back into Manhattan so my parents could spend a few days alone at the Waldorf Hotel. A vacation from the vacation?

Waiting by the gate for my flight to LA, I was kept company by my father's secretary, Violet Arase. Violet was a middle-aged Japanese American woman, who was my dad's lifelong personal secretary, and if being obsessed with my father made her good at her job, she was the best. Feeling nauseated, probably from the already too long flight back to the States, I sat with Violet until it was time to board. On that westbound flight I wrote in my diary, "When the stewardess asked me what I wanted to drink," heeding my now internalized mother's voice, "I didn't dare order a Coke." We were not allowed to drink "that poison," and though there was no one on the plane to rat me out, I dutifully ordered a tomato juice, even though a Coke would've most likely better settled my queasy stomach. I had this inner watchdog, my parents' opinions and rules. Their approach to everything was my lifeline. I assumed that if I played by their rules, nothing bad could happen to me.

My grandparents, Dacie (my nickname for my dad's mother) and Mickey, picked me up at LAX and drove me to their apartment in Westwood, close to my orthodontist, Dr. Baum, the entire reason for my trip.

When we first got to my grandparents' place, Mickey, an excruciatingly tentative driver, ever so slowly eased his black Crown Victoria down into the underground garage as the building's superintendent, a thirtysomething man in a putty gray work shirt, waved him painstakingly into his parking spot, welcoming my grandparents home with a broad smile. The patch on his mechanic's shirt read Jorge.

Mickey had an affinity for speaking Spanish any chance he could—with the busboys at Nate 'n Al's, or the short-order cooks at the counter of the Beverly Hills Hotel coffee shop, where they all knew and loved him. Dacie made up for her lack of Spanish with her own flirty familiarity, the warmth she exuded available to anyone crossing her path. Once we got out of the car, they enthusiastically introduced me to their favorite, friendly super, "Jorge! This is our *beautiful* granddaughter, Jenny, who's visiting us from New York!"

Jorge offered to help with my suitcase, lifting it out of the trunk and carrying it up to their apartment. In the elevator, Dacie proudly announced, "Our Jenny is here to get her braces off tomorrow!" Jorge smiled, swept up in their enthusiasm party. As we got out on the second floor, Dacie, never at a loss for hyperbole, with her characteristic dramatic, high-pitched inhalation—really more like a gasp—purred loudly for all to hear, "Oh, Jengie!! We are the luckiest! Jorge is the most wooonderful young man . . ." Acknowledging my grandmother's fervent appreciation, the super smiled politely, followed us into their apartment, and gently placed my suitcase down in my grandfather's study. We all thanked him effusively for his going the extra mile, and as he left my grandfather might have given him a few dollars.

Since I was moving to New York, this was my last possible chance to see my Oakwood crush, Steve Doran, and who knows, maybe without braces, I'd seem more grown-up. As soon as I was ensconced in the guest room at my grandparents', my first order of business was to do some detective work, get Steve's family's home number, and boldly ask him to have lunch with me after my orthodontist appointment.

The planets were aligning to be sure, as the next day a lot would be going on. President Nixon would be giving his resignation speech. I would finally be getting my braces off, and then me and my braces-free mouth were going to have lunch with Steve Doran.

I wore a favorite tank top with broad, diagonal navy blue and white stripes, paired with my best flared, low-rise Landlubber jeans, with just a ribbon of skin visible between the waistband of my cropped top and the horizontal slit pockets of the jeans. I wore Kork-Ease, the cork wedge platform sandals with crisscross leather straps worn by everyone and their mother, for extra height. Steve was tall.

I don't remember a single detail about our lunch, or even where we went, except that it was ultimately uneventful (see: disappointing). Steve was a good guy, and he knew better than to take advantage of a young girl's crush, so he respectfully dropped me off in front of my grandparents' apartment building on Wilshire Boulevard with just a peck on the cheek as I got out of his car. I waved to him as he drove off, kind of wanting to cry.

My grandparents lived in one of those apartment buildings from the fifties, with just two or three floors, and an intercom system outside. I pushed my grandparents' buzzer on the metal plate with the list of the other tenants. After there was no answer, I double-checked to be sure I had been buzzing the right apartment. And I had.

I looked all around for someone to help, but I was alone on Wilshire Boulevard. It was LA, so there were no pedestrians. Only a blur of cars rushing by. There was no pay phone (and it would be almost ten years before the world's first cell phone). I'd never been in a situation like this and had no clue what to do next.

I tried the Katz buzzer again, and again. At the bottom of all the tenants' names, I saw a buzzer labeled Superintendent or Manager, and I pushed it, thinking, "Okay. Maybe that guy can help."

Over a scratchy intercom, somebody mumbled something in Spanish. I immediately felt better, having made contact with a human.

"Oh! Hi! Um, I'm so sorry to bother you . . . Is this—? Uh, this is Jenny. The Katzes' granddaughter? I think I met you yesterday—"

After a beat, the voice warmed. "Oh. Yes. Mr. Katz's granddaughter. Yes."

"Listen, um, I'm so sorry to bother you. I've just been ringing and ringing my grandparents' buzzer, which is weird because they're supposed to *be* there . . . I mean at home, and uh, I don't know, not sure what to do."

"Okay. Come down through the garage, I'll open it. You can call them."

Flooded with relief, I ran down into the underground garage as the gate was opening. I walked straight back to the apartment at the far end of the garage, to where someone was standing, backlit in the open doorway. It wasn't until I was closer that I saw he was in his underwear, one of those wifebeater undershirts, stretched out yet snug on his protruding belly, and low-slung boxers. He was big, but not in a muscular or fit way. At first I thought it might not be the same guy I'd met the day before, or maybe he just looked different out of his uniform. He said, "Here, come. Use my phone." While I didn't love this, I forged on, judging myself for feeling icky. After all he'd been so nice. He'd probably just been taking a nap on his day off.

As he showed me inside and pointed to his phone, I apologized for disturbing him, and saw that his television was tuned in to Nixon's resignation. I gestured to his small black-and-white television set. "Wow, how's all that going?" He had shitty reception. Rolling horizontal bars interrupted the snowy image of President Nixon's face.

I dialed my grandparents' number, which, like all important phone numbers, I had memorized. My heart beat faster with every ring. Finally, I heard my grandmother's familiar birdlike phone voice.

My fear shifted in a flash to irritation. I snapped, "Jesus, Dacie! *You're home?*"

She kind of yelled back in her falsetto, "Jengie! Mickey, it's Jengie!"

"I'm downstairs."

"Whaaat?"

"Why weren't you answering your buzzer?"

She yelled to my grandfather, "It's Jengie—" Then back to me, "Jenny? I can't hear you!"

"I've been outside forever! Buzzing."

She yelled, trying to be heard over her blaring television, "WHAT? I can't hear you. We're watching Nixon!"

I could barely hear her over the president's voice, their TV's volume turned all the way up.

"Throughout the long and difficult period of Watergate, I have felt it was my duty to persevere—"

"I'M DOWNSTAIRS," I yelled back. "ANSWER THE DOOR."

"You're DOWNSTAIRS? Come up! NIXON'S ON."

As I hung up, I took a giant breath and released an audible exhale, realizing I'd gotten into quite a state. It had already been a day, chock-full of peak experiences. When I placed the receiver back on the phone and turned around, Jorge was standing there looking at me.

He asked, "So, did you see the doctor?"

I didn't know what he was talking about. Was he just making conversation, or confusing me with someone else?

He smiled and asked again, "Your braces, you got them off?"

Oh my god! This guy is so sweet. I just met him for a second yesterday, and he remembered the reason for my visit? No wonder my grandparents love him.

"Yes! I did!" I said sheepishly.

"Lemme see?" And like a little kid showing off her very first lost tooth, I proudly curled up my lips to flash him my perfectly straight chicklets. As he was quite a bit taller, I tilted my face upward so he could appreciate my newly minted pearly whites. I must've closed my eyes for a brief second. Next thing I knew, he was behind me, pinning my arms down by my side.

I was in shock. This couldn't be happening. This was the kindest, most lovely man. My grandparents adored this guy. He was now licking my neck, breathing harder and harder, pressing his body into me from behind.

Time suddenly became unrecognizable. Things were moving either very slowly or very quickly, blurred, but I knew one thing for sure: I was very much in trouble. I had no clue how to defend myself, having never even hit or slapped anyone. I started to speak from some other part of me. Then this calm came over me and I automatically began to channel some other animal, an awakened beast I hadn't known was inside me.

"Are you fucking kidding me? Is this the only way you can get this? You're pathetic. You can't get someone your own age to have sex with you, so you go after a fourteen-year-old? I just hung up the phone! My grandparents are waiting for me upstairs. You're going to get fired. You're so fucked."

The moment the words shot out of my mouth, they fried and shorted out whatever circuitry he was running on. He stopped licking my neck and released my arms without a word. With the calm of a zombie, I walked directly out of his apartment and into the elevator. *Just get into the elevator. Just push the button.* I noticed my hands shaking, my body starting to vibrate from head to toe. Once inside the chrome cubicle, I pushed the elevator button as the silver walls started to spin, nausea and adrenaline cresting.

My grandparents had left their front door ajar for me, and the sound from their television echoed down the open-air breezeway. I made a beeline for Mickey's bathroom, with the stink of stale cigars and pine matches, and promptly threw up. Crying and still breathless, I called my dad in New York and tearily told him what had just happened.

After a beat, he responded, sounding strangely cold and detached, "Well, what did you expect? You were probably all juicy from your date with Steve."

Wait. He *couldn't* have said that. There's no way my dad could have *meant* what I thought he said. That I had only myself, my horniness, my natural God-given desire to blame for this creep attempting to molest me? I was filled with shame as well as with a healthy dose of disgust. I was my dad's little girl. The last thing any girl wants to hear is her father referring to her as "juicy." I wished I could magically unhear that word.

My grandparents were glued to the television set, to the booming voice of Tricky Dick. Nothing could have prepared me for their blatant, blank dismissal of what had happened to me.

"Our Jorge? He would *never.*"

They seemed almost angry with me, and that was the end of the discussion.

I was fourteen years old, about to enter my first year of high school, had never kissed anyone, except for my warm-up session with Bonnie and a few boys at the spin the bottle party. This was a loss of innocence, but one that needed to be lost, especially with where I was headed.

There was a lot to process, because until this moment I had never known any man to be anything but protective and loving, and like all young girls, I had been warned about the bad, dangerous men in the world. The shock of being fooled by someone who seemed so safe, who had been such a gentleman and was adored by my grandparents, made me realize I just couldn't trust myself to know.

On future visits to my grandparents' place, I was always uneasy, wondering if Jorge was still working there. One time I remember suddenly dropping onto the parquet floor of my grandparents' apartment and slithering out of sight, as their beloved superintendent leered at me through their jalousie windows, slowly watering the potted plants in the breezeway.

There has never been any question in my mind that my grandparents were crazy about me, that my dad loved me beyond words. Yet how does the psyche reconcile the discrepancies? I felt perhaps I must've been somehow at fault or else had been mistaken about the entire event. Why else would the people I trusted most in the world disappoint me so profoundly? On another, much deeper level, I had to have made a subconscious mental note. I couldn't ever count on anyone, even if I was in real trouble.

7

Gypsies, Tramps, and Sleaze

There is a theory regarding epigenetics, which I think might apply to my family's roots. As the heat was being turned up in eastern Europe, the people with the overdeveloped amygdala—the ones with the most highly reactive fight, flight, or freeze response—were the ones who made it out, willing to risk everything when they fled to America. These more reactive people—not the chill ones who thought it was all going to be okay, but the nervous ones, the highly vigilant ones—arrived on Ellis Island. They moved into communities with the other nervous wrecks and made babies, inadvertently creating a genetically modified superanxious race. God forbid you make babies with the goyim, diluting the adrenally souped-up broth. You might lose some of that edge! Perhaps that's how we earned the reputation of being *nervous Jews*.

I'd sprung from this posse of hearty, albeit anxious, Jews who'd fled Russia and set up shop wherever they could, and many of my particular clan had chosen to pursue one of the most irregular of vocations. I grew up with the understanding that because I had been born into this band of gypsies, the ways our family ping-ponged from one coast to another, and the frequency with which Jimmy and I changed schools—those kinds of chronic disruptions were just the price you had to pay for getting to live the "never dull" life of an actor. And since I had no question that was the life I was headed for, on some level I put the endless upheaval into the category of lucky, early training for my future career.

I imagined that my little brother, Jimmy, having been plucked from a disparate reality and plopped into our weird tribe, might've experienced the lifestyle he found himself wedged into to be perhaps a less-than-natural fit.

Jimmy was a real boy, with a capital OY! He had a lot of energy, was naturally athletic, super smart, and while he without question possessed a true and gentle sweetness, he also had a temperament that was completely foreign to the three of us. Everyone has anger (and anyone who denies that they do is the one you really have to look out for), but flares of overt anger in our family were patently not tolerated. As a little boy, my brother was prescribed Ritalin for "hyperactivity." And for a while, my mother even hired this older kid as a "manny" to take Jimmy out to the park after school sometimes to throw a ball around, so he "could blow off steam," doing those things that dads typically did with their sons because our dad was not the sporty type. My beautiful and more "challenging" brother struggled emotionally, and who could blame him? Looking back, I can't help but wonder if perhaps another kind of family, with a more stable, less chaotic lifestyle, a family that could and would have adapted to *him* and his needs, might have been a better fit for his sensitive soul.

So, for a long time, I just assumed that the way our family functioned was no big deal for me. I think I minimized that going to eight different schools, constantly being uprooted, living in six or seven different homes as a kid might've been hard on *me*. I'd developed a certain pride in my resilience and adaptability. Wherever we were, whatever the challenge was, I could handle it, I thought.

But when I returned to New York after three years of California life, I was thrown into the deep end of a deep pool. Dalton. One of the more academically rigorous of the city's prep schools, where the rarified air was infused with unrelenting, privileged expectations from the high-powered parents.

Ninth grade was my first year at Dalton, though most of the kids had been there since first grade. And because I'd switched schools the way other people change their socks, and because each school I'd attended had such a varied curriculum, I'd arrived at Dalton with some pretty gaping holes in my education. I found myself having to playing catch-up at the exact moment when the academic pressure was shifting into overdrive.

In reading my journals from that fall, I can hear the panic, disorientation, and confusion about how many hours I spent doing homework.

Sept. 12, 1974

I know that I went through this last year, the year before, and the year before when I started in new schools, and I did somehow pull through, but that still isn't very comforting. It's just the whole feeling of starting over and adjusting. I'm not used to all of the work. The teachers expect so much of you! I suppose it's just a matter of time. I'll just keep reminding myself; don't get all frantic and overwhelmed. Deal with one thing at a time and do your best; that's all you can do! Have more faith in yourself!

Sept. 19, 1974

Referring back to what I wrote the other day, I still feel the same. Not quite as frantic, but there is still a ceaseless and overwhelming amount of work. I haven't had any time to myself lately. I don't do the things that I love and give me pleasure after school, like ballet or movies . . . or a nice leisurely dinner without rushing through because of the thought of getting to my homework. I really really like school a lot, but when it gets like this, I feel like it's an invasion of my privacy . . . I will give it a bit more, but if things don't even out a little I . . . I . . . I don't know what I'll do!

There was no balance, no downtime, no time to reset. No time for hobbies or anything else that can remind you of what it feels like to be a human being. At Oakwood, I had tasted equilibrium. I knew it was possible to work really hard in school and still be excited about learning. But at Dalton, the message was, "You have to step it up." With no time to relax, to get to know new friends, unable to fully wake up in the morning, having stayed up far too late trying to finish my homework, the despair I felt was palpable, as was the utter shock when I got the first C of my life. I couldn't reconcile how little progress I was making, considering how hard I was working.

Until then, much of my identity had come from being good. A really good student, extremely capable of accomplishing whatever was asked of me. I'd always been a curious person, excited to learn new things, but what I was being taught and the way I was being taught were definitely not working for me. I had no outside help or tutors, and could never quite get my footing. No one considered at the time that I might have learning issues. I was so verbal, so outgoing, I could fake it, and I prided myself on not asking for help. My difficulties were covert and confounding, even to me.

There was also the culture shock of being the newly displaced beach rat from Malibu that left me feeling woefully unprepared for this new chapter. Malibu had been all about being natural. Clairol Herbal Essence shampoo had been all I needed to feel bulletproof. One whiff of my intoxicating, earthy, floral-scented tresses was all the artillery I needed. I'd worn my naturally curly hair with a middle part that gradually expanded to a sloping pyramid around my shoulders and no makeup. I dressed in cutoffs paired with T-shirts silk-screened with your basic winged angels, moons, unicorns, rainbows. Right before moving east, my parents had sprung for my first pair of designer jeans—Sisley jeans—high-waisted with a wide leg.

I knew I very much wanted to start fresh with this move, to take advantage of the opportunity to rebrand myself without the stink of that good-girl persona following me from Malibu. Bonnie and I had been the outliers when all the local kids our age were getting high on the regular, but I had made a deal with my parents, who wanted me to "hold off" until I was a little older and not to "succumb to peer pressure." I had been secretly a little nervous about what getting stoned might feel like, and because I still had never lied to my parents, even by omission, I agreed to wait. My dad, who didn't usually partake, promised me if I kept up my end of the bargain, he would "get some grass from a friend" and we could get high together. It would be "safer" because I'd at least know what kind of stuff I was smoking.

Getting high for the first time with my dad was not exactly ideal. I did think it was a little weird, but I was more scared about having a "bad experience without supervision" and had heard stories about grass being "laced with stuff." These fears weren't quite as unfounded and lame as they now sound, as pot was unregulated and illegal. The fear of getting busted was a real thing.

One crisp fall afternoon shortly after our move back to New York, at the weekend country house we'd rented across the Hudson River in Snedens Landing, I got high for the first time, with my dad. I was stoked to finally catch up to my peers and know what all the fuss was about, and this was just more proof of how lucky I was to have a cool dad.

He had filled my mom in on our plan, and we told her and my brother we were going out for a walk. We scouted the area until we found the perfect spot, a little ways away from the house. The leaves and ground had turned a dull brown and we sat under a small bare tree on the property. I watched as he pulled the tidy little prerolled joint out of his pocket and lit it, inhaling deeply until he coughed, passing it to me. After we each had taken a few hits, I immediately regretted getting high with him rather than with my friends. I got thoroughly creeped out. I hated this feeling. I thought if this is what getting high feels like, it's not for me. I couldn't separate the feeling of being high from the feeling of being high *with my dad*. What I experienced might have been your garden-variety paranoia, but at the time all I wanted was to get the hell away from him, thinking, "This is just wrong."

The only academic support offered to me at Dalton was being placed in a remedial math class. It was at that round table of "math-fits" where I noticed one girl who seemed cool and was super pretty, with big, blue almond-shaped eyes and a warm smile. She stood out like Marilyn, the nonmonster family member from *The Munsters*. In that stale room smelling of teenage armpits, she was the only one who got my generally weird sense of humor. She snickered in solidarity at my stupid asides mumbled to no one. She had been a student at Dalton since forever, but because we had no other class together, we never really had any occasion to speak. Our little gang of losers met in a room the size of a closet. There was no opportunity for discussion or chitchat. But the mere presence of this one girl made me feel less alone, less bad about myself for being separated from the herd.

Socially, Dalton was a pretty cliquey place, but then again, cliqu- ishness in high school is akin to the wet aspect of the ocean. Kristina Loggia was in the grade below me at Dalton, the youngest daughter of my mother's very good friend Marje and the actor Robert Loggia. Kristina was one of those girls who was just born cool, and as with many cool kids, she had a robust social life. She was a bit of a tomboy, the guys all loved her, and she seemed to somehow always be sur- rounded by a pack of them. Kristina made being a teenager look effortless, her unbrushed straight, shiny brown hair held in a chignon with a pencil. Her style was very accidentally chic, old, oversized men's cashmere sweaters and Levi's. She had a confident, raucous laugh and was one of those people who made smoking cigarettes look unbelievably cool. Before she even had a driver's license, she looked like she was born knowing how to drive (a stick shift, no less) while smoking her Marlboros, Joan Armatrading blasting from the cassette deck. And maybe the most appealing thing about Kristina was that she didn't seem to care what anybody thought of her, a quality that simply mystified me.

With no particular fanfare, Kris regularly threw parties where there was a mix of friends and family, at her mom's Sutton Place apartment as well as at her family's place in East Hampton. Her mom, Marje, beloved by everyone, had made it a point, after splitting from Bob, to create a haven destination where her friends, her kids, and their friends would gather.

One weekend, a bunch of us drove out to Kris's family's sprawling house in East Hampton. It was off-season and just getting cold, and the beach town felt empty, finally reclaimed by the locals. The Loggia house was blessedly free of meddling adults and would be for the duration. By dusk everywhere you looked, teens were doing whatever teens do when left unsupervised. Kids from Dalton, Spence, Nightingale, Fieldston, and Collegiate, where JFK Jr. was a student, had converged there. John-John wasn't in attendance on this night, but it was that group.

The decor was your traditional WASPy country house aesthetic, with well-worn slipcovers hanging loosely on old, now shapeless couches and slouchy oversized armchairs, a style my parents would dismissively (or was it enviously?) describe as goyishe "old money."

On this particular night, the rambling home, familiar to me from when our families had splashed and jumped off diving boards in the pool in the deep green of summers past, had morphed into a dimly lit, slightly menacing make-out party. The automatic record changer, with its heavy stack of LPs, had been playing Bob Marley, Minnie Riperton, Van Morrison, and then, with a slap, the Isley Brothers' *The Heat Is On* dropped onto the turntable, the slow side of long-playing songs like "Sensuality" and "For the Love of You."

There were Heineken bottles everywhere, snacks strewn on coffee tables, half-eaten tins of Sara Lee banana cake, and crushed Pepperidge Farm cookie bags, with only the crunch of pleated white paper dividers remaining. The kid assigned to rolling the joints methodically separated the stems and leaves from the rogue seeds that threatened to roll away like tiny BBs. Ashtrays were chock-full of butts, roaches, and long-abandoned whole cigarettes left to burn like curling fat gray caterpillars. There was probably an elite group doing coke upstairs somewhere, behind closed doors.

Every piece of furniture seemed to be claimed, covered with barely moving, slowly writhing, interlocked bodies and almost imperceptible groans punctuating the steady mouth sounds that could be heard in the rhythmic, scratchy pause between songs. These human mounds, their jigsaw-puzzled limbs wound around each other like Escher drawings.

I found myself walking from one darkened room of faceless bodies to another, looking for a place to sit, or someone, anyone, who like me remained tragically unpaired, like a lone sock on top of the dryer. Some part of me thought, "C'mon, seriously? This can't be happening. Where's Kris? And where are the guys who want to mash with *me*? Where am I supposed to go? I can't leave, I'm sleeping here, and . . . what the fuck?"

Eventually, I spotted this one figure backlit in a doorway, and as I got closer, I saw it was the girl from remedial math class. Her name was Tracy. We cleaved to each other like sole survivors of a shipwreck in a sea of hormones. While I'd felt like I must be some kind of troll to have been singled out as the *only* one nobody wanted to get with, when I saw Tracy in what looked like the same humiliating boat, and she was without question one of the prettiest girls in the school, I was hugely relieved.

This angel sent by the math gods and I sat nursing our Heinekens on the front porch, laughing our asses off. We bonded not only over the fact that we both sucked at math, but over being equally gobsmacked and frankly a tad insulted to find ourselves in this situation. We really must not be as cool as we thought if in all the heavy-petting action currently in full swing, we were the only two outcasts left standing in this high school make-out game of musical chairs.

Finding each other amid the groping throng that fateful night immediately changed the narrative of how we saw ourselves. Not only did it save us from feeling like the biggest losers, because you can't really feel like a loser when you unexpectedly meet the person who'll be your best friend for decades to come. But truth to tell, there wasn't anyone there that either of us were into. Or at least that's what we told ourselves. I remember the palpable shift in perspective, that fortuitous moment when I knew I was not alone.

Because Tracy and I didn't have any classes together, except for our special math group, we'd had no idea how much we had in common. Like me, Tracy wanted to be an actress, and we shared a similar sense of humor, liked the same food, and were both Jewish. Her family conveniently lived in a Park Avenue apartment building down the block from school, so we went there for our free periods or after school to study and do homework. Tracy's mom, Corky, was a go-to Manhattan tastemaker, writing and curating the "Best Bets" column for *New York* magazine. She was also an amazing cook, so leftovers there were always great. Her parents were foodies like mine. Tracy became my best friend at Dalton, like a sister to me. We were both caretaker-y, slightly neurotic, well-liked "good girls."

But while Tracy was like an angel on one shoulder, I still had another shoulder. I could feel this pull toward something else, an undertow. There was another part of me lying in wait.

Maggie Jakobson, who later married and became Maggie Wheeler (who went on to be best known as Janice from *Friends*), had left Dalton the year I arrived for a more progressive school across town, but was missing all the pals she'd grown up with since first grade. She regularly came round just as school was letting out, and when we were introduced outside the iron gates of Dalton, we instantly clicked.

She didn't seem to feel any compunction about cutting classes. She was a year older than I was and had a lot of style. Her parents were New York socialites. Her dad, John Jakobson, at age twenty-five, had become one of the youngest people ever to buy a seat on the New York Stock Exchange, and her mother, Barbara, was a trustee at the Museum of Modern Art. There were major works of modern art throughout their four-story Upper East Side brownstone, and her parents went out even more than mine.

It was kind of a *Clueless* thing when Maggie took me on as her project. She knew exactly what needed to happen to get me up to speed as a city girl, though it wasn't going to be a quick fix. And it was going to involve a lot of painful tweezing.

She got me smoking True Greens, because menthol was a refreshing twist, like brushing your teeth and smoking at the same time. We might even have gone through a brief period of smoking the more elegant and ladylike Eve cigarettes, with the pretty floral design that wrapped around the filter. Whatever Maggie smoked, I smoked, but secretly, mind you. My parents would've killed me if they knew. My mom used to smoke when I was little, but when I learned that smoking could kill you, I found her stash of Kent 100's and crumbled them into the waste basket. But that was then, and this was 1974.

Maggie and I started smoking pot together, and that was very, very exciting. She taught me how to make a pipe out of an apple, carving a bowl into the top of the apple, gingerly lining the bowl with foil, then poking holes in the foil with a pin from our sewing kit, jabbing a chopstick or screwdriver to connect to the bowl (an early iteration of apple-flavored vaping). I don't remember where we got the woody, dirty-looking nickel bag, probably in the park, because Maggie had done some time as a "parkie"—hanging out with the sketchy kids who, instead of going to school would just smoke pot, play Frisbee in Central Park by the bandshell, and tag everything their spray cans could find.

There were these hole-in-the-wall newsstands in New York then, where you could buy Zig-Zag papers, tiny pipes, and little bamboo devices to help a novice roll professional-looking joints. Of course, my paranoia as a recovering good girl made me thrilled-scared that even buying the paraphernalia could somehow flag me as a felon to the authorities. As they handed me the thin booklet of rolling papers, the iconic bearded Zig-Zag dude on the logo winked at me in solidarity.

The teen hangout on weekends was a bar on East 79th Street called Malkan's, a well-known "kids' bar," packed with all the preppies from the private schools in and outside the city. It was where everyone went to drink. They served all the underage kids, even the thirteen-year-olds dressed to the nines, and when a cop "stopped in," like clockwork all of the gin and tonics, rum and Cokes, etc., got switched out for ginger ales, and as soon as the cop left, we went right back to throwing back our fill of the hard stuff.

My new *bad girl* big sister, in charge of corrupting me, was from some pretty fancy Upper East Side stock, but she and I bonded over our shared thirst for dangerous, edgy, sexy adult business. Maggie and I snuck in to see the X-rated, French soft-core porn movie *Emmanuelle,* playing at the Paris, the art house movie theater next to the Plaza Hotel. The tagline was "X was never like this." It was shot in steamy Bangkok, looking more like an exotic fashion shoot destination than one of those tragically tacky porno sets, and instead of the overinflated boob jobs bobbing like pool toys, the actresses were all small-breasted European beauties.

That film made quite the impression on us. *Emmanuelle* was hot, and women from all over the city were lining up around the block, snaking around Bergdorf Goodman to get into The Paris movie theater for their fix of something they might be turned on by. Probably the 1974 cinematic equivalent of the horny fervor created by *Fifty Shades of Grey.*

After getting our first taste of sexy magic, Maggie dragged me along to check out one of those hard-core porn movies in Times Square, and I'm not talking about your Disneyland Times Square, kids. Times Square in the seventies was *the icky sticky* center of sleaze-bags, lousy with lowlifes, the capital of sexual depravity. Maggie had a fearless rebellious streak I could only try to keep up with. I was the totally freaked-out scaredy-cat of the duo.

We were two uptown teenagers who had gone to great lengths to try to pass for grown women, but could've just as easily been mistaken for young prostitutes. Our signature look was vintage tramp. Mangy fur jackets from the forties over slinky rayon thrift-shop frocks and towering chunky platforms. Our lids, heavy with iridescent glitter from Il Makiage, borrowed or stolen from Maggie's older sister. Our scent, also "borrowed" from our mothers' vanities, Yves Saint Laurent's Rive Gauche. Our pouty lips, thickly glazed with strawberry gloss, its powerfully realistic scent of the ripest berries could make a dead man's mouth water. Sometimes we would glue a single, tiny, metallic gold star, the size of a lentil, to the outer corner of our lower lash, which would catch the light, flashing when we blinked. Maggie always had the bling o' the times and I was envious of all of it—her Elsa Peretti teardrop necklace, her Rolex. That time we found ourselves in that seedy porn house, she lost one of her diamond earrings, dropped down the drain of the grimy bathroom sink.

Was it *The Devil and Miss Jones* or *Behind the Green Door*? Once we took our seats and our eyes adjusted to the darkness, we were shocked to realize we were the *only* females in the sparsely attended showing. We had crashed a party that clearly had not been thrown with us in mind. It was tailored to suit the needs of these shadowy men with overcoats covering their laps. As the opening credits rolled, all I could think was, "This is not where my parents would want me to be," and I wanted out. Maggie made me stay a bit longer, but I eventually got us the fuck outta there.

I grew up keenly aware of the vast array of flavors of sexuality that existed in the world. I was raised in show business, specifically around dancers and musical theater, so "gay" never had any negative connotations for me. In fact, a lot of my early crushes were on gay men, though at the time I had no idea that was a common denominator.

One of my first memories of being completely lit up over a guy was when I was about ten years old, and I was introduced to Peter Allen, who at the time was married to Liza Minnelli, my dad's *Cabaret* costar. I just assumed he was straight. When Liza brought him to my parents' Central Park West apartment, I was wearing a wool, red plaid kilt from the Scotch House, adorned with one of those oversized silver safety pins. Peter made some playful comment, asking, in a benign, flirty manner if the pin was there to keep the kilt closed.

There's no way in the world his remark was intended to be anything other than charming, and I was *extremely* charmed. I immediately felt that spark of heat. I felt seen by a very attractive man with an Australian accent. I loved him.

Years later, when I saw his club act at the Bottom Line in Greenwich Village, he was electrifying and "gay as pink ink," as Elaine Stritch used to say. (Clearly, I wasn't the only one blinded by his pansexual appeal. Years later, Liza told a reporter for *The Advocate,* "I married Peter and he didn't tell me he was gay. Everyone knew but me.")

Then, when I was fourteen, I developed a killer crush on Mark Baker, the twenty-five-year-old playing the title role of *Candide* on Broadway. That revival was one of those life-changing, beyond thrilling theatrical events, magnificently and disruptively staged by Hal Prince, more experiential carnival than theater. The audience was positioned in and around the set, with the actors running past on drawbridges and roller coaster–like paths and parapets. The performers, so close, you might even receive a sprinkling of their "holy water," the sweat of these otherworldly creatures, or the "misting" of aerosols emitted as they belted out the operatic Leonard Bernstein score.

I was *that* close to young Candide's scantily clad, lily-white skin as the lovers clumsily ravaged each other. How could I *not* have an out-of-body experience? It was like pouring gasoline on my desperate yearnings to be part of this circus. A perfect nexus of my theatrical fantasies and my own hormonal ticking time bomb. *Boom!*

And what better way to amplify this "change everything" moment than to meet the man himself? I'd already made my parents spring for the glossy souvenir program, but that wasn't going to do it. Lucky for me, every time we went to the theater, I got to go backstage with my dad to meet the cast. In this particular instance, meeting Mark Baker in his dressing room triggered this phenomenon of craving, whetting my whistle for more. I repurposed that access and returned repeatedly to see the show with Maggie. Mark seemed to enjoy my super-fandom in the way any young actor might enjoy that kind of idolatry.

For me, my aggressive pursuit had a built-in safety net. There was no risk because there was no chance of anything happening between us. I was much more powerfully drawn to him than to any straight boy my age. Was it *because* of the impossibility that my feelings would be reciprocated, and that was all I was developmentally ready for at the time? It was built to fail. Or were gay men what I was programmed to be attracted to for some unconscious reason? I don't know. Either way, these full-blown obsessions seemed to include the insurance that I wouldn't be getting into any serious trouble. Part of the beauty of being a fan is that it is based purely on projection, founded on fantasy. This yearning, being unrequited, has nowhere else to go but to build on itself, and intensify these delicious longings, independent of the object of desire.

Maggie was my partner in crime for all things intense, dark, and gay. She and I were like two stage-door Jennies, basically stalkers, inviting ourselves to join in whatever after-show *festivities* Mark Baker was up to. As it turned out, this charismatic young actor was up to all kinds of underground shenanigans. Quite a different animal from the musical theater show folk I'd grown up around, but way fun nevertheless. Maggie and I followed him everywhere he went, to every skanky venue, and more than once to the sketchy Bowery neighborhood to see his good pal from back in Baltimore, Divine, in *Women Behind Bars*. At fifteen and fourteen, Maggie and I were more than willing to cavort with drag queens, fascinated and feeling very grown-up to be able to hold our own in this particularly adult underbelly of New York in the seventies.

When *The Rocky Horror Show* opened on Broadway in March 1975, Maggie and I became instant groupies. The conceit of the show, as *Playbill* put it, pretty well mirrored our journey: "Innocent Brad and Janet find themselves seeking shelter at a mysterious old castle on a dark and stormy night, where they encounter transvestite Dr. Frank 'N' Furter, his 'perfect' creation, Rocky, and an assortment of other crazy creatures." Tim Curry was Frank 'N' Furter, and Kim Milford, a close friend of Mark's, played the nearly naked flaxen-haired monster god, Rocky. This addition to our widening net of naughty, campy freak shows only ran for a month, but Maggie and I were there whenever possible, and it was over those weeks I turned fifteen.

Our initial dynamic, as I remember it, was this: I would introduce Maggie to the Broadway gay boys so I could share with her the torment of crushing on the impossible-to-attain but super charismatic, who felt infinitely more interesting and somehow *safer* than the heterosexual rich boys we had easy access to. And Maggie, more than game, gave me courage. Our thrill seeking led us away from what we were expected to do, far from the preppy pack.

Back then I didn't fully appreciate why I might have been so attracted to the overt sexuality of gay men, or why I resonated so strongly with them, but now I can see that the world they inhabited was where I could let my freak flag fly. Because I felt distinctly different from girls my age, more highly awake sexually, I identified with the way openly gay guys expressed their big sexual feelings and horny crushes. The soundtrack of my budding sexuality was in tune with their anthem. Uncensored, my erotic feelings didn't necessarily go hand in hand with having a boyfriend or being in love. Horniness and having a relationship were not a sweater set for me, though I identified my lustful feelings as "love," for sure. In "girl sexuality," as I saw it, at school and at school parties, the goal seemed to be to get a boyfriend. There was a lot of plotting with that result in mind, and the physical connection was secondary, the price of doing business. Or, for other girls, randiness begat getting a boyfriend, commonly fused as one and the same. I felt alone and perplexed about why my relationship to desire felt so different. I was relieved to find these kindred spirits in gay men, where I could finally exhale and not have to edit myself. My friends in those circles didn't dismissively roll their eyes at my being "boy crazy"; they appreciated my candor and got my raunchy jokes. I couldn't shock them. These were my people.

———

Back at home, the rules of the house were the same as they had always been. If I played my cards right and fulfilled my parents' high expectations of me, which I had done with aplomb for years, we'd all be good. But I was drowning at Dalton. So in tenth grade, I changed schools yet again, in hopes that I might settle down and thrive in a less high-pressured environment.

I enrolled in UNIS, the United Nations International School. But being in over my head at school had already coincided with my fortuitous discovery of forbidden fruits. My attachments to being a good girl and an exemplary student had begun to lose their appeal. Like Goldilocks, I was looking to land in a place that would feel *just* right, where I could feel good about myself again. I needed to find something . . . something I could excel in.

8

Good Headshot

I never considered becoming anything other than an actor.

My parents had always been adamant about me not acting professionally until I was out of high school. Having been a child actor, my dad knew firsthand how challenging it was for a young person. The developing psyche is particularly vulnerable to becoming dependent on the opinions of others for determining self-worth, and show business is a playground that more closely resembles Fight Club than Disneyland. Extreme, unnatural highs and inevitable lows go hand in hand with trying to get an acting job. Brutal rejection, far more common than adulation, is almost impossible not to take personally, because let's face it, it *is* personal. It's you. What you look like, what you sound like, your very essence, is what you're hoping they're buying.

I became a restless teen, desperate to get on with it, feeling like I was wasting my time in high school. Still, my parents would only allow me to take singing lessons and dance classes. These were considered safe enough creative outlets, where I could develop skills that might someday come in handy, but there would be no acting classes until I was older, and definitely no agents or auditions.

By the time I was around fifteen or so and had basically worn my parents down, I was permitted to dip my toe in. My mom agreed to set up an appointment for me to meet with a commercial agent she knew who repped young clients.

Dizzy with the expectation of what this could all mean, I was shown into the talent agent's unfancy office facing 57th Street. Marje Fields, white haired and maternal, looking like she'd stepped right out of *Broadway Danny Rose,* warmly greeted me and we chatted, interrupted every few minutes by her secretary's voice over the intercom, the row of little plastic lights on the phone blinking. Marje would politely excuse herself then take the call, her side of the conversation peppered with the household names of cleaning products, breakfast cereals, etc. This was big time. When she wasn't looking, I'd sneak peeks at the sloppy piles of black-and-white 8×10 glossies of smiling, almost aggressively perky faces. This was so cool, seeing up close how the sausage was made, while trying to seem like I did this kind of thing all the time. I assumed what I thought to be a professional stance, sitting on the very edge of my chair with my back unnaturally erect. Marje asked me to fill out a form on a clipboard and to list any special skills I might have. Juggling, skiing, skydiving, horseback riding. Hmmm. I really didn't feel like I could do any of those things well enough to list them. She asked me if I was interested in doing soap operas and I lied yes. I knew it was going well when she informed me that I would need to get a headshot so she could start sending me out for commercials and soaps.

As soon as I got home, I booked my photo shoot with the popular headshot guy at the time, whom a few of my older pals, the ones who were studying at Juilliard, had used. This was like a dream come true, my own private nirvana. Entry into a world that pulsed with the possibility of everything I knew to be good, everything I'd been patiently waiting for. Relegated to living at such close range to the action, my lifelong proximity to the pungent aroma of the greatest meal on earth had me more than ready to sit down at the table. I just needed a shot, a way in, and then it would only be a matter of time until I was where I wanted to be. That place where I had always known I belonged.

I had taken what I understood to be the necessary steps to be "camera ready." First and foremost, the hair had to be dealt with, and as it was the midseventies, it was all about the smooth pageboy.

There were no such things as blow-dry bars back in the day, so blowouts (and manicures) were only available in proper upscale beauty salons. You got a blow dry after your haircut. Rich ladies were the only ones who ever got their hair done independent of the cut.

The heavy swing of impossibly shiny tresses was every Jewish girl's obsession, an instant upgrade every time. I had gone to great pains the night before my shoot, methodically "wrapping" all my hair around my head, using my skull like a giant oversized roller (or the world's craziest comb-over) save for the crown, which had been wound around an empty Minute Maid frozen orange juice can, to give it height.

The following morning, I had finished off this endeavor by blow-drying my now limp hair into a pageboy. The ends flipped neatly under around my jawline with my Denman brush, the kind that was popular in the sixties, with sharp, off-white, spiky plastic bristles that sprung out of the red rubber bed of the brush.

I was intimately acquainted with their sharpness, because the only time I remember ever being really hit was when my mother had left me with a perfect arrangement of raised bloody dots, like braille, on my butt. I have no recollection what precipitated this rage and corporal punishment from my mother, and when I asked her recently, she had no memory of it, but briskly snapped, "All I know is you must've done something *pret-ty* bad to deserve it." To which I posited, "Really? Like what? Is there *anything* a kid could possibly do that would warrant hitting them so hard with your brush as to draw blood?"

Most kids from my generation and before were spanked, hit on the regular, and much, much worse, and nobody thought twice about it. Funny how these experiential, sensorial imprints are indelibly memorized by the body, like a silent movie with no storyline, just the ruby red welts lined up in tight formation, like a military troop as seen from an airplane.

Once I'd arrived at the photography studio, and had hung up my two changes of tops, I diligently applied the most minimal of makeup in the brightly lit changing room. After a coat of mascara, I smoothed Clinique's Eye Treat, in "mushroom," across my lids and daubed the milky glaze of barely pink lip gloss in Meadow Flower.

I had attended to, and done away with, what was considered not commercial about my look at the time, namely my naturally curly hair. But it was on that maiden voyage I first became aware, almost as soon as we had begun, that my smile was also a problem. Or something about my happy face was somehow casting a shadow over the scene.

"Give me a smile," the photographer's disembodied voice echoed through the studio. That was easy. My excitement and joy were hard to contain, so with his permission I felt confident to loosen the reins a bit.

"Okay, not that much," he blurted out, like I had spilled grape juice on his freshly starched tablecloth. I immediately turned down the volume on my exuberance, quick to comply, demonstrating my adaptable emotional rheostat. I was like a jukebox, eager to play whatever tune was asked of me.

The photographer's irritability couldn't help but bleed through his professional demeanor. "Okay, maybe . . . just a *hint* of a smile." Sensing his impatience, I quickly downsized to a more coy, lowercase glee. His silence and the sudden inactivity of the camera and strobe told me I was still off the mark, as I could feel my smile dissolving into an aching lie.

Resigned, the photographer finally uttered, "Hmm. Maybe. Just . . . smile with your eyes." It was like that game where you're blindfolded and the seeing person is trying to guide you, acting like your operating system on a remote-control toy plane, trying to keep you from crashing via hints of, "Warrrmer, colder, cold. Warm. Oooh, you're hot! Hotter, hot-hot-hot. Ouch! You're burning up!"

Based on his coaxing and thinly veiled frustration, it became apparent that maybe I just shouldn't smile. At all. Which was confusing and odd, because my default face is pretty expressive, its true north, joyful and open by nature. Particularly in this instance, considering how thrilled I was to be finally living my dream, lost in imagining my future career unfolding as I tried my best to channel, at breakneck speed, all the colors and textures I knew I was capable of portraying. A wide spectrum, ranging from comedy goofball to my most deeply felt secret pain, all while gazing deeply into the camera's black lens, like the eyes of a lover who could see into my soul.

I just assumed all of who I was, this internal bonfire of my hopes and dreams, the palpable electric magic I felt, couldn't help but be seen and captured. This would soon serve as my calling card, a personal mandala.

I *felt* beautiful. Not cookie-cutter beautiful, but my own kind of beautiful, unlike anyone else. It was based more on a feeling that lived inside me than what I actually looked like. So if I could just connect to that feeling, it had to be registered by this stranger obscured by his camera, backlit by the strobe's blinding pops, like lightning against the arctic white, seamless backdrop.

The snarky input from this photographer was making it increasingly challenging to imagine my glorious future of going to an audition and proudly presenting them with my headshot. This guy lacked the acting chops or charm to disguise his disinterest in shooting me. Or perhaps, it was just too challenging.

I got it. It was going to be a neat trick if he could somehow capture me, but not so much . . . my nose. My smile was somehow causing a chain reaction. The outward pull of my cheek muscles created a tension that inadvertently caused the tip of my nose to dip down, catching the light, and not in a good way. This most natural expression of joy would have to have some guardrails to avoid killing the mood.

Those original headshots could have been captioned, "Hi, it's me. Can I please be enough for you? I will be so good. I promise, you won't be sorry. Oh, and my friend here . . . she's cool. You'll see once you get to know her." Dying to be invited to the "big dance," yet beginning to suspect that I might not be let in with my "friend," posed a dilemma for me. I didn't want to be *that* girl who'd ditch my friend just to gain entry. But I was confident that if I could somehow slip her in without too much of a fuss, we could hang with the best of 'em.

My takeaway from that brutal photo shoot was the three-quarter angle was the *only* angle for me. Smiling was too risky. Limiting myself to merely pleasant thoughts was about all my face could contain before all hell broke loose. The exposure would have to be "blown out" to fade the schnoz and pop the eyes and mouth, which would float in a mist of dreamy nothingness, framed by a lot of hair. Money and time would be spent on retouching. This was the basic formula for every shoot I did going forward.

The big day had arrived, when I was to pick up my proof sheets at the lab, waiting in line alongside working actors and models, trying to act like I did this all the time. I inhaled the strange air, heavy with the stink of chemicals. Professional headshots papered the walls, a giant checkerboard of airbrushed black-and-white faces, their intense eyes trained on me, with looks designed to hypnotize.

When it was my turn, I was handed the oversized envelope and as I slid the contact sheets out, my heart pumping like a lab rabbit, something inside me sank like a stone. This amorphous energy that naturally emanated from my being like I was lit from within bore no resemblance to the less-than-glowing young girl looking back at me in this grid of miniature half-smiling faces. Everything about her read as awkward, tentatively seeking some kind of permission or acceptance. I really didn't know who that girl was from the confines of her little square frames. A muted, strange alter ego. A twin I'd been separated from at birth, who didn't know half of what I knew to be true, had been rendered porous and defenseless against absorbing this hack's opinion of her. The abandonment of self, the relinquishing of her fire and spunk so complete.

I certainly wasn't going to cry there in front of everyone, though inside, I was crushed and shocked, frankly. I had never entertained the possibility that I looked anything remotely like that. I didn't know who that person was looking back at me. It just wasn't me. I reassured myself that at least the shots looked professional and that was going to have to be good enough for the time being.

When I look at the images from that first photo shoot now it hurts my heart. The look in my eyes, full of hope and longing, painfully innocent, clueless as to who I was, like some unformed lump looking to be squeezed through the Play-Doh Fun Factory to finally discover my intended shape.

If I could time travel back to that fifteen-year-old now, I'd reassure her with complete and utter confidence that this was going to be a real adventure. The road ahead was going to be rocky, but also super fun. It was going to take a while, but someday she would come to understand so much more, feel so much more solid and more comfortable in her skin. Beautiful, much more beautiful than she could possibly know, but not in ways she would be able to fathom at this moment, and that it would all be worth it. She would eventually have a sense of her true value and purpose that no one—no man, parent, or outside force—would be able to take away from her. One day she would finally own and know, really know, how amazing it is to be her. Exactly as she is, in every perfectly deeply imperfect way, inside and out.

9

I Started with Men

One Saturday after the first cold snap, halfway through my sophomore year at UNIS, my parents and I popped into San Francisco Clothing on Lexington, a shop that catered to the well-heeled who understood the cachet of a Fair Isle sweater vest. The start of a new season often prompted New Yorkers to hit the stores to pick up a few key pieces to "freshen up" their winter wardrobes. My parents and I had the same taste in just about everything—food, clothing, movies, even a shared appreciation for attractive humans. Not only did we have similar styles, but the three of us were also roughly the same size, so luckily I could freely borrow from both of their closets. And since everything at this place was out of my budget, if I could tag along offering my two cents, it could be a win for me.

On this particular afternoon while my parents were perusing the merchandise, I made a beeline for the extremely cute guy in horn-rimmed glasses behind the counter. I was fifteen and a half, but that didn't stop me from brazenly flirting with this guy, clearly well into his twenties. His name was Frank Mills, and when he wasn't selling Harris Tweed riding jackets, he was, though a few years older than the rest of the student body, studying acting at Sarah Lawrence. I was like a heat-seeking missile headed for this impeccably styled, lanky charmer from Kansas, with hair like corn silk that hung across cornflower blue eyes. I wasn't blind to the fact that this guy fit one of my types—WASPy, lanky, bookish (see: bespectacled), and older. Our meeting just so happened to coincide with my resolve to lose my virginity. I hadn't yet dated a single soul, and was on the prowl for someone who would take care of this virginity problem of mine.

Reassured that my choice was on point, as both of my parents also seemed to be energized in the company of this handsome young salesman, I became "terribly interested" in his school's drama program and what they were working on. He told me the following week his class would be performing down at the La MaMa. La MaMa was *the* experimental theater lab, real avant-garde stuff, too abstract for fifteen-year-old me, but I feigned interest. "Ooooh, La MaMa? Very cool. I'd love to come see the work."

When we'd first moved back to New York from Malibu, we'd briefly returned to our Central Park West apartment, but by the time I was at UNIS, we had moved to much tonier digs on Fifth Avenue and 93rd Street. It was a grand, old prewar building, with two door-men in attendance in the echoey, all-marble lobby. There was only one apartment on each floor, so when the elevator door opened on the eleventh floor, you were in our sprawling three-bedroom (plus two small maids' rooms off the kitchen) apartment overlooking Central Park and the reservoir.

The week after I'd set my sights on the cute guy working at San Francisco Clothing, I took a cab way, way downtown to the Bowery, and as I paid the cabbie, he peered at me through the rearview mirror to make sure the girl he'd picked up from the swanky doorman building was meant to be dropped off in this desolate no-man's-land. He slowly drove off, leaving me on my own on the dark sidewalk in an extremely tight-fitting, burgundy, Swiss-dotted, vintage '30s frock, with its own Bakelite deco buckle, and high-necked, white-lace-trimmed collar, as if I'd squeezed myself into one of my dolls' dresses. And as the fabric was pretty much very sheer, the winter wind whistled through the diaphanous material, so I might as well have been naked from the waist down. Fortunately, on top I had my ratty, fabulous, cropped fur '40s jacket with big shoulder pads, smelling faintly of animal with prominent notes of tired. I teetered in my high-heeled Mary Jane wedges with the textured gum sole and scuttled in short, mincing steps, due to the narrow cut of the dress and the steep incline of my shoes on the uneven cobblestones, into the tiny black-box theater.

It was *definitely* avant-garde theater—minimalist, confusing, every-one in black turtlenecks—but then, I hadn't come for the theatrical experience. After the performance, Frank and I went down the block to the funky corner bar, Phebe's Tavern, for drinks. I was drinking greyhounds at the time, smoking Merits. Frank smoked Parliaments.

After a few drinks and some flirty chitchat, it became apparent we needed to find someplace where we could go, and he had gotten the keys to a place from his good buddy whose parents were out of town in their second home in Florida.

I knew what I'd come there to do, and as I barely knew this guy, lovely as he seemed, he didn't need to know any more than was necessary. We started kissing in the darkened living room of the Upper East Side high-rise apartment building, illuminated only by the lights from the city coming in through the grimy storm windows. As things heated up, Frank carried me (like a bride over her matrimonial threshold) into what seemed to be maybe a guest room and laid me on one of the twin beds. I tried shimmying out of my dress, which wasn't cooperating, acting more like a Chinese finger trap, and because I like to think of myself as helpful, I lifted my butt up so he could peel me out of my shimmery nude pantyhose, like glittery sausage casings.

I watched in awe at how speedily his clothes flew off him, noticing so many things I didn't know what to look at first. Once naked, even in the near dark, I could see he had a fan-*tastic* body. I've always had pretty spot-on X-ray vision.

I liked this guy. He was cool, smart, handsome, nice, and when he took his glasses off and his silky blond hair swung forward, tickling various parts of my face and body, that was good, too. As he lowered himself on top of me, I couldn't believe how shockingly good, how otherworldly his warm and impossibly smooth skin felt against mine. As each part of his body made contact with mine, each new territory awakened, lighting up the skin on my arms, my breasts, my belly, and thighs until I barely recognized these body parts as my own. My first-ever skin-on-skin experience. *This* was something. I really, really liked this sensation, the beautiful slip of his skin coupled with the heavenly pressure of his weight bearing down on me. All this new information flooding my senses, exceeding my expectations.

I was grateful for the darkness and this guy's apparent preoccupation with whatever he was so focused on, so when he pushed into me and the sharp burning took my breath away, I could gut it out without him being any the wiser. I did some of my best acting afterward, utterly confused when he noticed the blood on the bedding, and, thinking fast, made like I had just gotten my period. He rearranged the Lilly Pulitzer–style bedspread to cover up the telltale tracks as I played back my undressing in reverse, only this time, the way I saw it, I walked out a woman.

I lost it on a weird, floral, quilted polyester bedspread in the dark of a random guest room in a stranger's apartment with a guy I barely knew, but it worked out fine. Frank became my boyfriend for the next year, until I was sixteen and a half. It wasn't until years later when we had become good friends that he even knew he'd been "my first."

Let me back up a little.

Early in 1975, February to be exact, a month before my fifteenth birthday, *Shampoo* came out. This movie revolves around a promiscuous Beverly Hills hairdresser who sleeps with every woman who sits in his chair. Warren Beatty, at the time pretty much everyone's idea of the sexiest man alive, starred as the hairdresser. His clients/lovers, each thinking they are the only one he's sleeping with, were portrayed by Julie Christie, Goldie Hawn, Lee Grant, and a teenage Carrie Fisher, in her film debut as Lee Grant's daughter and another of Beatty's conquests. Or was he the teenager's conquest? Fisher's character flips the power dynamic, beautifully outmaneuvering Beatty's character and her mother.

Shampoo shattered the archetype of the gay hairdresser, and from the moment the movie hit the theaters, getting a great haircut suddenly had new meaning. It was open season for straight hairdressers, experiencing a sharp uptick in clientele looking for a quick beauty upgrade with a little extra bang for their buck. Unconsciously, it probably set the stage for me, as the Carrie Fisher role was my tailor-made avatar: a precocious adolescent, trying out her newfound sexual powers in a twisted, "like mother, like daughter" trope.

The notion that a girl could go to a flirty, heterosexual hairdresser capable of increasing her stock by upgrading her look while giving her his undivided male gaze, the possibility that thirty minutes in his chair might drown out a lifetime of negative voices like a vigorous shake of an Etch A Sketch, was also an appealing proposition.

In my coming of age, this delicate recalibration of self, in figuring out who I wanted to be now that I was eschewing the restrictions imposed on me by my parents, finding myself just such a hairdresser felt like a no-brainer.

Vincent Tribiani was a twenty-four-year-old hairdresser and rising star in the magazine editorial world, as well as at Enzo, the anointed "it salon" in 1976. I was a sixteen-and-a-half-year-old rising junior at the Dalton School (don't ask, I transferred back for my junior year) and was getting itchy to see what else might be out there after Frank and I had broken up.

Being a straight male hairdresser is actually a genius enterprise for a street-smart hustler, preying on the palpable vulnerability of women and girls in the decidedly *power down* position, wanting to feel more beautiful. Seeking some*thing*, some*one* outside of herself to cull, procure, tap into, add, or reveal what, until now, had been overlooked or invisible to the world.

Vincent and I first met when he cut and styled my hair from the slavishly blown-dry pageboy into a definitely upgraded, foxier rendition of me. He gave me his signature layered shag, "The Sauvage," because one couldn't help but look wild and "just fucked" with this do. Generally, I'd never trust a haircut with a name, but this haircut was the exception.

Now, through the lens of #MeToo, I can see red flags waving hither and yon. There was plenty not to trust.

When I was first shown to Vincent's chair, it was obvious from the back-to-back bookings of clients, and the flirty rapport he had with every single woman in the salon, that this guy thought he was pretty hot shit, and I, of course, immediately needed him to want me. He was playful and cocky, and right off the bat made some critical comment about how I had been wearing my hair, which made me instantly want to curl up and die, ashamed that I had ever even left the house sporting such an ordinary and unflattering style. He gestured to the young, braless shampoo girl to take me back to the sink. As she was sudsing up my scalp, her breasts practically skimming my face, I couldn't help but wonder if they had fucked. I figured they probably had. (I saw everyone through this lens now that I was a card-carrying member of the sexually active club.) I was returned to my chair looking like a little drowned rat, suddenly wishing I'd worn more eye makeup.

Vincent was a wiry, ambitious Italian kid from Brooklyn, back when it was still a dees, dems, and dohs borough. But thrown into the mix with his native *GoodFellas* accent was a confusing twang from some unspecified faraway locale. Random flourishes he'd picked up from the French and British star hairdressers he emulated. It was weird. Strutting around like a bantam Mick Jagger, Vincent reflexively couldn't resist looking at himself in the mirror while he was doing his clients' hair. Pursing his lips in that way that everyone seems to think makes them look their sexy best, but to anyone else, only looks insane. Walking through the salon like the duke of some country I'd never heard of, smoking Merits, playing air guitar or drums intermittently while, again, half glancing at his reflection in the floor-to-ceiling mirrors. I thought, "Who is this freak? This skinny Italian guy totally thinks he's some kind of rock star." I just wanted his eyes on me and for him to fucking fix me already.

Vincent started to roughly comb my hair in front of my face, so I couldn't see anything through the blindfold of sopping wet hair. Then he suddenly became very stern, like I was maybe in trouble or something, or he was about to perform a risky surgery, ordering me to, "Sit up straight," "Chin down," "Uncross your legs," "Don't move." I nervously obeyed, holding my breath in the hopes that this major storm of hair flying around me would not end up being something I would regret for a long time to come.

He would occasionally stop and assess his handiwork, putting his face up close to mine, looking at us both in the mirror, murmuring, "*Beauuu-ty,*" and then he'd mess my hair up again. The more he cut, the more into me he seemed. Like he was Michelangelo removing everything that wasn't the *David,* that is, if *David* was a Jewish girl in 1976. He would grab fistfuls of my curls, roughly finger my bangs to frame my face, then he'd measure the sides, double-checking for evenness with his pointy chin balancing on the top of my head. When he was satisfied, he made it clear he had done me a major solid, telling me I'd "never looked this good," then he winked at me as he fired up another Merit with his Bic lighter, moving on to his next client.

I had to admit, this dude was not wrong. I had never entertained that a haircut could so dramatically reinvent my whole look. The way he'd layered my natural curls was a radical change for the better, plus it was wash 'n' wear—I would never have to blow-dry my hair again.

A few days later, ol' Scissorhands treated me to a tortellini dinner at Fiorello's, across from Lincoln Center, which was conveniently a block from his high-rise one-bedroom. I remember Vincent marveling at his own handiwork while fucking me on that first date, impressed with how his layers framed my face in every position. He was simply giving it up to himself, admiring his artistry, but for me, essentially a kid, that was okay by me. The intensity of his attention made me feel the closest I'd ever felt to being a *Vogue* model, even if I was just the vehicle, a walking wig stand, to advertise his skills.

When I left his apartment that night, I remember thinking, "Well . . . that happened." In the taxi ride home, I felt like I carried within me these still-smoking, glowing embers, in possession of a fire so hot, a kind of power that set me apart from my high school girl-friends. At the time I thought I'd probably never see him again, at least until I needed a bang trim. But surprisingly, Vincent became my boyfriend for the next two-plus years.

Pretty regularly I'd go out to Studio 54 (but no one cool ever called it that, we said either Studio *or* 54) with my hairdresser boy-friend, who I was basically living with. I would try to get whatever homework I had done at his apartment, then take a nap. After a light dinner, the preparations for the night out began, which was a bit of an ordeal. Quite a bit of thought went into the outfit (see: costume) for that evening's festivities, and the elaborate pro-level makeup and hair styling would complete the look.

The night would begin at Vincent's boss, Enzo's, modern high-rise apartment on 58th Street and the East River in a building called the Sovereign, where Calvin Klein also lived. The usual crew consisted of the other stylists from the salon—including iconic makeup artist Sandy Linter, big-time fashion photographers, *Vogue* editor Vera Wang (who'd years later design my off-the-rack wedding dress). I mean, c'mon! What's more fun than that for a sixteen-year-old girl? Fuck math. Fuck astronomy and fuck the French Revolution in its face!

We'd start the night snorting rails of coke off the stainless steel coffee table or a passed silver tray using someone's rolled-up hundred-dollar bill. We'd drink champagne or red wine, pass joints (that good sticky Thai stick), and everyone chain-smoked cigarettes. Once we were fully locked and loaded, we'd pile into a fleet of taxis to head across town to 54.

Before even getting out of the cab, you could feel the city block quaking with frenetic energy and the insistent throb of the bass pounding like thunder into your nether regions. No sooner had our gang snaked its way into the dense dressed-to-kill throng of hopefuls, tightly holding on to each other's hands in single file like preschoolers (or a monkey chain), than the packed crowd parted, as Mark, the charmless power broker behind the velvet rope, waved us in.

Once past the burly bodyguards flanking the swinging doors, upon hearing whatever song happened to be playing, despite the initial shock of ear-splitting decibels, whether it was The Trammps' "Disco Inferno," "Push, Push in the Bush," Grace Jones, or Sylvester, we knew them all. If it was one of my particular faves, not wanting to miss it, I'd break into as much of a jog as my stilettos would allow and wedge myself into my tiny plot of dance floor before the song was over.

We'd stay out till the wee small hours, dancing with abandon in the mob scene, soaked in sweat, only intermittently and, when absolutely necessary, idling just to the side of the dance floor long enough to have a few drags off a cigarette or joint, a hit of coke, or to throw back a cocktail from one of the shirtless waiters in micro gym shorts. I'd pop into the ladies' room, with *all kinds of ladies* filing out of the stalls like a conga line, to reapply my lip gloss, attempt to touch up the smudged kohl ringing my eyes, primp the wet ringlets now glued to my face, then jump back into the fray.

Just as the sun was beginning to think about rising, my limbs rubbery as Gumby, I'd limp barefoot out of the club, my feet swollen and filthy, soothed by the ice-cold concrete of the sidewalk, my torturous bronze Charles Jourdan strappy sandals hooked on my index finger. We'd go for breakfast at our regular after-hours spot, Ruskay's, on Columbus Avenue, where whoever had left the club with us would collapse in a booth, gobble up eggs, toasted English muffins, and coffee as the sky began to brighten. Vincent and I would slink back to his apartment to shower, and I'd get ready for school.

Looking back, so many disturbing images flash in my mind, a montage of depravity, of putting myself in harm's way, in way over my head. One night, lying on Enzo's shiny black marble bathroom floor after eating hash brownies and unable to lift my head, I made a pact with God as I pictured my poor parents' heartbreak and shock in hearing the news of my pitiful demise.

How does such a darling girl, growing up with all her earthly needs met, adored by her parents, a girl with so much spunk and moxie, find herself in situations I wouldn't wish on my worst enemy? The adults not on the receiving end of my risky behaviors were, I'm sure, scared for me. My parents didn't really have any idea of the kind of trouble I was up to, and though they weren't thrilled about my current romantic situation, they didn't feel like they had any recourse. Plus Vinny was very charming with them and cut their hair for free. Yes, his haircuts were that good.

When I try to imagine my own daughter at sixteen, playing house, essentially living with a grown-ass man, doing tons of blow, popping Quaaludes, and going to Studio—not to mention being lied to, cheated on, then gifted with various and sundry STDs and unwanted pregnancies, it makes me feel physically ill. No teenager should be swimming in waters that dark, at the mercy of grown men who know better, but when you're a sixteen-year-old girl, nobody's going to tell you to put your clothes on and go home to your parents. Well, the predators certainly won't. Yet I saw *myself* as the predator and the men as my targets. I ferreted out trouble.

In rereading my deeply personal, raw, unexpurgated journals, I only now realize I survived these soul-crushing indecencies by minimizing them, dusting off my broken self, thinking, "Hey, I brought this on myself." I thought I could handle some of the gnarliest, most messed-up shit. In retrospect that naïveté simply breaks my heart for my younger self. I thought of myself as an adult. The last thing I wanted to be was a child.

10

Acting "As If"

I may have been the only one in my entire graduating class at Dalton who had zero aspirations about going off to college. I felt I had already wasted too much time and enough of my parents' money doing the least possible amount of work in high school. Which pains me from where I sit now, but back then, I had been pretty beaten up by the academic rigors and had no clue as to why this highly competitive prep school had not been the right fit for me. The support of a really good tutor or educational therapist probably would have done wonders for me, not to mention some ADHD medication, but we didn't know about that stuff then. I had started out as such a bright and hardworking kid, a committed pleaser and perfectionist, so that early on, my issues in school hadn't presented in ways that would've sent up flares.

While all my high school friends were fretting over their SAT scores and application essays, I struck a deal with my parents that in lieu of college I would enroll in a full-time conservatory to study acting.

Billy DeAcutis, one of my close pals from the mosh pit that was New York, was in his first year in the acting program at Juilliard and offered to help me prepare both the classical and contemporary monologues for my audition. I was flatly rejected—on two separate occasions, six months apart.

Only now, looking back, can I see how delusional I had been. The hubris and cluelessness of youth! To think I could simply commit to memory an *As You Like It* monologue, have my pal give his "notes," and assume that the premier acting conservatory in America would fling open its doors to welcome the glory of me. I had zero experience doing Shakespeare, and no idea what it meant to be prepared for an audition at that level. What I did notice, in the wake of those rejections, was that there seemed to be a "look" that Juilliard had a penchant for. There was an Anglo type, a vocal quality, and carriage that seemed to be their ideal for doing Ibsen, Chekhov, and Shakespeare.

By high school graduation, when all my friends knew what colleges they would be attending, I was still unsure where I was going to be come fall. Fortuitously, that summer I was accepted into the Neighborhood Playhouse School of the Theatre. I was the youngest person admitted into the program. Most of my classmates had already spent at least some time in college. The Playhouse was a full-time, nine-to-five, five-days-a-week, *potentially* two-year program. Just as when my mom went there, the first-year class was made up of a hundred students, with only twenty-five "invited back."

The curriculum at the Playhouse was rounded out with classes in speech, Linklater voice work, along with dance classes and movement for actors. But the primary focus was on getting a solid foundation of the Meisner technique. There was the fundamental "repetition exercise" that Sandy Meisner, who founded the Playhouse, had invented, which was designed to force you to take the focus off yourself and put it 100 percent on your partner, which would eventually train you to "really listen to" and "work off" the other person. The *reality of doing* puts your focus on whatever you're doing. Everything was designed to get you out of your head, hence freeing you of self-consciousness (the enemy of good acting). Meisner said, "Acting is doing. Meaningful acting is *doing* under emotional circumstances. Acting is the ability to live truthfully under given imaginary circumstances."

Meisner's strategy was to first rid the student of any misguided ideas or bad acting habits picked up from bogus high school or college productions. His style, which set the tone for his protégés, was Draconian, and involved "breaking you down" when necessary, which sometimes meant humiliating you in front of the class, rendering you, in this shattered state, more malleable and teachable. Meisner would say, "You can't learn to act unless you're criticized. If you tie that criticism to your childhood insecurities, you'll have a terrible time. Instead, you must take criticism objectively, pertaining it only to the work being done."

By the time I became a student at the Playhouse, Meisner had retired and was living on the island of Bequia in the Grenadines. But even from that distance his presence loomed large. Our teachers—his protégés—quoted him daily, like he was the patron saint of actors. It was never *not* terrifying when it was your turn to "go up" in front of the class, whether it be for the teacher to prove a point, to do an exercise with a partner, or to present a scene. No one was safe from being torn to shreds.

When I was the one in the crosshairs of this ego-shattering event, it felt like I was getting mugged, but from the safety of my folding chair in the audience, when watching the teacher mercilessly go after one of my classmates who was unknowingly doing some "bad acting," this correction, as brutal as it was, somehow seemed to justify the means. Inevitably, this devastated student became more beautiful, more real, instantly more compelling. If you could take what they were dishing out, the reward was doing good work.

My own mother had not been able to take it. The story about how she'd walked out of the Playhouse never to return was part of our family lore. I asked her years later if she regretted having left. She did.

She wondered why she hadn't been able to walk back through those doors. As a kid, I remember thinking, "If someone had said that to me, I wouldn't have quit." And then, there I was. This hazing was not for sissies. The Playhouse did not play.

It was a morning class. I was standing center stage, facing the three tiers of wooden platforms crowded with metal folding chairs that lined the back wall. The teacher sat behind an imposing wooden desk off to one side so he could be seen by both the person on stage and the other students leaning forward, hanging on to his every word.

My teacher, Bill Alderson, silently studying me and slowly rubbing his fastidiously groomed, big-boned head, asked in his robotic, gravelly voice, "Are you spoiled?"

You could see the pulse beating just above his cheap shirt collar and tie, as if he were in a coiled rage. I was wearing a pale pink T-shirt that I'd cut the ribbed neckline out of. It was stretched out and hung loosely around my collarbone, and I wore a long gold chain with a medallion of St. Genesius, the saint who protects actors, borrowed from my dad's armoire. I was feeling pretty good about myself, I thought. Then someone pulled the trapdoor.

"Am I spoiled?" I sputtered.

"Are you spoiled?" he repeated with calculated cool. I felt like he was going for my carotid artery. Surely, he saw on my face that I was trying not to react, not to cry. *No one had ever spoken that way to me.*

That I was the daughter of somebody famous preceded me into every room, without my permission, without having anything to do with me. Always somebody's daughter first, never myself. Was being my dad's daughter the most valuable thing about me? At the Playhouse, my snake of a teacher hissed confidently, looking for his target, my profound and secret stash of shame and worthlessness. Bull's-eye. Knowing what he was trying to get me to do didn't alleviate the horror, but I refused to let him win, and met him head-on, intent on proving him wrong about his shitty assumptions, that I had grit.

In some ways that autumn, my first semester at the Playhouse, my life went on as it had been before. I was living back at my parents' apartment, without a boyfriend for the first time in years. On Saturdays I worked as a salesgirl at Henri Bendel in the women's clothing department, I took singing lessons and dance classes a few times a week after school, and I'd see my friends from Dalton whenever they came home on their school breaks.

At the Playhouse, the youngest in my class, I regularly struggled with feeling less than. I wasn't with other teenagers, a coddled freshman in some sweet college town, but in New York City, studying among adults, getting the shit beat out of me by teachers who wore psychological brass knuckles.

That program was the hardest thing I had ever done. The pressure was great. Every exercise. Every scene. You did not want to fuck up. If you didn't do the work, it was obvious to everyone. Every day was brutal. And exciting. And I was committed to it. I was willing to put myself in the eye of the storm because, having drunk the Kool-Aid, I believed in the goal. As deeply as I feared the emotional flogging in the name of making me into the kind of actor I wanted to be, I preferred the thrashing to being a shit actor. I was not going to be cowed by the fight I was having with my own ego. I wanted for myself what Meisner's gospel wanted for me.

The school's expectations around being on time, being prepared, and not making excuses were serious. Being held to these high standards was good for me. I liked the structure and the boundaries. I was a different kind of student here. I would never have dreamed of cutting class; I was always prepared. It never got easier, but I never stopped wanting to get it right. If I could hang on, I knew I could leave there with a tool kit that would get me where I wanted to go. They made it very clear that once we left the Playhouse, more often than not we would be left on our own, as good directors and good material were the anomalies. The realities of the business would conspire to make it easier for us to do bad acting, instilling in me a very real fear of this slippery slope.

The Playhouse enforced a strict edict, forbidding students from taking any acting jobs, or even auditioning, until they had graduated from the two-year program, and if you didn't comply with this rule, you were instantly expelled. They didn't want their students falling prey to "outside influences." The Meisner technique and its tough love not only trained us to be truthful as actors, it prepared us for the blistering rejection that lay ahead. The message was, "If you can't stomach what we're dishing out here, you'll never make it in this business. And the sooner you find out, the better."

Back when I was in high school, and my parents first let me go out on auditions set up by Marje Fields, I tried out for dopey commercials and even dopier soap operas, but I didn't care. I felt so grown-up and beyond cool to be one of these young women seated on the folding chairs lining the hallways of ad agencies. Those waiting areas were jammed to the gills with the competition, all studying "the copy," holding their black-and-white glossies with résumés stapled to the back. As I snuck glances, I marveled at how they could come up with so much to type there, seeing as how hard it was for me to think of anything at all to put on mine beneath the letterhead from my agency. They must've started as babies.

Each arrival stepped out of the elevator dressed in her professional finery, the tidy, conventional outfits you'd see girls wearing in commercials, one step down from what would be fitting to wear to church. Needless to say, I didn't have much in the way of those looks in my wardrobe.

Until then, for the most part I had felt pretty good about myself, as attractive as was necessary. I had no problem with not being the prettiest girl in the room, but those auditions were a fresh hell. In these clusterfucks of young professional actresses, I understood, for the first time, feeling "other." They all resembled the squeaky-clean girls you'd see in print ads, commercials, or sitcoms, like they were made in the same factory that made Marcia Brady. Then there were the more modely-looking ones, made by the Brooke Shields fabricators. I felt like some weirdo, an interloper crashing their pretty-girl party.

As I looked around, I began to realize I'd never seen a girl who looked anything like me in a commercial, or in a print ad for that matter. Then what were my chances? What was I even doing there? While I didn't particularly care for that look, I *was* fascinated by the symmetry of their features, how they were just born that way with all their pieces fitting together so perfectly. As a way to comfort myself, or just to keep myself going, I began to seed this secret feeling of superiority, a belief that somehow I was in fact cooler *because* of my difference.

When I'd hear my name called, I'd march toward the casting assistant with the clipboard, determined to defy the odds as she led me down the hall to a cramped office where they'd hung a roll of seamless background paper to create a makeshift studio. I'd "slate"—stand on the line of gaffer's tape, look into the camera, smile, state my name, height, agent—and then we'd read the copy. Corny, old-school commercial material, artificial and mind-numbingly inane. In the brief time allotted, I'd try to impress upon the huddle of others in the shadows that I was the kind of person they'd probably want to be friends with. I was so much more human than those robots out there in the waiting area.

I never booked a job. *Ever.* I just kept getting rejected, but like those Rock 'Em Sock 'Em Robots, or the inflatable clown you'd punch in the face that just reflexively bounced back up, I never tired of the thrill of possibility, the hope that one day I would be "the one" they were looking for.

I knew then that my nose was most likely an issue, but since I was never going to have surgery, I was just gonna have to wait 'em out. I figured it was a numbers game, so I just kept slugging. My nose was never anything I could really experience firsthand unless it was in photographs. It's a perspective thing, like when you're looking everywhere for your misplaced glasses that're stuck on your head. Your eyes, being situated on either side of your nose, are by design focusing ahead of you, so the nose—I can only speak for *my own* nose—was right smack in the middle of my blind spot. Out of sight, out of mind. I would forget about it because I couldn't see it. Unless I was seeing it reflected back to me through the eyes of another.

Both of my parents had fixed their noses before I was born. I can't remember ever *not* knowing they had had them done. My mother told me she'd gotten a nose job because she "wanted to be an actress." She was beautiful, and her new, and I guess improved, nose looked like it very well could've sprouted from her face of its own accord. She was striking, with blue eyes, silky dark hair, a gorgeous smile with big white teeth, and a petite, shapely body. If she was insecure about her looks, as a kid I was not aware of it. Her new nose felt so natural to her it was like she'd forgotten she'd ever had a different one.

I never knew my dad with his original nose, either. And on my father's side of the family, the nose jobs went back even a generation further. My grandmother, my great-aunt, pretty much all the gals, had acquired diminutive noses, obviously the preferred style in the fifties.

Thinking about it now, I can't help but notice that the roles my dad was being cast in were decidedly *not* Jewish. The part he became most identified with, the Master of Ceremonies in *Cabaret,* was most likely a Nazi, or Nazi adjacent. His character personified the decadence and darkness lurking at the epicenter of Nazi Germany, obviously a role he would never have been cast in if he'd looked Jewish. In one of the musical numbers from *Cabaret,* a seemingly whimsical, lighthearted love song, "If You Could See Her Through My Eyes," my dad's character beseeches the audience to understand his unlikely and undying love for the oversized, girly gorilla he is waltzing with. Watching the stage version as a little kid, I was only enchanted by my dad's brilliant theatrical antics and showmanship. But by the time Bob Fosse directed the film, the lyrics of the song were changed, delivering the knockout blow as my dad hisses maniacally into the camera, "If you could see her through my eyes . . . she wouldn't look *Jewish* at all." It's a pivotal moment, when the audience realizes the insidiousness of normalizing this conceit: that Jews are the definition of ugly.

How deep the vilification, to be the *punch line* of such a joke.

———

Once I hit puberty, and even more so when I began to think about pursuing a career as an actor, I found myself supremely distracted, basically *consumed* by assessing peoples' noses. This was not a conscious choice. I certainly did not want this issue to loom so large.

From what I could tell, my dad's amended profile afforded him and his career much improved latitude and range. But having spent years adoring his face, studying the evenhanded distribution of his features, I had made a mental note that while his nose fit his face to perfection, I did not want that for myself.

If I'm being really honest, I had developed a quiet disdain for people who chose the plastic surgery route. If I, or anyone, chose to get a nose job, I interpreted it as a tell. A sign of weakness, lack of character, evidence of their low self-esteem and desperation, to throw ones's Self under the bus in the hopes of an upgrade.

In my parents' cases, my theory did not apply. Theirs was a very different time—the obligatory cultural assimilation was on trend and necessary—but I held myself to a different standard. As part of the next, more evolved generation, I shunned such self-inflicted transgressions, and I rejected outright the implied anti-Semitism. My taking this stand clashed badly with another part of me that knew, in no uncertain terms, that what people looked like and what they chose to change or not change about themselves was nobody's fucking business but their own. This same part of me was determined to hold my ground. I was actually making a case for myself, resolute about never succumbing to peer pressure or groupthink.

I felt this covert shame for having such a lame mission, which felt embarrassingly almost political, like my identity and character were somehow riding on it. My job was to show the world that I was enough as I was, and to ultimately believe and feel that myself. Since all I wanted to do was be an actor, I would just have to man up and suffer however much relentless rejection would be heaped upon me and keep going. Committing to myself, accepting, and loving myself as I was born.

I kept searching for role models in movies and on television, for actresses with prominent noses who'd been able to break through. There was Barbra Streisand, a giant star with a big nose, the only Jewish movie star I knew of growing up.

"Honey, she had a major singing career first," my mother said.

"What about Cher?"

"Also, a singer. And don't forget, she had Sonny."

Then, in my sophomore year of high school, a young actress came on the scene, recently sprung from the Yale School of Drama, who, in her first year in the city (three years before I began classes at the Playhouse), played six female leads in six different major theatrical events with every one of her performances earning rave reviews. She was even nominated for a Tony. As far as everyone in the know was concerned, Meryl Streep was the Messiah. She was everything my parents hoped I'd be.

And this Meryl had a prominent nose.

I could barely notice her brilliance, barely be wowed by her seemingly infinite range. I couldn't see that she was the second coming. All I saw was that beautiful, aquiline, prominent nose.

11

When My Baby Goes to Rio

It was the winter of my first year at the Playhouse, five months out of high school. I'd broken up with Vincent, the hairdresser, and was living full-time back at home with my parents, my brother, and Nellie on Fifth Avenue.

I had met and started dating a guy named Patrice de la Falaise, a thirty-nine-year-old filmmaker who had just broken up with the wild older sister of a friend of mine, a huge presence in my small world. A bed still warm from this spectacular woman was incentive enough for me; I was thrilled to pitch my tent wherever she'd recently been. Patrice, who would later become an architect as well as a filmmaker, was from a wealthy and industrious French family transplanted from Luxembourg to Dallas in the forties, bringing high art and progressive political ideas to Texas. The de la Falaises weren't just major collectors and patrons, they were known as the Medicis of modern art.

I met Patrice at a party, I don't remember exactly where. He was as close to European royalty as I had ever encountered. He lived in a townhouse on the Upper East Side, and on the walls hung some of the most important art I'd ever seen outside of a museum. While he was by far the wealthiest person I'd ever been intimate with—or had probably even shaken hands with—he was nonetheless decidedly low-key. Soft-spoken, with an enigmatic confidence. He had a mop of curly, brown, unkempt hair parted on the side. He wore aviator sunglasses, a Saint Laurent blazer over a silk shirt, Levi's, and cowboy boots. With Patrice, I was on an exploratory mission. Perhaps I had been shortsighted, rash in unfairly writing off the very rich just because of their bank accounts. To this day, wealth is probably the last thing that rings my must-have bell. I've always had a penchant for grittier types, as long as they are charismatic and ooze untapped genius.

When I met Patrice, I had been having an affair—if you can call what I'm about to describe an affair—with an out-of-work actor who'd attended the Playhouse a few years before but was still living in his hovel down the block from the school. One morning, walking down 54th Street between First and Second avenues on my way to class, I clocked this guy in his midtwenties, hunched over on a stoop, smoking a cigarette, and sipping coffee out of one of those blue-and-white deli cups. He was wearing Levi's and Converse high-tops, his muscled arms and back conspiring with a thin, faded T-shirt to drive a red-blooded woman insane. His hair hung messily over one side of his face like it could give two shits. Clearly he'd just rolled out of bed, his hooded blue eyes still adjusting to the daylight kinda squinted up at me as he took a long drag off his cigarette and gave a half smile as I walked past him. I could see a gap between his front teeth just beyond his pillowy lips, and I felt his eyes burning into the back of me as I kept a pace, looking straight ahead, my pulse quickening, blood vessels expanding.

I signed in once inside the entrance of school, turned around, and made a beeline back down the street to sit alongside this sleepy sex machine on his stoop, the smoke curling around him in the rays of morning light. I introduced myself, and hearing his voice, as low as thunder, I knew I was cooked. A few hours later, I saw my name scrawled on a folded scrap of paper left under the glass just inside the entrance of the school where students left messages for each other, with just his apartment number.

We'd fuck periodically during my lunch break on a mattress on the floor of his studio apartment. In lieu of postcoital cuddling, he would take these huge ornate Japanese swords down off the wall and perform some psycho martial art, slicing and dicing the musky, smoky, postsex air, while I lay on the mattress beneath this well-endowed madman, feigning awe at his swordplay.

With Patrice, I was hoping to be turned on by someone who had a more reasonable lifestyle, even though the sex was muted by comparison to my down-and-dirty lunch beast. Patrice was not really my type, but I was trying to broaden my reach, and I enjoyed being courted by this elegant, hard-to-read cat.

Coke was everywhere back in those days in New York. But the nose candy was super expensive, so I couldn't buy it myself. Looking back, I think it's pretty safe to say cocaine played a pivotal role in my relationship with this guy, though at the time I was too coked up to make that connection. It was different doing blow with someone like Patrice; it felt more refined, snorted discreetly, neatly set up in fat rails on the gorgeous leather desk of his sumptuously appointed home office. Cocaine had a habit of exponentially enhancing the talking portion of any personal connection. Whoever you were doing the coke with became infinitely more fascinating.

Patrice was inviting me to be his date to whatever was the A-list, happening place to be on any given night, at a time when the city was as electrifying as it's ever been. Our first date was a press screening of *The Deer Hunter*. Other nights we'd dine at Parma (which would later become Elio's), the clubby Italian restaurant on the Upper East Side that was like Elaine's but with better food. There were gallery openings with the Warhol gang, and he was chummy with the *Saturday Night Live* people, specifically with Lorne Michaels himself.

A few weeks after we'd begun seeing each other, Patrice invited me to come to Rio de Janeiro, where he'd rented a house for the Christmas holidays. Initially, I declined, because we'd only been dating for a short time, but after some long-distance coaxing from my new beau, already ensconced in Brazil, I decided, "Oh, what the hell!" And Patrice's office sent over a first-class round-trip ticket.

When I told my parents that I'd changed my mind and would be joining Patrice in Rio as I had nothing better to do over the vacation and it was such an incredible opportunity, they promptly forbade me to go. I can't remember exactly what transpired then, except that the conversation suddenly escalated into a vein-popping screaming match between my father and me. My mother helplessly stood by, unsuccessfully trying to extinguish the flames of this grease fire that threatened to engulf their lovely apartment. I shrieked at them in a full-blown, repulsive teenage tantrum that surprised even me.

"You can't tell me what I can or can't do. I'm eighteen years old!"

I may even have thrown in a good old-fashioned "FUUUUCK you!" to really secure my position as every parent's worst nightmare, emptying my chambers of rebellious toxic rage as a cornered skunk expels its noxious fumes.

Surprised I hadn't burst every blood vessel in my head from the forceful exertion of my autonomy, I stormed out with a few items thrown into a bag: string bikini, cover-up, shorts, flip-flops, twenty-dollar bill, and my Varig Airlines ticket. It was the old kind of ticket, a rectangular flimsy booklet of multicolored, superthin sheets, one for each leg of the trip.

The flight departure time was late in the evening, which only added allure and sophistication to the adventure. As I settled into my luxurious and impossibly plush first-ever first-class airplane seat, pampered like an oversized royal baby, I excitedly set about outfitting myself in my adorable Varig socklets and trying all the little sample bottles of lotions and potions offered expressly with the jet set in mind. It seemed to me that these glorious extra little touches, along with the cigarettes I was chain-smoking and the unlimited free booze, were just what the doctor ordered to soothe my crackling nervous system.

I felt free from my overbearing parents, who I thought used my financial dependence to exert control over me. Well, I'd finally cut the strings, and was on my way to see my new man, who was richer than Croesus. Another way I might've looked at it, though of course I didn't at the time, was that my parents, while they got off light by not having to foot the bill for college, *were* paying for my drama school and allowing me to live rent-free with them in their apartment. If I was going to be living under their roof, it would not have been unreasonable to assume that I should abide by their rules. And how in the world could they not be completely terrified for me and my safety? At the time, I was unable to see their point of view and took zero responsibility for my part. (PS Dearest Mom and Dad, I am truly so incredibly sorry for what I put you through when I was a teenager. I know I've said it before, but it pains me, filling me with healthy shame every time I think about it.)

It was one of those overnight flights, so I took a Valium or something like that, drank wine or Jack Daniel's, and passed out. (By the way, do NOT do that.) Those intercontinental night flights have a particular vibe. Shuttling through the inky black sky into eternity. Chock-full of humans, pretending, en masse, that it's normal to be trapped in a metal capsule flying over the ocean. Right up against total strangers, drooling and snoring as if asleep at home in their beds.

But the morning was as heavenly as the night was dystopian. With the new dawn streaming into the cabin, which last appeared shrouded in darkness and artificial light, one can almost hear the angels singing amid the gentle clatter of porcelain coffee cups and saucers. I was awoken by the heavenly aroma of freshly brewed coffee. In first class, a bevy of beautiful Brazilian stewardesses, like sky nannies, served up an actually delectable breakfast.

I freshened up with the goodies from my travel kit, brushing my teeth with extra vigor with the doll-sized toothbrush and toothpaste, anticipating my arrival in Brazil, the capital of hedonism, knowing nothing more than the cliché of hot-blooded Latin lovers.

When I stepped off the plane, Patrice met me at the gate looking relaxed, tan, and happy to see me. He'd already lost his winter pallor, having dropped into a laid-back, beachy vacation mode. This was *definitely* the right decision. The hot Brazilian sun was blazing as we jumped into his red convertible sports car and began the dramatic drive up into the mountains, arriving at the palatial villa with a breathtaking view of the ocean.

Patrice had invited two other friends from New York. The tall, socialite, downtown gadfly writer, Chase Schermerhorn, and his fashion model girlfriend, Suzi Quant. I remember her saying, as she admired my pretty petite feet at poolside, that I "could probably be a foot model." Uh, gee. Thanks?

Patrice showed me to our bedroom, and after a quick make-out session, we got ready for the beach. Before leaving, we snorted the purest cocaine straight out of the bulging sandwich-sized Baggie that sat on the dining table in the living room, as casual as a sugar bowl.

The four of us took off for the famed Ipanema Beach. It was super crowded, but crowded with people who were hot as fuck. We set up our towels, enjoying the view, and to me, an American teenager, these Brazilians were more than living up to their reputations. Their bodies were better than I'd imagined, their bikinis so small I wondered what the point was.

We hadn't been there very long when out of nowhere a pack of wild dogs descended upon us. All four of us jumped up, screaming, terrified, trying to fend them off with our towels and kicks. We quickly hightailed it back to the car in a cloud of sand and adrenaline.

Safely back at the house, we showered as the cooks prepared our dinner. We drank and ate what we could, though our enjoyment of the extraordinarily pure cocaine took a bit of the edge off our appetites.

I woke up the next morning to find my bed empty. It was almost

Christmas Eve, and as I got out of bed, I spotted a small, gift-wrapped box from Fred Leighton (the most incredible antique jewelry store located around the corner from Patrice's townhouse) in a half-open carry-on bag next to the dresser. I was never much of a jewelry hound, but I couldn't help but wonder if that perfect little square box perhaps contained a trinket for *moi?*

Still groggy from jet lag and the festivities from the night before, I wandered around in my underwear through the open-air, white-washed sprawl of the villa, a bit confused as to where everyone had gone. My voice echoed through the cavernous empty house. A warm breeze came in off the ocean as I looked everywhere for my guy. Or anybody.

At the table in the main hall, I saw the plastic bag of coke from the night before just sitting there, still swollen like a puppy's belly after a big feed. I proceeded to snort some of the greatest coke ever snorted, not even bothering to make lines, just sticking a rolled-up bill straight into the fluffy white powder, as we all had done the night before.

I didn't do much, but I didn't need much.

One of the cooks bid me good morning, and I assumed was offering to make me breakfast. As I spoke no Portuguese and she spoke no English, I asked if she wouldn't mind making me a Cachaça (the only Portuguese word in my vocabulary), Brazil's national cocktail, and now my new favorite morning beverage.

I drank the Brazilian rum with muddled lime, smoked a cigarette, and snorted a bit more coke, even though it wasn't really my drug of choice. I was always too anxious a person by nature. I preferred downers, like Quaaludes, to settle my nerves, plus I couldn't afford the expensive habit. But *this* coke was . . . it's hard to describe, except to say that it was just much, much better.

I heard something and looked to where the giant wooden front door had swung open. I squinted to make out the silhouette of a backlit group, my host and his houseguests. With the unbridled joy of a dog gazing at her returning master, I welcomed them home, asking where they'd been. It was then that I noticed some luggage, along with an addition to the gang. Turns out they'd been to the airport to pick up Gilda Radner, my idol, my queen, from *Saturday Night Live*. The four of them stood there in the doorway for a beat, Gilda's face as waxen as one of Madame Tussauds' replicas, clearly surprised to find a half-naked teenage nymphet throwing her arms around the host.

I, on the other hand, completely unaware of my nakedness (or was I just comfortable with my body?), was beyond excited to welcome our newest camper to this dream vacation that, to my mind, had gotten exponentially better with this greatest of surprise arrivals.

Everything suddenly slowed down, with the dawning realization that my comedy hero was perhaps less than happy to see me. With a sudden shift of energy, a bitter cold wind blew through the open-plan luxury destination. Within a split second, I was a paranoid, coked-up teenager, sleeping with a middle-aged man I barely knew. I had no idea what was going on. Nobody was explaining to me what had happened, but it was clear that I was stuck in some alternate reality, and no one had any intention of helping me out.

I put a shirt on. I did some more coke, smoked some more cigarettes, drank another Cachaça, smoked the joints being passed around, and tried with everything I had to regain Patrice's amorous gaze, or even catch his eye. I tried to convince myself that everything was cool, that I just needed to relax and that things weren't really as bad and weird as they seemed.

But I endured hours of the most wretched silent treatment, of trying to get Patrice to tell me what he was feeling, because if he was upset over something I'd done, I wanted to know. I wanted to fix it, but I couldn't reach him. He seemed made of stone. Hadn't he begged me to come all this way? Hadn't he seemed happy when I'd finally decided to come? I couldn't think of what I had done. If he wasn't going to look at me or talk to me, how was I supposed to know what was wrong, or how to make it better? It was super scary to be on the other side of the world, so far from home with only these grown-ups I really didn't know, who had all, on a dime, decided to ignore me.

Finally, Patrice begrudgingly intimated to me that perhaps my favorite funny lady of all time had mistakenly assumed his invitation to come to Brazil was one of a romantic nature. Oh great! But what did *I* do? Why was I being punished?

Once the cat was out of the bag, I was relieved to finally be let in on what had gone down, and I felt terrible for Gilda. I was sure we could all figure it out, or laugh about it, or something. But Patrice's disclosure to me didn't appear to alleviate any tension. They still seemed to be talking among themselves, nobody willing to let me back in.

I withdrew to our bedroom, where I lay in bed crying until my eyelids had swollen shut. I'd made a pact with myself to keep my face down in the sopping-wet pillow until Patrice came in, apologized up and down for being such a monster, and made everything all right again. He'd been so crazy for me only the night before, and now no one was talking to me. *Please, please, please make it go back to how it was before.*

After what felt like at least an hour of hard-core facedown crying, Patrice finally appeared and curtly announced, "Dinner is ready. Go splash some water on your face," and walked out. Not exactly the kind of sympathy or apology I had been holding out for.

With my head throbbing and unable to open my eyes, I had to literally *feel* my way, following the smooth stucco walls up the steps in the bathroom, designed on multiple levels, to make it to the sink. I splashed and splashed with the coldest water possible, trying to bring down the swelling. Eyes still sealed shut, I felt around for the plush white hand towel, and as I gently dabbed at my thickened rubbery eyelids, I noticed an odd, scratchy, prickly sensation. Like someone had left a squirt of dried toothpaste on the towel that I was now rubbing into my numb lids.

When I forced my slits open enough to assess what was what, all

I could make out was a blur—was it fur?—a colorful something. As I leaned in closer, straining to focus, I saw the yellow and black hair of a large tarantula, the size of the palm of my hand. I started screaming. I threw the towel with the drowsing spider still stuck to it to the stone floor.

Hearing my bloodcurdling cries echoing through the villa, Chase Schermerhorn came running, swinging his tennis racket, with the rest of the gang following suit like an episode of *Fawlty Towers,* except nobody was laughing.

After the dust had settled from this surreal chain of events, we sat down to dinner and Gilda made some crack about how she had planted the tarantula in my bathroom. And they all laughed.

After dinner, I wanted to talk to her and followed her into her room, to let her know that I felt terrible about what had happened. And that if she was interested in Patrice, she could have him. She was my last hope for some shred of human connection. And she was Gilda. Fucking. Radner. She, of all people, *had* to see the humor, the utter ridiculousness of the situation. She was someone I had idolized and *so* related to on *Saturday Night Live*. She was brilliant. And bananas in the best possible way. The most humiliating part of this whole drama was to find myself cast as the idiot bimbo. I was sure that in any other situation there was a good chance Gilda and I would be friends. I knew I was her kind of girl. I was sure of it.

I was hoping she'd say, "Oh, gurl! C'mon! Let's get outta here! The *fuck're* we doing with these people? They're nuts." And we'd escape this freak show, laughing all the way home. Friends for life.

Instead, Gilda began packing her suitcase while not really looking at me, assuring me she would be leaving for the airport in an hour.

I said, "Oh, no, no, no. Please. I beg you! *I'm* leaving. I *really* have to get out of here."

She insisted she was the one who'd be leaving and said something about how dumb she felt for having come in the first place.

I blurted out, "You can have him. I swear. I don't want him. I want to go home."

As she finished putting her things into her bag, she said, with remorse tinged with shame, "I have a really nice boyfriend back in New York. I don't even know why I came here. So I'm going to go back and be with him."

Gilda walked out of that very same large wooden door about twelve hours after she'd first walked in.

Patrice's icy demeanor remained unchanged by Gilda's departure. Later that night, I crawled into bed, disoriented and panicky, stuck in some horrible dream. I lay there in the darkness trying to think of something to say, hoping he would say *something*. Finally, I whispered that in the morning I wanted to fly back home.

The silence was deafening. He offered no rebuttal, no shred of leftover warmth. He wanted me to disappear, and figured if he ignored me, I'd eventually do just that. I was stranded in Rio de Janeiro on Christmas Eve, lying next to someone whose tides had changed, a stranger.

Without an ounce of protectiveness or the tiniest shred of compassion from any of these adults, I felt as alone as I'd ever been, with only my twenty-dollar bill and my return plane ticket to get me back to Kansas.

The following morning, my host drove me to the airport in silence. I never saw or heard from him again.

If I hadn't just been beaten to an emotional pulp, my collect call home from the airport pay phone, hysterically crying, begging my parents' forgiveness, would've been the worst fate and eating of crow to befall me. But considering the relentless mind fucking I'd just endured, it was nothing shy of manna from heaven to hear the soft comfort of my dad's voice behind the static of the overseas line. "It's okay, honey. Just come home. We're here. We'll see you soon. We love you."

When I got back to my parents' apartment, between the jet lag, coming off the coke bender, not to mention the emotional hangover, I became almost catatonic. It was the most depressed I'd ever felt.

I put the whole experience away in one of those hard-to-reach places in my unconscious, only occasionally pulling it out to share at parties. A crazy tale of my wild youth, rife with hair-raising details and boldfaced names, never once considering the ramifications, the psychic damage incurred. I just moved on, thinking, "I'm sure this kind of thing happens to everybody when they're young."

Twenty years later, I was hired to play Gene Wilder's wife in a pilot for a sitcom, and he told me that *Dirty Dancing* had been the one movie Gilda watched on a loop when she was going through her cancer treatments. I wondered what she'd made of that whole fiasco in Brazil, or if she even knew that Baby was the same tragic panty-clad teenager who'd stolen her billionaire in Rio. Who knows if she even remembered that whole debacle?

But, in the first days of 1979, a week after my forty-eight hours in Rio, battered and bludgeoned, I resumed classes at the Neighborhood Playhouse, where, in a few months, I would be asked back. I would go on to be their youngest graduate.

PART TWO

12

Reasons to Be Cheerful

My agent, Philip Carlson, toils in tight, airless quarters, walled in behind stacks of scripts, contracts, résumés, and a *Moon for the Misbegotten* coffee mug stuffed with dull pencils and leaky pens. I've stopped by to drop off an oversized envelope of my 8×10s to restock the agency's supply, and Philip tells me he's just received this casting breakdown for a *very* low-budget movie, with a part I could be "really right for."

Philip hands me the breakdown he's just read, and as I gaze down at the two stapled pages, reading the summary of the storyline and descriptions of the cast of characters, I almost can't believe what I'm seeing. Trying to refocus, blinking, my heart quickening, I distinctly think, "Is this really happening?" The description of the lead in the movie, the protagonist, reads as if it had been written for exactly me.

Okay, so the part was written as a seventeen-year-old, and I was now twenty-six. Also, she was a stone-cold virgin, and at this point I don't think I need to remind you that I was not. But aside from those two *minor* details, everything else was as if it had been written expressly with me in mind. I couldn't think of anyone else who would be more right for it, followed almost immediately by the thought, "If I don't get *this* one, I'm never gonna get *anything.*"

Both Baby (aka Frances Houseman) and I were raised in upper-middle-class, Jewish New York families. Both of us were born-and-bred daddy's girls. Baby's father was a successful family doctor, mine a revered actor. And like Baby's, my parents were liberals, passionate about social justice, pillars of their community. I was trained to be *just like them,* and to make sure to never embarrass them. I knew what it took to please them, and I wanted to. Like Baby, I, for a long time, didn't feel compelled to rebel, or even question my parents' authority, which was easy for the better part of my childhood, as they were pretty much perfect in my eyes. My family had been the nest I never, ever wanted to stray too far from.

"I thought I'd never meet a guy as great as my dad," Baby says as part of her opening monologue. I'd spent my youth feeling, and even saying, those same words. Like Baby, I'd taken certain pride in having never lied to my parents, well beyond the age where that was developmentally appropriate or considered cool.

My dad was my hero and he, in turn, idealized me, which was easy for me, good as I was at playing by the rules. But when I got older and would do something he didn't approve of, it didn't go so well. His tsunami of adoration would vanish. It was frightening and confusing to feel the balmy atmosphere suddenly frost over. Baby experiences that same big chill when she finds herself having to make the choice between her allegiance to her father and his polar opposite, in the form of an irresistibly smokin'-hot Adonis. Of course, her biology wins out. In the movie, as in life, when the body says it's *go* time, it's time to fly. Ya gotta fly, baby. Come what may.

The character of Frances "Baby" Houseman was decidedly more "interesting-looking" than traditionally pretty. It was actually a plot point. Not only was Baby Jewish, but she had to *look* Jewish (see: nobody this

Adonis of a sexy, gorgeous dance teacher would ordinarily ever look at twice). At the same time, she was the female lead of the movie. It was her story. So she'd have to be at least *somewhat* attractive for the movie to work, right? My girl, Baby, and I were like two peas in a pod.

It was uncanny the parallel lives Baby and I had been living, and not only were we similar to an almost ridiculous degree, but it was a love story, and its "love language" was dance. And it just so happened dance was one of *my* love languages! I was five years old when I started taking a ballet class in the studios next to Carnegie Hall. Just your Saturday morning kiddie class, nothing serious, but from then on, I was always going to some dance class or another. I would tirelessly try to coax and drag my girlfriends to come with me. I took tap, jazz, modern, and ballet from some of the greatest teachers in New York—the Alvin Ailey School, Broadway Dance Center, Finis Jhung, Maggie Black, and David Howard—and though I could never keep up with the "real dancers," I loved class just the same. I guess I had enough natural talent, or something, to blend in and not completely stick out.

Learning choreography was always my Achilles' heel. I'd take the barre right alongside some of the principal dancers from American Ballet Theatre and New York City Ballet, trying my best to pass for one of them. I'd study these beautiful silent waifs, emulating their every move. The proximity of these ballerinas' numinous energies to my body made it feel almost possible that I might receive a transmission of their virtuosity. Like Baby—mesmerized by the otherworldly grace of the dance pros Johnny and Penny doing their showstopping dance routine—I understood firsthand this deep longing, an almost animal hunger to be inside the experience of a great dancer, to live and breathe that rarified air.

As soon as the barre portion, maybe forty-five minutes into the hour-and-a-half class, was over, the dancers would reconfigure themselves in the center of the room to learn the adagio for that day or file into the corner to, one at a time, go across the floor. That was always the moment of truth for me.

My mom, as a young actress at the Playhouse, had Martha

Graham herself as her modern dance teacher. On one occasion, as their class was "going from the corner," the legend leaned into my mother, giving her own chest a hearty smack with the palm of her hand as she urged my mother to, "Cross the floor as if your heart is waiting for you on the other side."

While I never forgot that image and tried to use it to rouse my courage, every class I'd have to decide whether I should stay and suffer the potential humiliation of dancing solo across the room—or split. I almost always fled. Because you can't hide from dance. Dance can't help but reveal everything about you.

Perched on the arm of a dilapidated couch in my agent's tiny office, devouring every word of this mouthwatering breakdown, my mind racing, armpits tingling, I struggled to shush the stern schoolmarm of a voice reminding me of my already pretty long history of being disappointed. Who was I kidding? I was never going to *get* this. It was the lead, and I didn't get leads. And if I *did* get it, there was no way it was going to be any good. Not with a cheesy title like *Dirty Dancing*.

In October 1980, six years earlier and a few months out of the Playhouse, I'd auditioned for an Off-Broadway play called *Album,* to be directed by Joan Micklin Silver, who was hot off the movie *Hester Street*. It was a four-character play, divided into eight scenes, chronicling the coming of age of two teenage couples during the sixties, struggling with impending adulthood and their awakening sexuality. The music of Bob Dylan, the Beatles, and the Beach Boys served as the soundtrack of their last few carefree years together. Originally, I read for the part of the popular, pretty, stuck-up cheerleader. It was easy for me to embody the energy of that girl, and I could tell I did a really good job, yet I could also see in the director's eyes . . . this *look*. The "trying to fit a square peg into a round hole" look. After a beat, she perked up and said, "Hey! Why don't you have a look at this other part." Soon after, I effortlessly slipped into the skin of the quirky, insecure girl. Still, there was that look. Again.

Over time, I would become the master of reading this unspoken thought bubble, as it was the most consistent feedback I would receive for the lion's share of my auditioning years. Not quite "pretty enough" for the popular girl, but not awkward enough to pass for the loser. This neither/nor situation landed me the job of understudy for both parts in *Album*. I would most likely never get the chance to go on for either girl, my pay was less than half what a full-fledged cast member was paid, but I was totally psyched to book my first professional job.

The play was a hit, popular as well as critically acclaimed, and once it got the rave review from *The New York Times*, every show was sold out. The young actors were Kevin Bacon, Keith Gordon, Jenny Wright, and Jan Leslie Harding, all exceptionally good. I couldn't blame anyone for casting them.

Bruce MacVittie, the boys' understudy, and I were kept backstage for eight shows a week, until maybe a half hour before the curtain came down, just in case one of the actors fell sick during a performance. In a windowless prop storage room that stank of cat piss, Bruce and I were to run lines, a speed-through of the entire play, each playing two parts. From the purview of our peeling vinyl couch, we could hear the actors on stage delivering the dialogue we'd been reciting, interrupted by howls of laughter and the crack of applause through the scratchy backstage monitor.

Not long after that rave review in the *Times,* Jenny Wright called in sick thirty minutes before curtain for a packed Saturday night house. I had never before set foot on any stage in front of a paying audience, nor had I ever even tried on the costumes or rehearsed with the actors. But there I was, standing in Jenny's dressing room with someone furiously safety-pinning her white denim shorts on me while the stage manager, script in hand, drilled me on my lines with the ferocity of a ball machine. This frenzy of theatrical paramedics followed me down the stairs and into the wings until I was thrust out onto the stage, where the three main actors took over, nudging me to and fro, like wide-eyed, slightly panicked shepherds. In this haze of adrenaline overload, I had my first out-of-body experience. Years later, I would understand this to be a

kind of panic attack, a disassociated state that feels like you've gone
suddenly mad, where everything looks distorted and unfamiliar. At one
point I remember looking down at these strange, unfamiliar white
shorts and wondering whose legs those were.

I got through the performance fueled by enough stress-induced
chemicals that I could've easily lifted a car off a child. After the curtain, the cast and crew gathered for a victory lap at Montana Eve
around the corner, where we did tequila shots, toasting and celebrating our shared near-death experience by getting pretty loaded. I later
went home to my fourth-floor walk-up studio apartment above the
Madison Avenue Bookshop and promptly got wicked sick.

I knew how unusual and lucky it was that my very first gig was
this long-running, popular, and critically acclaimed Off-Broadway
show, working with, if not directly, this bunch of wildly talented people at the historic Cherry Lane Theatre in Greenwich Village. It was
not an easy job, or particularly satisfying on the ol' ego front, but I
learned a lot from the experience, and it got me my Actors' Equity
card. After I waited for the better part of a year for the chance to
finally replace one of the girls, the producers asked me to be in a
Chicago production of *Album,* playing the awkward one (pictured

here with, from left to right, Adam Baldwin, Megan Mullally, the playwright David Rimmer, and Alan Ruck).

My next big break came in 1982, back in New York. I'd just come home from my busboy shift at the Cottonwood Café, when I received a phone call that made me feel like my head was going to explode from excitement. My good friend, the wonderful casting director Gretchen Rennell, was calling to ask me for a favor. The next day, Francis Ford Coppola was going to hear the cast do the first read-through of his next movie, *The Cotton Club*. But Diane Lane, one of the leads, was stuck on location, shooting *Streets of Fire,* which had gone over schedule. Gretchen asked if I wouldn't mind helping out by coming to Kaufman Astoria Studios in Queens the next morning to read the Diane Lane part opposite Richard Gere. The rest of the cast was extraordinary—Gregory Hines, Lonette McKee, Gwen Verdon, Bob Hoskins, Maurice Hines, Tom Waits, Fred Gwynne, Laurence Fishburne, Giancarlo Esposito, Honi Coles, and more, if you can believe it, as well as Francis's teenage nephew, Nicolas Cage.

The cast was like a legend lasagna, layer upon layer of geniuses. From the crème de la crème of gangster types, to the best choreographers, to tap dance royalty. There was no performer alive who wasn't dying to work with Francis at that time. The jazz music, dance, and vocals of the Cotton Club would serve as the backdrop for parallel Black and white love stories. An ambitious movie musical period piece meets *The Godfather,* with the ample budget necessary to make it all happen.

Before the read-through on the soundstage, at least fifty people had gathered nervously around a series of very long folding tables pushed end to end, while big daddy Francis held court. He announced that the script was very much a "work in progress" and that he would be relying heavily on improvisation to flesh out the story in the weeks of rehearsal leading up to the start of principal photography. He explained that we'd be reading through the script, and then immediately following lunch, he would start rehearsing scenes with the cast. He planned to videotape the rehearsals, so by the time filming began in earnest, he could cut together the footage to use as a blueprint for the film.

What Francis described that morning was—and I think I speak for most actors in the eighties—a thespian's Nirvana. After the extraordinary achievement of *The Godfather* and the legendary fallout from *Apocalypse Now*, this irrepressible auteur was due for another big win. To be a part of his comeback movie would be the greatest opportunity and honor.

When the table read was over, they broke for lunch, and having served my purpose for being there, I sadly took that as my cue to leave. I was packing up my gear to jump on the subway back to Manhattan just as everyone else was about to embark on the creative adventure of a lifetime, when the assistant director informed me that I needed to stay to play Diane's part until she could join the production, which they hoped would be any day now.

Lunch was the fanciest catered meal I have ever seen on any movie set to date: tablecloths, silverware, crystal, china, wine— a proper Italian meal. After lunch, I was used as a human love prop, a stand-in for the romantic interest of Richard Gere, who in the year of *An Officer and a Gentleman* was every living being's erotic fantasy man. In other scenes, whenever they needed a white female body, I was game and joined the improv party, eager to be whatever Francis needed me to be.

For weeks, it was more of the same. Time was elastic in Francis's world. When they started filming, the enormous cast was brought in and put into "the works," full hair and makeup, dressed in their elaborate twenties costumes every single day for months on end. It wasn't unusual to sit around the actors' holding area, all dressed up with nowhere to go, just hanging out waiting to be used by Francis, and then at the end of the day to be released. He seemed to want everyone there in readiness, just in case he got inspired so he could pick up that doll and throw it into his dollhouse. The sequestered gang began to grow increasingly restless and irritable.

Jennifer Jason Leigh had been cast as Nic Cage's gangster moll fiancée, but soon after filming began, word circulated around the set that she had been offered another movie, *Grandview, U.S.A.,* and had decided to jump ship and take it. When I asked Fred Roos, Francis's longtime producer and in-house casting guru, who would be replacing Jennifer, he said I could audition for the role, so I did. And I got it.

They had me do a makeup and hair test to establish my character's "look," my face reimagined, painted anew, eyebrows plucked into 1920s submission. My body would have to be whitewashed to match my face, painted the ghostly hue of a powdery china doll. My hair was bobbed, then bleached and rebleached, never quite attaining the desired platinum. Beneath the bob and layers of makeup, I was brimming with nervous excitement while trying to act cooler than I felt.

Nic Cage was playing Richard's kid brother, and Gwen Verdon, their mom. My very first scene was with Nic, Richard, and Gwen. Nic was young, maybe seventeen? Intense and brooding, a method actor, who would only answer to his character's name.

As the four of us gathered on the set to read through the scene, Francis looked distracted, rubbing his head, tugging on his beard, then he looked at me and asked, "Can you sound like Judy Holliday?" Of course, I was a fan of the "dumb blonde" from *Born Yesterday,* with the high-pitched voice and even higher IQ. I nodded hesitantly, and Francis said, "Let me hear you say, when Richard congratulates you on your engagement, you correct him, and say: 'You don't congratulate the bride, you congratulate the groom.'"

I spoke my new line in my best impersonation of Judy Holliday, and still Francis looked like something was not quite right. Then he gestured to no one in particular. "Somebody. Somebody, run out and get her a kitten!" His commandment sent production assistants scurrying, sprinting to the nearest pet store in Queens to fetch me a live prop.

A kitten? Okay. That sounded like it could be *promising*. Who can forget Brando rhythmically stroking a cat on his lap in *The Godfather?* Maybe my presence was activating something in Francis. Everything had come to a halt because I needed a kitten. This could be good.

Meanwhile, the four of us were put back into "the works" for finishing touches—makeup, hair, costumes—as the crew began to light the set, creating that dreamy amber glow. Milena Canonero, the Italian Academy Award–winning costume designer, one of the most sophisticated and stylish women I've ever seen, had dressed me in gorgeous vintage peach lingerie with off-white silk stockings.

Back on the set, I was handed this tiny, fluffy Balinese kitten, a blue-eyed, cream-colored fluffball tipped with gray. As we were getting close to filming, my nerves on edge, petting this kitten like a good-luck charm, and silently running my new line like a mantra in my best Betty Boop New York–ease, Francis said, pointing to Nic and me, "You guys are in the bed."

We got into the bed. I was in my silk teddy and stockings. Nic was in a sleeveless undershirt and boxers, and we rehearsed the scene one last time before "picture."

Francis yelled, "Cut!" Then to Nic and me, "You guys are under the covers, so take your clothes off."

The assistant director called out, "Okay, picture's up. Last looks."

Thinking back on it, it all happened so fast I never even had a chance to consider how I felt about it, or that I might have any say. I was informed by Francis Ford Coppola, in front of the whole crew, that I would play my first scene naked, as offhandedly as if he were telling the waiter to make sure the calamari were crispy. But if I couldn't trust Francis to take care of me as an actress, whom could I trust?

I could sense a maternal protectiveness from Milena, catching the sideways glances between her attendant wardrobe crew and any woman within earshot, as I was shuttled back to my dressing room. I stood there buck naked, assuming a starfish position as instructed, as the two makeup artists, kneeling on either side of me, vigorously washed me down with giant sponges dipped into a pail of baby pink body makeup, then buffed and powdered me like a baby in a cloud of talcum, making sure my coverage was seamless, as it was now all the costume I would be wearing.

The one good thing that came out of that day was that Nic, sensing my vulnerability and discomfort with being suddenly starkers on the set, became chivalrous and protective, taking care of me by pressing me tightly against his bare chest to keep my tits covered.

Right before Francis called, "Action," he told Nic to get on top of me, and we started kissing, naked. (It's possible we had covertly retained something of our vintage underwear without Francis being any the wiser.) Richard and Gwen entered the room, with a couple of thugs in tow, and Nic and I played the scene from the moment our coitus was interruptussed.

No one closed the set, which is the usual protocol when an actor is naked, or partially clad. I didn't know to ask for anything that might've made me feel safe. I was mostly concerned with not being a problem, and it felt like so many things seemed to point to me not being quite what Francis had envisioned. I wasn't sure how much more frustration he could tolerate. I wanted more than anything to be Francis's muse, one of the actors in his gang, and here I was with the man himself. But instead of feeling that I was his creative inspiration, it seemed like he was trying to make the best of a stepchild he felt stuck with.

It quickly became quite warm on the set, as brilliant cinematographers with bloated budgets tend to light the shit out of everything. I also had a big ol' boy on top of me under the covers. Our skin was growing sticky. It would have been a neat trick to have been able to deliver my new dialogue in my newly minted voice and accent, keeping my boobs glued to my scene partner, while willing my pores to close. But I couldn't hide my sweat. Once it started, it was on. They had to keep stopping between every take to reapply my white body makeup, as my true colors were bleeding through.

I spent quite a bit of time at Kaufman Astoria Studios aboard that now well-documented runaway train, with its ballooning budget, producer infighting, and all manner of shady business. (Look it up!) And while my character appeared here and there in plenty of scenes, I also sat around, fully made up and in costume in my dressing cubicle, for days on end, unused.

My character's only other important scene was when her husband gets machine gunned down in a telephone booth right in front of her, in a bloody gang-related attack. I had been waiting for this payoff scene for months, and I felt a certain pressure to come up with the emotional goods—to weep uncontrollably, as written, over my brutally slain husband's body.

By the time they got around to filming this scene, it was at the tail end of a night shoot. I had been waiting around since the day before. In the wee small hours of the following morning, semi-incoherent from the day-night confusion, my makeup had become thick from too many touch-ups due to false starts throughout the night, and my hairdo looked more like a "hair don't."

They shot Nic's close-up first, with all the necessary special effects—exploding squibs, splattering blood, earsplitting machine gunfire, smoke. But by the time the camera was turning around to grab my close-up, it was the last shot of the probably fourteen-hour day. Nic had been wrapped and did not care to stick around to feed

me his lines from "off camera," so I tried my best to repurpose my
built-up frustration and anger, screaming and crying over his dying
body, which was, in reality, just a pile of dusty, twisted electrical
cables on the floor of the telephone booth. My only cue to start
screaming and crying was someone from the crew, off camera, calling
out, "Bang! Bang!" And that, my friend, is why it's called acting.

I did get another gig, even before *Cotton Club* had wrapped. *Red
Dawn*, the right-wing propaganda movie about a handful of small-
town Colorado, AK-47-toting teens fighting a Russian invasion, would
at one point be declared the most violent film of all time by the *Guin-
ness Book of World Records*. But it was an opportunity, an ensemble
action movie where I got to be a badass guerrilla fighter, and amid the
carnage my character got two juicy acting scenes—one love scene
and one death scene.

The actor cast as my love interest was a good-looking, big-hearted
cowboy from Texas named Patrick Swayze. At thirty-one, he was the

eldest of the "high school students" in the cast, and was by default the designated boss of everyone. After weeks of relentless running, screaming, and killing, I was very much looking forward to shooting our tender postcoital love scene. It was shot at night inside a pup tent, and once Patrick, shirtless, slid into the sleeping bag alongside me, I could smell booze on his breath. Was this burly, manly man nervous? He couldn't remember his lines. The script supervisor kept feeding them to him, but we could never get through the scene. John Milius, the director, finally gave up, saying he'd reshoot it another day, which never happened. I was crushed, but there was still my death scene to look forward to.

We'd all been put up in a motel in a remote area of New Mexico so sketchy we weren't even allowed to walk around. The night before we were scheduled to film my last hope for redemption, I'd smoked a joint, my nighttime ritual, and had gone to bed early, in preparation for what I considered to be my most important and difficult scene of the shoot. Hearing what I thought were gunshots just outside my motel room was not ideal. My paranoia spiked and I couldn't sleep a wink. The more I couldn't sleep, the more anxious I got that I was not going to be able to deliver the goods the next day.

In the morning, when I found out that the "gunshots" had been a prank—played by Patrick and his pack of restless "Wolverines" setting off firecrackers they'd stuck in the frame of my door—I was so angry I couldn't even look at him.

In the movie, my character has been mortally wounded, shot up by a machine gun, and she decides to blow herself up with a hand grenade so as not to slow the others down. In a *Soldier of Fortune* take on *Romeo and Juliet*, she begs Patrick's character to "pull the pin" for her. This scene was obviously crucial to the melodrama of the movie and hence to me. At twenty-four, I was still quite green as an actor, and young to be playing a death scene. I knew I'd be pretty much on my own, as emotional sensitivity was not the director's strong suit. (See: Conan the Barbarian.) And this already tricky scene was made

even trickier because I was furious with Patrick. I felt like he'd sabo-
taged my performance.

From the late seventies through most of the eighties, I supported
myself waitressing. Before that, I had been a temp secretary, a salesgirl at Henri Bendel, and had worked behind the counter at the gourmet deli Mangia, when it first opened on 56th Street.

My first waitressing job was at the Saloon across from Lincoln
Center, where I lied on my application about having prior experience.
How hard could it be? I'd been eating at restaurants all my life. Most
of the servers at the Saloon were really experienced, and many waited
tables on roller skates. The only thing I was worse at than waitressing
was roller-skating. Like it wasn't stressful enough to have gone from
never having waited tables to working the favored destination across
from Lincoln Center with the intense theater rush, but then you put
skates on me. And don't forget my math issues. I also worked at Jeze-
bel in the Theater District, where I got fired after dropping some
bigwig record producer's ham hocks on the kitchen floor. I waitressed
at 65 Irving Place, and later worked around the corner from my apartment on Bethune Street as a busboy-waitress hopeful at the popular
Tex-Mex joint the Cottonwood Café. The singer Shawn Colvin waited
tables there, and also gigged in the back room. I was part of the original crew that opened Tortilla Flats before they got their liquor license,
and between jobs, I was always looking to grab random shifts with
caterers, passing hors d'oeuvres at parties, often for people I knew in
the business, or friends of my family.

My first real paying acting gig was a national commercial for Dr.
Pepper, with the catchy jingle tagline, "Wouldn't you like to be a Pepper, too?" I did. I was. A Pepper. Ka-ching.

The dance audition was for the well-known modern dancer and
choreographer Louis Falco. The choreography was, as usual, impossible for me to learn, and at one point I just started going off, dancing

like I do (nowadays they'd call it "freestyling"). Falco stopped me and said, "Oh, that was . . . Can you do that again? Just—whatever it was you just did." I was the only one exempt from having to do the choreography. My sheer unbridled joy, as it was expressed through my personal style of movement, was what they hired me for.

It was my first taste of, "Oh, maybe I could someday, actually support myself doing what I've always dreamed of," and though I only got paid scale, the Screen Actors Guild minimum, it was way more than I ever made as a waitress. You shoot the commercial for one day and then the money just keeps coming in for years! The checks came in dribs and drabs, always unexpectedly, and always just when I was really strapped for cash. Every time I saw one of those envelopes in my mailbox it felt like a miracle—not to mention, I got hired as a *dancer,* even though I couldn't remember the choreography. Who does that?

It seemed that dance was dogging me. Every job I got or got close to getting seemed to involve dance, which was ironic because I couldn't remember the most rudimentary routines in class. But I still couldn't resist imagining that maybe this time I would be able to conquer this odd brain glitch and get to join in the fun. Because I loved it.

The first time I danced for Adrian Lyne, I wore a leotard, tights, and high heels, as per the casting director's instructions. *Flashdance* was his first feature, though he was already a very successful commercial director in England.

I was trying out for the lead role and there was an immediate flirtatious, sexy energy between us. When he pulled me aside, like he was giving me a hot stock tip, and suggested I lose the tights, with a bit of a stinky face that said, "Yeah . . . they're not sexy," I was in a bit of a bind. I certainly didn't want to be "not sexy" for this very groovy director who clearly knew from sexy, but taking off my tights felt like a big step. Like a contortionist in the cramped restroom stall, I peeled out of my opaque nude Danskin tights, which suddenly looked to me like geriatric hose.

Now extremely exposed and insecure, my thighs blotchy and jig-gly, like Jell-O still loose in the mold, I made my way back to my director, feeling particularly naked as I strode through the corporate halls of the Gulf and Western building where Paramount had its offices, passing the raised eyebrows of receptionists at their desks.

Adrian was so obviously pleased when I reappeared having ful-filled his request that I almost forgot I hated my legs. Ordinarily, the casting assistant runs the video camera, the director watches the audition from behind a desk, set back from the action, but on this occasion, Adrian would be filming me. (It's possible it was just us in the room, but at the least it felt like that.) He pressed play on the boom box at his feet, blasting Tina Turner's "What's Love Got to Do with It," and I gyrated for him as he growled in his sexy English accent, "Oh yes, fuuuck me, dahlin', oh yes, like that. Oh my god, you're so fuuucking hot."

Adrian was, in fact, fucking hot. He had that English rocker vibe with a longish blond shag, a dirty mouth, and I did not mind one bit having to return to the Paramount offices to read for him again and again and, especially, to dance for him, appealing to my darker nature. With every callback, feeling more and more confident that the part was mine, I wanted so much to be invited along to join this sexy rocket-ship of a ride I didn't have the self-esteem to even consider that I should be fed up and disgusted by being brought back in again and again. When I learned that I didn't get the job, I was shocked. I'd never been so close to being cast as the lead in any movie, so when they ultimately threw me a bone, some stripper-adjacent "friend" part, I was devastated. My agent at that time, David Guç, was so offended on my behalf he told them that they "could go fuck them-selves." *Flashdance* felt like the closest I'd come to getting something I felt born to do.

The Cotton Club was eventually released in 1984. The night of the cast and crew screening was the first time I remember someone, unsolicited, acknowledging that I might go on to have a career. The lighting was low, rosy in hue, and the energy of New York's most rarefied crowd buzzed around us. Standing toward the back of the small, packed screening room, Richard Gere told me that he thought I was talented, and he hoped for me to have enough opportunity to explore and experiment as an actress before becoming a star. I was stunned and encouraged that he thought I might possibly go on to have a career. Not lost on me was also a wistfulness, perhaps his own feelings of being creatively thwarted on the other side of stardom. This bona fide movie star seemed to see something in me, even if he was just making polite conversation. I clung to this shard of validation, hoping that if my talent was evident to Richard Gere, with whom I wasn't particularly close, it would also have to be perceptible to my father.

The lights dimmed, and I sat down next to my dad feeling anticipation and immense pride about being a part of this movie, in such spectacular company. No one had any idea what to expect, because Francis had shot enough footage to make four films. As I watched the movie, my high hopes, held at bay for a year, began to deflate one scene at a time. Sequences that had taken a whole week to shoot now passed through the frame in a flash. Whole storylines were gone, as if they had never happened. Had I made it all up? Or was I cut out because I wasn't any good? I felt embarrassed, like I had lied to my loved ones about the extent of my involvement. Even I couldn't understand how I could have been on a movie for that many months, most every day, and not have much to show for it. At all.

Despite this disappointing blow, I was pretty confident that at least my dad, having just seen the apple of his eye in a big-time Francis Ford Coppola film, would find something positive to say about my performance, see some kind of "it" factor, even if only an "it" detectable by a loved one. When we left the screening room, it was night, the streets in Midtown were quiet. I walked alongside my dad; his pace was brisk, his eyes focused ahead of him. I oriented myself toward him, crabbing sideways, then buzzing around him like a bee, anxiously awaiting his feedback as soon as we were out of earshot of the others.

"So? Whadja think?" I asked excitedly.

His overall assessment was, "Well, it's all over the place. And verrrry long. Ultimately, not really satisfying."

When I couldn't wait another second, I blurted out, "But what did you think . . . about *me*?"

I was pressing him for an answer he didn't readily have. He reluctantly admitted, "Well, you know, there wasn't—I mean, it was hard to tell." And, almost protectively, "They really didn't give you much to do."

To my mind, my dad was the arbiter of all things. He has always been extremely candid and vocal about what was, in his opinion, good, and I had fashioned my opinions and tastes after his. He suddenly, uncharacteristically, had no opinion. Unwilling to let it go, I began feeding him what I wanted to hear, "What'd you think of the moment when . . . ?" I was looking for something, anything, the subtlest nod to my having made an impression, but there was a penuriousness, as if he needed to hold himself to a certain standard, his allegiance to some unwavering truth, his integrity eclipsing my need for his approval. My takeaway from that evening was, "The one thing I know for a fact is that my dad loves me more than anyone in this world, so if there was anything good to possibly say, he would've said it. At least I can trust him to tell me the truth."

When I went into Janet Hirshenson's casting office in New York to audition for the new John Hughes movie, I had just seen *Sixteen Candles,* and frankly didn't quite get what all the hype was about. I had perused his latest script, scanning it for my scenes because I could barely follow what was happening in the story. What was up with all the monologues of Ferris Bueller talking to camera? I didn't get it. (Somebody, notify the ADHD police. Clearly, we have an actress sorely in need of a stimulant.)

In the waiting room of casting offices, next to the sign-in sheet, there's typically a stack of mimeographed scenes for whichever roles they're casting on that day. When it was my turn to go in to read, I had the scenes marked "Jeanie" in hand, which I'd hardly worked on, and John Hughes was there.

He stood up when we were introduced, and he was over six feet tall. He dressed like a big overgrown kid, but a well-outfitted one in Air Jordans, jeans, and fancy leather jacket. He wore glasses, frosted round plastic frames, his thick blond mane styled in a mullet, and he chain-smoked Carltons.

I was the anomaly, not being a crazed fan. I was cool as a cucumber. My default mode has always been pretty sunny, ebullient, trending perhaps toward annoyingly friendly, but because Ferris's sour sister called for a more prickly vibe, my poor attitude on this occasion worked in my favor. I gave off the kind of shitty energy that would befit a Jeanie Bueller. I got the part.

What I wasn't prepared for was that I would become creatively besotted with John. And while he was nowhere near being my type, I couldn't deny being "a little in love" with him. Was it his brain, or was it that I felt seen by him, appreciated? The more hilarious he thought I was, the freer I became. The freer I became, the more I was this new version of myself. John praised me for inhabiting everything that had been strictly verboten in my family—exploring and playing in the more shadowy side of my psyche. It was a relief to be given utter permission to let my darker freak flag fly. It was sheer bliss.

The majority of Jeanie's scenes were of her alone—ruminating, burning up with frustration, and seething with jealous rage, so John, from behind the camera, was in essence my scene partner. When I was shooting my scenes, he was right there, either calling out impromptu lines for me to parrot back as they occurred to him, or enthusiastically yelling out "pieces of business" for me to do. I never knew what was going to happen, nor did he. There was no room or time to be self-conscious or insecure because it was all happening so fast and in the moment. Afterward I'd have no clue what had just happened, it was like being in an improv blackout.

Matthew Broderick was cast as Ferris, and at twenty-four, this kid had the world on a string. He'd won a Tony for Neil Simon's *Brighton Beach Memoirs* and had just starred in the hit movie *WarGames*. And while he was very talented, he didn't present like your typical movie star, more like your grumpy grandpa. He looked like he'd just rolled out of bed, with crazy chapped lips and sleep in his eyes.

Matthew and I hardly had any scenes together until the very end of the shooting schedule, and I don't remember how or when we first got to know each other. But I was as surprised as anyone when our relationship morphed from on-screen sibling rivalry to off-screen illicit romance.

When you're engaged in monkey business on location, you're in this make-believe bubble away from your real life. The entire company is staying in the same hotel, and suddenly you're living one of those bedroom farces, padding down the carpeted hallway, barefoot in your robe, or in various stages of undress. The row of peepholes on the other guests' doors can feel like an army of eyeballs watching your every move. Then you get a grip on yourself. *Oh, please! No one is*

pressed up against their door waiting to catch a fish-eye glance of some
scantily clad actress. Nobody cares. They're busy. Living their own lives.
This paranoid phenomenon could also be construed as a conscience.
And I *should* have been feeling guiltier than I was.

When Matthew and I were having our secret rendezvous in his
hotel room, inevitably, just as it was getting good, the hotel phone
would suddenly burst into a cacophonous jangly ring. Imagine my
shock and disbelief the first time Matthew bolted upright to pick up
the phone. Seriously? The interruptus was only made worse by his
sudden change in demeanor. Deadly serious, his eyes bugged wide,
he pressed his index finger to his lips, those same lips I had just been
having my way with moments before. A soundless "Shhhh!"

From what I could suss, there appeared to be some girl he had
failed to mention, who was or was not, in fact, his girlfriend. And if
she *wasn't* his girlfriend, then why was she calling him and why else
would he be shushing me? When I questioned him about this mystery woman, he assured me she was not his girlfriend but more of a
close family friend who fancied him.

My denial was clearly working overtime to obfuscate at this point.
It boiled down to: I wanted what I wanted. Ah, to be young, reckless,
and a total jerk. And I'd have to add hypocrite to the list, as I had
always been a self-proclaimed "girls' girl," but this particular situation
seemed to require that I make an exception to my rule.

By the time we wrapped the movie and our clandestine set
romance was over, it was Thanksgiving, and I went home to my West
Village apartment, where I lived with my roommate, Meg Burnie,
who would become a lifelong friend. I realized I was in love with
Matthew and told him I couldn't see him anymore. He promptly
broke up with his "close family friend" and we were together.

Matthew just felt like my guy. We were both Jewish, New Yorkers,
actors, with actor parents. We loved the same theater, Chinese food
on Sunday nights, and he made me laugh. I loved his humor, his
brains, his talent. Being with a crowned prince of Broadway also felt
familiar. He felt like home.

The night before my audition for *Dirty Dancing,* I begged Matthew to come out with me to Heartbreak, a club just below Canal Street in Tribeca where you could dance to music from the fifties and sixties, but Matthew wasn't in the mood. He was a twenty-four-year-old who could easily slip into the persona of a cranky old guy when it suited him. After I pleaded with him and finally convinced him, he said this odd thing, as if to reassure himself, like he wasn't aware he was using his "out loud voice": "I don't know what I'm worried about. There's no way you're gonna get it. I'm sure they're seeing everybody for this part."

The following day, I took the subway to a skyscraper in Times Square, 1515 Broadway, at 44th Street, and rode the escalator up to the Minskoff studios—the cavernous, airy rehearsal spaces with floor-to-ceiling windows, where auditions for the biggest Broadway shows, as well as commercial auditions, were often held, in the same building as the Ailey School where I had been taking dance classes.

I had worked on the couple of scenes, and if the reading went well, I was told to bring along some music I liked and be prepared to dance. I don't remember much about the scenes or who I read with, except that it was for a handful of people, I assume the usual suspects: Emile Ardolino, the director; Eleanor Bergstein, the writer; Linda Gottlieb, the producer; and Bonnie Timmermann, the casting director. They seemed very pleased with my reading and asked me to dance.

I was thrilled that I could pick my own music and that there would be no choreography to learn. I'd brought along my boom box, cued up to the exact little groove I'd marked with a pen in the mini window of my cassette of *Jackson 5 Greatest Hits.* My song was "I Want You Back." I knew I had to have a song I could depend on to take me where I needed to go, to that place I was very familiar with, that place where I'd just *go off* into my own dance trance. Something about that song, even today, involuntarily plugs me into my body and out of my head, an "on" switch that transports me to my wildest, unchained happy place. If a song is not one of those silver bullets that shoots straight to my core and leaves me no choice, I can become almost paralyzed. I need all choice to be removed, to be securely under the spell of a master, and Michael Jackson—not to mention the single greatest chord progression of all time—was that master.

I remember turning my back on the group, and the awkward silence as they waited for me to pick up my boom box, position it in the middle of the immense rehearsal hall, and bend down to press play. I can't tell you what happened after that, because the next thing I knew it was over. I had no idea what I'd done. I'd had no plan or choreography, no moves I was particularly fond of or knew to be crowd-pleasers. I just went there. And when the song was over, my heart felt like it might explode from the intensity of exertion. I stood there sweating and shaking, and I pretty much knew without even looking at anyone that I had the part.

13

The Time of My Life

I'm not sure if it was the next day or a few days after my audition for *Dirty Dancing* when I got the call from my agent saying that they loved me, that I basically had the part, as I was the only one that would be screen-testing with their top choices for the guy's part. The choreographer, Kenny Ortega, had just flown in from LA and brought along his collection of old 45s for us to dance to. Kenny, who happened to have worked on a bunch of John Hughes movies, including *Ferris,* would demonstrate basic Latin combinations for the potential Johnny Castles, while the rest of the creative team, sitting in a row of folding chairs, checked out what level of dance game these guys had. The other key component was: When paired up, did the guy and I look hot together?

It proved to be a very elusive creature they were searching for; maybe he didn't even exist. A guy with serious animal magnetism, a young Brando who could *really* dance. Dance was the DNA of the story, and it could not be faked. Johnny was originally written as a young, working-class Italian American gigolo whose bread and butter, when not at Kellerman's Catskills resort in the summer, was teaching women to dance at Arthur Murray. There was not an enormous pool of first-rate actors who were also strong dancers and convincingly heterosexual.

Billy Zane, a top contender, came in and danced with me. Scott Plank was an actor-dancer who'd done Broadway musicals. But the second any of the guys who came in put their hands on me, I just knew.

Enter Patrick Swayze.

Patrick had grown up playing football and was also the son of a passionate, kick-ass, respected dance teacher and choreographer in Houston. His mother had her own dance school where Patrick had studied, and where he'd met a ballet dancer, Lisa Niemi, who eventually became his wife. Patrick and Lisa had moved to New York to pursue careers as dancers. He'd studied at the Joffrey and Harkness schools and danced with Eliot Feld. He'd even been a dancer in one of my dad's Broadway shows, *Goodtime Charley*.

The powers that be in that audition room were all extremely high on this Patrick idea.

Please, no. Not him.

"Anybody else. Please!" I begged.

Bonnie, the casting director, beamed enthusiastically. "Jennifer, he used to be a professional ballet dancer."

"Oh, I know. Believe me, I know."

Emile, the director, pitched in. "Male ballet dancers are trained specifically to partner. Pas de deux is all partner work."

He had a point. Having zero experience doing ballroom or Latin dancing, I was in an especially vulnerable position, and utterly dependent on the skills of my costar. This guy, whoever it ended up being, needed to know how to lead. The bunch of auditioning actors I'd danced with had either been too tentative on the dance floor or had flung me around too roughly, trying to prove themselves.

I felt it was in everyone's best interest to be transparent about my history with this guy. "I've worked with Patrick. We did *Red Dawn* together. I spent every day for two months with him. Trust me, it's not right."

It didn't matter what I said. They were bringing him in for this part.

The role of Johnny Castle was the big break Patrick had been waiting for. By the time he came in to audition, he knew that I'd already been cast, and that he might be a tough sell for me, in light of our history on *Red Dawn*.

After the initial hugs and greetings from the lathered-up welcoming committee, including yours truly, putting on my most convincing friendly face, the hunky actor asked if he and I could step outside so he could have a moment alone with me. He took my hand and led me down the hall a little ways. Once out of earshot, we turned to face each other, each perfectly mirroring the other, leaning against the wall. Patrick scanned me in my cut-off black tights, dance briefs rolled down, a sports bra and vintage blue satin high heels, and said, "Whoa. You clean up good, girl."

"Thanks."

"This is a great part for you. Congratulations."

"I know, right? It's crazy." This *was* softening me up. It felt good to be able to share my news with someone I knew.

"I know, you're probably thinkin', 'Aw, no, not this idiot again.'" Then his eyes started to well up. Real tears. And with the most earnest delivery imaginable, said, "You know I've always loved you." He stared into my eyes. "And I've been really workin' on gettin' my shit together. So, if I get the chance, I swear I'm gonna make it up to you. You will not be sorry."

I said, "Uh-huh."

He smiled and was working hard on getting me to smile back. "C'mon, you know if we did this together, we'd kill it."

I started crying, too, but not for the reasons he thought. I had imagined this character, Johnny Castle, as this street-smart, gritty

Italian. A guy that I could see myself being hot for, maybe even fall in love with. This was my first leading role, and I knew how crucial the casting of this part was to the movie's success. The sexual chemistry between Baby and Johnny was everything, and I was not feeling it. How was I supposed to trust this guy? Next thing I knew Patrick was hugging me super tight. I could feel his heart beating against my chest.

We went back into the rehearsal space.

The YouTube clip of our screen test says it all. Patrick was far and away the best dancer who'd come in. He was strong, manly, and confident. Having never danced with him before, I had never experienced him in this way. There was no question that our bodies liked each other, in spite of what my head was saying. There has never been anyone with Patrick's combination of grace, brawn, sensitivity, and fearless, reckless gusto.

The *Dirty Dancing* shoot was famously beset with problems. Extremely chaotic. You could almost say, cursed.

The fictional story of Frances "Baby" Houseman's awakening took place over the Houseman family's summer vacation. Two resorts in tandem—one in Virginia and the other in North Carolina—would serve on screen as the singular Kellerman's Catskills destination. But production had to put off shooting until after each resort's real-life seasonal guests and campers had left. The movie's summer had to be shot in the fall, and the art department, in a race against the change of seasons, began madly spray-painting the leaves green as trees slipped into their natural autumnal glory.

It also rained. A lot. When a movie is shot on a location where the weather is changeable, it becomes trickier and more expensive, especially if your story and scenes require being drenched in the warm glow of summer.

And when it stopped raining? There were mosquitoes.

Because I'm basically a mosquito magnet and this wasn't a movie about a girl battling smallpox, the makeup artist had to cover up the red welts on me between every take (including during Baby and Johnny's love scenes, dabbing makeup on pretty much every part of my nearly naked body).

There was another issue with the locations. In the fifties and sixties, bungalow colonies like Kellerman's catered exclusively to Jewish New Yorkers escaping the sweltering summer in the city, because Jews weren't welcome at the other resorts. For the movie to capture the authenticity of the Borscht Belt (or the Jewish Alps, as the Catskills resorts were also called back then), the extras in the movie needed to look identifiably Jewish. And there wasn't exactly a surplus of Jews in the Appalachian South. There were precious few people in the area who could even pass as Jews.

Dirty Dancing had an Academy Award–winning documentary filmmaker as its director, its crew was overall top-notch, there were veteran New York actors filling out the cast, and everyone worked their tits off, devoted to making the movie the best possible version of itself. But it was an extremely low-budget production, and there remained a very real possibility that passionate dedication wouldn't be enough to save the movie from an embarrassing B-movie fate. The $4.5 million budget came from Vestron, a home video company based in Stamford, Connecticut, that had never before made a movie.

The schedule was impossibly tight, the whole thing had to be shot in forty-three days, and while the premise of the movie was appealing, the script was not exactly ready to go. The melodramatic, fairy-tale structure was also riddled with plotlines that didn't track and dialogue that didn't exactly roll off the tongue. The story and language initially read a bit like a bodice ripper. For two weeks before the start of principal photography, in a cavernous studio in the Mountain Lake Lodge in Pembroke, Virginia, Patrick and I learned the building blocks of mambo for the better part of every day, and in the afternoons we rehearsed key scenes with Emile.

Over lunch when we were alone, Emile and I combed through the script, scene by scene, line by line, trying to make it sound a bit more natural. There were passages of pitch-perfect dialogue in the original script, but there was enough off-pitch stuff to scare me as an actor, afraid I might not be up to the task of selling the melodrama. Lines like, "Me? I'm scared of everything. I'm scared of what I saw, I'm scared of what I did, of who I am, and most of all I'm scared of walking out of this room and never feeling the rest of my whole life, the way I feel when I'm with you." Patrick had similar issues with his dialogue, and strenuously resisted saying the now-famous line, "Nobody puts Baby in a corner."

Emile took full responsibility for the script changes that we had arrived at together; he never threw me or Patrick under the bus. Each evening, the cast and crew would receive revised script pages.

There was also a long-running contest on set to see who could come up with the movie's new title, because surely *Dirty Dancing* was never going to last. In the eighties, it sounded too scandalous to be able to reach its mainstream target audience. Censorship officers assumed it was a porn film.

The second day of shooting, the woman who was playing my mother fell ill and had to be recast on the spot. A rehearsal space was burglarized, heavy flooding blocked the roads, and among the cast and crew, there was a serious fall from a ladder, a broken toe, a fractured wrist, an outbreak of food poisoning. A ninety-year-old actress fainted from heatstroke. Patrick had an old football knee injury but insisted on doing his own stunts. In the scene where Johnny teaches Baby to balance on the log over a creek bed (the only scene in which I used a stunt double), Patrick fell, reinjuring his bad knee. Periodically after that, his knee would blow up like a grapefruit, and he'd have to take time out to have the fluid drained. The shooting schedule had to be rejiggered without adding days to accommodate recasting, injuries, illnesses, and the weather, which included not only the rain but a sudden cold snap and then a crazy heat wave.

I had my own problems, the kind I would have killed for before this gig. For one, I was in almost every scene of the movie. When I wasn't shooting, I was rehearsing. When I wasn't rehearsing or shooting, I was in a costume fitting. Very early on in the shoot, my makeup artist, who made me look great without looking like I had any makeup on, had a personal crisis and had to quit. I was desperate for her to stay on, but no matter. I did my own makeup for two weeks, until they were able to hire someone else. Later, that new makeup artist also had to leave.

And then there was a little costume problem. When you have your initial costume fitting, the designer lays out the road map for your character's arc, as told through the clothes you will be wearing. In this instance, Baby's entire wardrobe would be limited to whatever items she'd fit into her suitcase for her family vacation. Her look was "bookish daddy's girl," with a dash of "Peace Corps" for flavor. Somehow, with only the no-nonsense contents of her Samsonite, this duckling had to believably transform into a swan capable of snagging a streetwise, heart-stopping stud—without so much as a pal to borrow from and nary a trip to the mall. (And remember, friends, at that time, Amazon was only a river.)

Unfortunately, the reveal of the costumes the designer had assembled for Baby freaked me the fuck out. I had to maintain a game face out of respect for her best efforts, and she was an excellent designer, but I could see that the outfits required for Baby to make this pivotal transformation just weren't there. All I had to amend the situation were the contents from my *own* suitcase. We were stuck in the Allegheny Mountains in 1986, in desperate need of clothing specific to 1963. Trying to mask my distress, I knew it was on me to step in and collaborate to make Baby's look work.

Anytime I'm on a job where it feels like it's all falling apart and the production is utter mayhem, I'm always reminded of how incredibly chaotic and challenging the filming of *Cabaret* was. In my house growing up, in moments of similar "the sky is falling" crisis, part of the family lore was the story of when the "only gorilla suit in Germany" wasn't gonna cut it. Gwen Verdon jumped on a plane to New York to fetch what they needed and flew back with a superior gorilla head on her lap in the nick of time. I'd grown up on plenty of "the show must go on" stories, like when Liza Minnelli doing her nightclub act, performing her heart out, working up a sweat singing and dancing like her life depended on it, if one of her signature spiky strip lashes started to come unglued, she'd just yank 'em both off and toss 'em onto the stage. From childhood, I'd absorbed the knowledge that when you're in the eye of the storm, the play's the thing. All vanity and perfectionism must be abandoned. Do whatever you need to do to make it work, to survive. Get busy finding a solution to whatever the challenge is, and what you'll come up with is often better than if all had gone swimmingly. In a pressured situation like on a set, every limitation adds heat, and conflagration is required to forge metal. Nobody wants their hair on fire, but in my family—and in my extended Broadway family—the unspoken motto was, "When the going gets tough? We fucking kill it." Okay, I don't know if that exact language came from my upbringing, but that was my takeaway.

The only way to change this costume situation was to hustle.

The designer was working with a seamstress to build the hot pink chiffon halter ballroom dress that Baby would wear to perform at the Sheldrake (the venue where she makes her debut as Johnny's dance partner). The wardrobe team was also building the sleeveless, pastel going-to-a-restaurant-with-her-parents dress Baby wears when she first sneaks off to the staff quarters, and, of course, the pale pink party dress for the movie's finale. The designer also had made a modest dusty rose cotton bathing suit. There were a couple of good vintage tops, an embroidered peasant blouse, the bulky long pale blue mohair cardigan, and a madras sleeveless shell. But there weren't the kinds of pieces that would lend themselves to be more convertible, to be able to be restyled as more adult or sexy.

Just a few weeks before, while vacationing on Martha's Vineyard with my friend Tracy, I'd made a mental note about a pair of shorts Tracy had worn. She had bought some jeans from the vintage store in Oak Bluffs, and cut them off just below the knee and cuffed them up to hit right above the kneecap. I asked the designer if she wouldn't mind getting some high-waisted jeans that we could turn into long shorts. One of the tops I'd brought along with me was my L. L. Bean red-striped sailor shirt. I loved Jean Seberg's look in Godard's *Breathless,* which I figured Baby could've easily been enamored of. And nothing said sixties to me like tight, high-waisted white Levi's cropped to just above the ankle. I asked the designer if we could get some of those and some of the old-school white lace-up Keds we all used to wear.

The designer and her assistant made a trip to the nearest big city, returning with boxes of the classic sneakers and a pile of jeans. She was such a good sport, and I was very grateful. On Baby's clothes rack of vintage pieces, I saw your basic, white button-down that could easily be turned into a midriff-baring top if I knotted it above the waist. I paired it with the long jean shorts. I believed that Baby could have owned and packed these pieces, and that as she became more comfortable in her own skin, she could gradually modify them to reveal more, and the more Baby risked exposing, the more willing she became to be seen, the more vulnerable and attractive she would become. Wardrobe solved.

Unfortunately, the actress I was trying to help costume (i.e., me) happened to be on the verge of starving. I had been a vegetarian for a few years at that time, and in those days, in the South especially, there weren't a lot of vegetarian options. The catering on movie sets is famously lackluster. Back in the eighties, if you didn't eat meat and were shooting a movie in Virginia and North Carolina on a shoestring budget, your options were grits or canned vegetables—and maybe a sad old salad. On a nutritional level as well as on a fuel level, I was running out of gas. At one of my low points in the shoot, the set medic gave me a B_{12} shot. My vitality surged. I felt lit up, like I'd sprouted wings. (Why had no one before told me this miracle supplement was an option?)

The Caesar salad offered daily was often my go-to. I'd have it for lunch, and sometimes pack up an extra helping in a Styrofoam box to eat later in my room as dinner. One night, though, I became deathly ill and spent the whole night sick. The only culprit I could think of was that I must've gotten food poisoning from the raw egg I hadn't known was used in the Caesar dressing.

The following morning I'd planned to sleep in because I had a late call, which was almost unprecedented for me on this movie. But at the crack of dawn, I got a call from the choreographer, Kenny, asking if I'd be willing to come in before I was called on set because he was shooting some montage footage for second unit. (The second unit director is responsible for shooting supplemental footage, often action sequences or stunts, and usually not with the lead actors.)

All I wanted was to say yes, because I knew this was an opportunity for Kenny to show his directing skills, and I would have done anything for this man. Unfortunately, I was super sick, and I told him so. Which didn't sway him. He wanted to grab some footage of Baby practicing her dance moves on the outdoor stairs. He promised it wouldn't take long. With the last ounce of chi in my body I arrived on the second unit set and threw on my costume. The entire time we shot that sequence (later brilliantly set against "Wipe Out," that classic instrumental by the Ventures), all I was trying to do was *not* throw up. Kenny shot me practicing my dance moves over and over. "Go back up to the top of the stairs. Let's go again. Still rolling!" It wasn't choreographed, I was just winging it. This beat in the montage sequence was never scripted as "Baby loses her mind and has a tantrum"; it was simply "Baby practices dance steps on her own." But I was weak and exhausted, and the frustration I was experiencing was real. The Play-house had ingrained in me to use whatever was happening in the moment, so I just let the line out, as Kenny kept rolling, "Do it again." My struggle (to not be sick) became Baby's struggle (to learn to dance).

One area, though, where my problem almost identically aligned with Baby's was in my abject terror of practicing "the lift," that daring flight into Johnny's raised arms that is the satisfying, emotional, romantic climax of the movie. I knew I wasn't going to be able to get out of that one. Postponing it was all I could do. I wouldn't rehearse it. I refused to. I was like a horse that wouldn't take the jump. Like the girl who climbs the ladder all the way up to the high dive, walks to the end of board, then slowly climbs back down the ladder. She just can't. And then she has to face everyone who watched the whole embarrassing ordeal. My fear made me feel like a total baby, but still I couldn't move past it.

From the very first day of rehearsal right on through the whole shoot, Patrick wanted us to rehearse the lift and I just wouldn't do it. He would say, "C'mon now! I've been doing this forever. I've never dropped anyone yet. And you're *tiny*." I knew he was telling me the truth. He'd been lifting ballerinas into the air since he was a kid. But I took no comfort in that fact. I wanted to let go of the fear, but the fear wouldn't let go of me. Hating myself and feeling shame wasn't enough to get my body to take the leap.

Meanwhile, all I wanted was to get along with Patrick. Every morning I would have a new resolve and a new approach. I would focus on all his great qualities, and they were plentiful. He was handsome and a great dancer, had a great body and was strong. But something would happen to throw a spanner in the works every day. Whatever progress I'd made internally to shape my desire by accentuating the positive would be undone. Patrick was chronically late, and the crew and I would have to wait for him. Every day, all day, for every scene. By the time he got to set, my hopeful emotional preparation for that scene would be spoiled. It's hard to fake it when the whole screen is your face. Looking back on it now, so what? I should have simply accepted him for who he was, had a sense of humor, and expected him to be exactly who he was. Instead, my efforts to stay upbeat by having unrealistic expectations set me up to be freshly disappointed every day.

Being cast as a romantic couple in a movie is a little bit like entering into an arranged marriage. You're trapped in an intimate situation with someone not necessarily of your choosing, which can trigger a person to be regressive, regardless of their age. And the accumulated stressors of an already challenging project, with the added pressure to perform "romantically" on demand, can kick up some fight, flight, or freeze response.

When Patrick's attention was on taking care of me, and when we were in a situation when I had no choice but to *allow* him to take care of me and see him as my protector, we were really good together. This happened while we were shooting the scene where Baby and Johnny practice the lift in the lake. The weather had suddenly turned, it was a serious cold snap. Underwater in the horrifically cold lake, the frogmen setting up the platform for Patrick to stand on wore full wetsuits to insulate them. Medics stood by on shore to check our vitals between takes. And Patrick and I were freezing, in real danger of hypothermia. So we clung together with the fervor of wannabe survivors on a sinking ship.

In the scene where Johnny and Baby drive off in his car and she is supposed to be laughing, exclaiming, "You're wild, you're wild!" I was having a hard time laughing on cue. In my opinion, nothing kills the funny like being told you *have* to laugh. For my close-up, Patrick was off camera, and I asked him to help me out. "Just do *something*, okay?" When they called, "Action," we started to drive, and with his eyes sparking, Patrick indicated where my something would be. He had taken his dick out of his pants. He knew me, and knew this couldn't help but make me squeal and laugh with genuine abandon.

I'm sure Patrick wished I were a better dancer than I was. It would have made it much easier and I'm sure more pleasurable to lead someone who could really hold her own. In partner dancing, the connection is so sensitive, and so much information is transmitted through the body. It's like a lie detector test. You can feel when someone is frustrated or dissatisfied, as I did, and I'm sure he felt my hurt feelings coming back at him, as I was trying to convey, "You think I'm not doing the best I can? I'm not *trying* to be a shitty dancer."

But the difficulties and challenges in making this movie were, for me, merely annoyances. I didn't for one minute lose sight of the fact that everything I had done up to that time had been in preparation for this opportunity: for my soul and the soul of this character to meet. I arrived already fluent in her language. There were so many points of connection, layers of common ground that I'd already traversed. I went before Baby. Shooting the movie was like traveling back in time and processing the stuff I had previously gone through. I was no stranger to feeling alone, different, and not enough, drawn to the dangerous gigolos, desperately wanting to be a better dancer than I was. I understood what it was like not to be considered beautiful, and conversely, to feel that surge of feminine power. I was the perfect steward for Baby.

Of all the music in the world, the music from that period set my soul on fire, which had a lot to do with Nellie. She was the one who'd played that music for me growing up. That music was a part of us.

And can we just talk about the Catskills for a minute? It's one thing to be Jewish, but to be the granddaughter of Mickey Katz? I was raised more on Borscht Belt shtick than Torah.

Everyone's mettle was tested on this film. Nobody was having an easy time of it. Most of the cast and crew struggled with as much as I did, if not more. We were all in it together. Some people dropped out, some got hurt, some got blind drunk. But through it all, pretty much everyone showed extraordinary fortitude, heart, and determination. We prevailed.

And more than likely we were buoyed by some power greater than ourselves.

No one could ask for a better human to play the good father than

Jerry Orbach. He was the ultimate pro—*haimish,* hilarious, generous, and present. And when the actress originally cast to play Baby's mother fell ill and had to leave, we hit the jackpot with Kelly Bishop. I'd been a fan ever since I'd seen her in her Tony Award–winning role of Sheila in *A Chorus Line.* Honi Coles, whom I knew and adored from *The Cotton Club,* a bona fide legend, played the musical director at Kellerman's. Jack Weston was Kellerman, Lonny Price, Kellerman's son. These were all hugely talented, revered Broadway actors, each one more perfect than the next to breathe life into this story's particular place and time. Hats off to Bonnie Timmermann who assembled this inspired cast.

Kenny had recommended Cynthia Rhodes for the role of Penny, Johnny's dance partner and the female dance teacher at Kellerman's. He'd worked with her in movies and music videos. She'd been in *Flashdance* and *Staying Alive* and was not only an exquisite dancer but also an angel. Kenny handpicked each of the dancers, every one of them perfection, distinct in their individuality and earthy hotness.

I was surrounded by excellence.

My hairdresser on the movie was a six-foot-tall Icelandic goddess named Fríða Aradóttir. *Dirty Dancing* was her first movie, and she and I were joined at the hip from day one. She was not only a great hairdresser, she was also my rock. It's no surprise she's now sought after by every gigantic movie star to be their personal hairstylist on a film. Fríða and I have been close ever since.

Emile Ardolino, the director, was a deep human being with a big heart. He was gentle, grounded, and kind. He had won an Academy Award for directing the moving documentary *He Makes Me Feel Like Dancin'*, about the New York City Ballet dancing legend Jacques d'Amboise. With his National Dance Institute, d'Amboise brought joy through dance to children in underserved communities. Emile had a way of controlling the set that was never bombastic. He didn't raise his voice. And beyond all of this, he was my ally. I trusted that he wouldn't let me be bad in this movie. I trusted his ear, his sensibility, and his barometer for truthfulness. It was a huge comfort knowing that he and I saw eye to eye on the task at hand. I knew he had my back and that we were a team. He heard every note I had, and with grace could subtly elevate the script without alienating anyone.

Emile and Kenny Ortega together were a powerful duo. Each brought to the project an unshakable belief in the transformative power of dance, in dance as a language that could layer levels of emotional storytelling—about intimacy, eroticism, and identity—that a scripted narrative alone couldn't have provided. Baby, for example, transformed from being one sort of person into a very different one, not solely because of what was indicated in the script but also through the more visceral, physical intelligence the movie revealed through dance. Emile and Kenny instilled in the production a purity of heart and truth, in the way they organically wove dance into the fabric of the movie.

The two weeks of dance rehearsals before the start of principal photography were, for me, the high point of the entire shoot. Kenny, one of the most generous of spirits, lovingly taught me the basics of mambo. In partner dancing there's an almost electrical current, transmitting everything that exists between the leader and the follower. Within this closed system, there is an intimate, improvisational, wordless conversation. From the outside it looks deceivingly simple, but inside there's a lot more going on.

Kenny's confidence in my ability as a dancer had a powerful influence over how I felt about myself. His appreciation for what I was intuitively bringing to the table, by just showing up as I was, turned down the volume of a long-standing, brutal self-appraisal. All those years in dance class, an inner voice had said that I wasn't a real dancer because of how much I struggled to learn choreography—and that I shouldn't even try because I would just embarrass myself. But dancing with Kenny, I learned that my job was to follow his lead. Completely in the moment, attuned, and at the ready to receive his signals, from a centered place of autonomy. Neither overly reliant on him, nor competing for control. He taught me the importance of being able to stand on my own two feet, while remaining alert and loose enough to be able to go wherever he led me, taking me out of my busy, thinking head, and dropping me into the calm, infinite wisdom of my body, where pleasure lies. Patiently waiting for me.

I had a crazy crush on Kenny. There was probably nobody on the set—not a man, not a woman—who didn't have a crazy crush on Kenny. But I was the one who got to dance with him, up close, with him grabbing me and grinding with me.

Kenny brought in his peer and good friend Miranda Garrison, as Patrick's Latin dance coach. Once Patrick and I had gotten the hang of the basics, Kenny and Miranda began to string together what would become Johnny and Baby's mambo for the Sheldrake, choreography they reworked into a "dirty mambo" for the movie's finale.

Eventually, after Patrick and I had learned the choreography with Miranda and Kenny, we started to rehearse together. But our bodies were having a very different conversation than the one I'd been having with Kenny. While one of Kenny's fortes was working with actors who move well, Patrick had only danced with professional dancers. He was especially used to partnering his ballet dancer wife. They'd been dancing together for fifteen years, since he was nineteen and she was sixteen. I couldn't help but sense Patrick's impatience with me in rehearsals. It freaked me out to feel I'd finally gotten it with Kenny and was ready to go, only to find that with Patrick, I didn't have it at all. It was suddenly much harder. I'm sure Kenny's expectations were more realistic, hence lower than Patrick's, plus Kenny was a really gifted teacher. He made me dance better. The unspoken conversation between Patrick and me was,

"Seriously? You're going to dance like that?"

"Seriously? You're going to act like a total dick?"

Fear was now in the room. Fear made me a worse dancer, made me forget what I knew. Patrick and I had both gotten used to dancing with these two choreographers, who were patient and particularly gifted at giving. Now we both had to learn to dance with someone who was at the same time trying to save their own ass. In the end, the tension between Patrick and me, which might've read as sexual tension, was more complicated than that, but energy between two intense people is still pretty interesting.

The whole premise of the movie is a bit hard to swallow, as fairy tales often are. But I think one of the things that possibly helped this movie override the implausible bits was that tension between us. The movie was working on us. Johnny is annoyed by being saddled with a girl who has no clue what she's doing, and he's accustomed to dancing with his very excellent partner. It would stand to reason that Baby could be feeling Johnny's annoyance, just as I felt Patrick's. The stakes were high for Patrick and me, and that raised the expression of the stakes for Johnny and Baby. This worked for the film. If the movie had featured two equally great dancers and it was all easy, with a big budget and longer shooting schedule, it would've been a different movie. The tension between us fed a certain real-life struggle and energy into the movie, which fed a desire in both of our characters to overcome something. Drama is conflict, and our real-life struggles infused the movie with real life. We were mismatched, and that served us. There was something under all the ego and fear that was somehow hot. And when you get to that hot lava center, it's more dramatic and more compelling than love. Tension is energy, and if you build up enough energy, it can transmogrify into whatever you please.

Shooting a love scene is always a nerve-racking affair. There's a pressure on everybody. The crew is excited and nervous, as it's both hot and awkward for everyone involved.

The director has some idea of how they imagine the scene playing out, of what "the action" is going to be. As an actress, you're in a decidedly *power down* position, vulnerable to the riptide of a director's whim or salacious intent, or to the studio's desire that you disrobe. You're wondering, "Will they still like me, be angry with me, or even recast me if I don't abandon my personal boundaries?"

Keep in mind, there was never any guarantee that our little movie would be getting a PG-13 rating. And there was the title.

Before we got around to shooting our first "proper" sex scene, we'd shot a scene in bed, a tame, postcoital, morning-after love scene. I had decided it wasn't necessary to be totally naked, so I'd kept my panties on under the covers. A few takes in, someone—the cinematographer or script supervisor—caught what they thought was a flash of pink floral something in the shot. I had to lose the panties.

A few nights later, I had a nightmare that I was being raped. I don't remember the specifics, only that I woke up terrified.

Patrick and I had clocked a lot of hours together on *Red Dawn*, as well as on this movie, and I was keenly aware of him as a flirty, sexual being who was used to women fainting over him. I, too, was a flirty, sexual being, but Patrick and I were sometimes like oil and water. I think he assumed I would automatically be more into him than I was, which would make sense, since I might've been the only woman alive who didn't melt like butter on toast when he walked into the room.

Because I wasn't feeling it in real life, I didn't know how I was going to make myself feel it for this sex scene, which I wanted and needed to do. I didn't know how I was going to get myself there, but I knew that the scene needed to work. It had to be hot, and it had to look real.

Sex I knew how to do. But I didn't know how to fake sex in front of a crew of men, who, in ridiculously close quarters, were practically on top of us. And I knew that whatever I would be feeling, the camera was going to be right up in there to capture it. It was practically a three-way. At the least.

Coming from the Playhouse, where it was all about the reality of doing, I was more than a tad nervous about what we would in fact really be doing. What exactly was going to happen? What if the guy gets hard? What if he doesn't? In either scenario, where does the dick go? Plus, the threat of a Groupon issued for an all-access pass to intimate parts of me was probably what my unconscious was trying to communicate to me in my dream. I realized that I needed to find some way to take my power back, to feel more in control of the situation.

I was powerless over having to shoot a sex scene, but not powerless over my *experience* of shooting that scene. My fear wasn't about sex. It was about choice. So I made a very conscious choice. Instead of colluding with the idea that what I needed didn't matter, I would make the scene *all about my needs*.

I was going to put myself in the catbird seat and make this scene so fucking hot for myself. And why wouldn't I? (Why wouldn't anyone *anytime* they had sex?) It was my job to figure out what it was I needed to make myself feel safe and taken care of. And why not make the most of it? Why leave the casino cheered to have not lost your shirt? While I'm there, I might as well win big. Cherry, cherry, cherry.

Since I didn't have a choice about a bunch of guys on the set seeing me simulate having sex, I decided instead of resisting it, I'd lean into it. This scene wasn't happening *to* me, it was happening *for* me. I'd make it a good thing. *A very good thing.* The more they watched, the more I'd get off on it. So that's what I did.

Whenever young actresses ask me about shooting love scenes, I basically tell them, "Just turn yourself on. Do whatever it takes to feel you're in the power position, because you are. No one's taking anything from you that you don't want to give."

Patrick had a gorgeous body. He had natural machismo. He was kind. Once I got going, in charge of my own experience, he became quite the asset. As soon as they said "*Cut!*" Patrick gasped, "Will you marry me?" And I said, "Definitely."

So that happened.

Still, there was this elephant in the room, the dreaded "lift."

Doing the lift is *not* a passive ride. It's nothing like just hanging on for dear life on a roller coaster. To be lifted, you have to run from a good distance to get momentum, then the instant you arrive at your destination, you propel yourself up as high as you can, jettisoning yourself into space, aiming for over your partner's head. You hope your hip bones meet the flat palms of his hands and that he will have the strength to deadlift you up over his head, nine feet above ground, balancing the full weight of your body on his wrists. Once aloft, your job (not over yet!) is to shoot your arms wide like airplane wings for balance, cross your ankles, and point your toes, maintaining your gaze on the horizon. And don't forget to smile. All these things happen simultaneously. Granted, he's doing the heavy lifting, but it's not solely his responsibility to keep the two of you safe. It's also on you. You must maintain length and balance. And, whether you feel it or not, maintain your fucking cool.

I knew I had to actively make good on my deal, and that it wasn't as easy as everyone thought it would be. I feared that if I didn't do my part perfectly, there might be sudden death, paralysis, or at least some broken bones. For either or both of us.

I come from physically fearful stock. Both of my parents were extremely nervous about getting hurt, as were their parents. My mom never learned to ride a bicycle. My dad can barely spell the word "sports."

Patrick, though, was fearless. He insisted on doing his own stunts. Breaking bones for him was just the price of doing business. He was an athletic phenomenon who craved extreme physical challenge, a thrill seeker who loved meeting his fear. It wasn't the most comforting thing for me to put my body in the hands of someone who ate calamity for breakfast. But you can't fling yourself into the air and have someone lift you nine feet off the ground if you don't trust them.

Again, if this lift had been solely about me trusting Patrick to do everything perfectly, that would have scared me a lot less. It was *me* who had to balance and not freak out, overriding my family's fears going back for generations, facing long-standing, limiting beliefs about myself. I was scared that my fear would make it so Patrick couldn't do his part. In Patrick's screen test, you see me try the lift just a little. But that was as far as I had ever gotten. Throughout the shoot, fear had me in a grip of static refusal. Can you imagine how anxiety-producing that must have been for Patrick? For the director, for the producers, for everyone? This climactic moment of the film—*and I just wouldn't do it.* Practicing in the water (hypothermia aside) was a brilliant way to avoid the peril of gravity. But on land? The way I pictured it, I was going to keep going, just keep flying over his head and crashing beyond him. Or I was going to collapse on top of him, taking us both down.

Everyone began to pressure me. *Oh my god. Would you just do it?* I didn't like being that person. It wasn't as if I liked holding people hostage. I couldn't help it. "Do the thing you fear the most and the death of fear is certain," Emerson wrote, but that's a whole lot easier said than done. What if I failed?

The first time I did the lift was the moment we shot it, which was probably in the middle of the night. We were all exhausted. They were using more cameras that day, to grab as many angles as possible on each take. There was a huge crowd. All the cast members. All the dancers. All the extras.

In this case, peer pressure was working in my favor. It was go time. I climbed up on the metaphorical fucking high dive and ran toward the end of the board. I leapt into the void—and the net appeared.

You ever have a flying dream? It was kind of like that. Glorious and exhilarating. Emerson was right.

After balancing me up there with preternatural strength and prowess, Patrick slowly, and with superhuman control, lowered me down until I was safely in his arms. What you see between us in that scene was also real. Real gratitude. Real pride. Real respect. Real care. If that's not love, what is?

I knew in that moment that Patrick was the only person who could have played that part. If I had the guts to jump, he was always going to be there to catch me.

I wish Patrick were alive. I wish we could get together. I wish we could reminisce about how, even though neither of us were kids, we were still very young . . . and dumb. In the chaos of it all, I couldn't see what we had in each other. I wish I could tell him I'm sorry for the times I was judgmental, or ball busting, for not treating him with more empathy and compassion, for not trusting that a man would actually show up for me. I wish I could tell him what I know now. That I was so scared and in over my head. I wish I could tell him how lucky I feel to have had him as my Baby's one and only Johnny.

14

Back at the Ranch, a Triptych

In 1979, while I was a student at the Playhouse, my family had made yet another move back to the West Coast, but this time, for the first time without me. I remained in New York, going to acting school and starting my adult life, living on my own.

My parents' new home was a modest, two-bedroom bungalow in Brentwood, a single-level house, except for my dad's office, which was an open loft suspended over the living area, where I slept on a daybed set up for me with sheets and a pillow when I came to visit. This was yet another home my parents couldn't help but put their imprimatur on. They had befriended and hired a young English interior designer named Paul Fortune, who had a knack for making every space he touched look effortlessly chic, reupholstering found vintage pieces with unusual textiles, while allowing my parents' place overall to remain specifically them.

Everywhere your eye landed in their new California nest was a visual feast, yet never contrived. It was chock-full of familiar objects—paperweights, vases, African art—touchstones that followed our family from house to house. Their home felt like the most comforting embrace, with freshly cut flowers and the fridge bursting with delectable goodies.

My parents' style was probably more of my dad's vision, but because they had been married so long, their partnership so enduring, their sensibility in lockstep, it was hard to tell where one of them ended and the other began. They seemed fused, like twin cherries, Jo and Joel.

In June 1982, I flew to LA for Jimmy's high school graduation from the (at that time) all-boys Harvard School. The day after graduation, to take advantage of this opportune moment when all four J's were briefly gathered under the same roof, my parents had asked their designer, Paul, to snap some casual family portraits in the backyard. The whole endeavor felt strained and unpleasant. We were all tense that day, just "at each other." I remember not understanding why we were having to do this photo shoot when no one seemed to be feeling it, yet the overriding expectation was that we needed to fall in and cooperate. I'm assuming the whole purpose was, ironically, to chronicle our "still happy after all these years" family.

The following morning was like most Los Angeles mornings, with great golden shafts of sun streaming through the floor-to-ceiling windows, bathing the house in a positive light. Birds chirping like they invented it. When I came downstairs, the house was oddly quiet, devoid of human activity. I found my mother still in bed, with an odd look on her face. My first thought was that perhaps she was sick, so I asked if she was okay. She made a half-hearted attempt to sit up a bit straighter, repositioning a pillow for support. Her eyes puffy from sleep, she uttered, "I told your father, I can't do this anymore."

I almost couldn't hear the words she was speaking. It was as if someone had muted the sound. She went on. "I woke up this morning knowing that if I didn't say something, if I didn't get out, I might not be able to. And I felt if I stayed another day, I was going to die."

In the rumpled sheets on my dad's side of the bed, I could see where his form had pressed into them. I asked the only thing I knew to ask, "Where's Dad?"

She said, "He left."

My brother was sleeping in his room across the hall. And I was unable to even imagine where my dad would have gone so early in the morning.

The brightness of the new day had been blighted.

Quietly, my mother said, "I just can't—can't do it anymore."

They never really quarreled, or not that I'd witnessed. They were so similar. They would say almost the same words to me on separate occasions. They liked and referenced the same things. They echoed each other's every thought. They were joined at the fucking hip. They had been married for twenty-four years. As I was growing up, it had never occurred to me they would get divorced. But when I heard the words "I can't do it anymore," somewhere deep within me, I understood exactly what she meant. She was tired of being Mrs. Joel Grey. She was making a last-ditch effort to reclaim her Self.

My mother packed a small bag and left that afternoon to stay at the Chateau Marmont. My parents began living their separate lives, my dad back in New York and my mom in Los Angeles. They divorced a year later.

• • •

Starting when I came back from the run of *Album* in Chicago, I had a roommate, because I couldn't not have a roommate. The rent for my apartment, the floor of a West Village brownstone on Bethune Street, was about a thousand dollars a month, and I just didn't have it. I was still waitressing and passing hors d'oeuvres for caterers. Matthew had been living in his mother's apartment rent-free, but our relationship was progressing, so for a time, Matthew moved in with me and my roommate, Meg, and paid his third of the rent.

Matthew could be moody, but he could also be charming and hilarious. His humor was dark and Jewish and smart. He'd turned me on to *The 2000 Year Old Man* and *Young Frankenstein*. He was unaffected and disheveled. On the outside, he had the boyish, Irish good looks; on the inside, he was more of a cranky old Jew. And I was crazy in love with him.

With the new John Hughes movie in the can, Matthew had become one of those in-demand actors with a slate of movies booked back-to-back. Soon after we wrapped *Ferris* and were officially a couple, Matthew went off to California to start shooting a movie called *Project X*.

He flew me out to LA to visit him on location. As part of Matthew's deal, the production had rented him a condo on the beach in Santa Monica and a Jaguar. On his days off, we'd take hours-long bike rides on the path along the ocean all the way down to Palos Verdes, go for dinner at the Ivy, spend evenings in bed, working our way through the complete *Fawlty Towers* VHS collection.

That year, Halley's Comet was making its highly anticipated return, and as luck would have it, there was a telescope in the condo. Matthew was shooting on location in Oxnard, so our plan was for me to drive the Jag an hour north, with the telescope and a bunch of blankets in the trunk, pick him up after work, and we'd head out into the desert.

But when I arrived on set, excited to meet everybody, they were still shooting, and I immediately noticed that Matthew seemed extremely uncomfortable. He stiffened when I leaned in to kiss him hello. I knew he sometimes could be socially awkward. That wasn't unusual. But something felt definitely off. He introduced me in passing to Helen Hunt, the other lead in the movie (aside from Virgil, the chimpanzee). In past conversations he had dismissively described Helen as someone he "got along with fine," and she seemed nice enough.

The next day, after our night in the desert, when Matthew and I were soaking in the motel's hot tub in Oxnard, Helen and her friend strolled by, and I thought I caught a vibe that was less than friendly. Sometime much later on in the shoot, Helen and a couple of her friends organized a day trip to a water park at Magic Mountain and invited Matthew and me to come along. It was a super fun day. We all got soaked on the water flume ride, and I thought Helen and her friends were great. It felt like we were all part of a gang.

Later that year, after *Project X* had wrapped, I was in LA without Matthew and called Helen to see if she wanted to get together. "Oh," she said. "I threw my back out. I can't leave the house." When I mentioned to Matthew that I'd tried to get together with Helen, but she'd hurt her back, he said, "What? Why would you call her?" I thought it was a strong reaction, but chalked it up to him being possessive. "Why wouldn't I? I wanted to hang out. I like her."

Then, after I came home from shooting *Dirty Dancing,* Matthew's next gig was *Biloxi Blues,* and they'd cast Penny Miller to reprise the role she'd played as Matthew's love interest on Broadway before he and I had met. His tales about this crazed young actress who had become unhinged over him had become legend from his reenactments. When I heard this same actress who had been so wonderful in this part had been cast in the movie version, I couldn't help but feel a little flutter of dread. But I also took his well-worn shtick about how "crazy" she was as some kind of guarantee that my relationship would be safe. (Little did I realize how likely it was that I was next in line to be referred to as "a close family friend" or the crazy bitch who just couldn't get over him.)

I was having pizza and beer with Maggie at John's, the old-school pizzeria on Bleecker Street, the night before I was flying to visit Matthew, who was shooting *Biloxi Blues* on a military base in Arkansas. I was telling Maggie I'd just gotten off a call with him where he'd said, "I don't know. Maybe you shouldn't come."

And I was, like, "What're you talking about? I'm supposed to get on a plane first thing tomorrow morning!"

He said, "I don't know, I guess Penny heard someone in the production office discussing your airport pickup and she totally freaked out. She said if you come here, she's quitting."

I said, "What the actual fuck."

He said, "I know . . . She's insane."

I asked, "Well, are you *fucking* her?!"

He said, "Of course not! Are you kidding me!? You know—she's *nuts*. She's just jealous. She's still got this weird thing about me."

"Oh, for fuck's sake. Well, if you're *not fucking* her . . . then I'm coming. I'll see you tomorrow."

I remember sitting in this hard wooden booth opposite Maggie as I was repeating this bizarre conversation I'd just had, feeling this particular queasiness in the pit of my stomach that was making it hard to enjoy my pizza.

I asked her, "So what do you think is going on?"

Maggie said, "I don't know."

"But, c'mon. That's so crazy sounding. She's going to *quit*? Who does that? I don't get it."

Maggie said, "I don't know. But . . . it doesn't sound *great*."

"He asked me to come. He arranged everything, sent me the ticket. And now he's telling me I shouldn't come? The night before?"

My conversation with Maggie went around in circles like that for at least an hour.

When I arrived at the military base the next day, I was introduced to Mike Nichols, who was directing, and Carrie Fisher, who was there hanging out with Mike, writing the screenplay for *Postcards from the Edge*. Carrie and I became fast friends, and Mr. Nichols more than lived up to the hype. He was one of the most spectacularly brilliant and seriously funny humans I'd ever met. That first day he instantly endeared himself to me. Right out of the gate, he said to me, "Yeah, I heard the whole story. *Everyone* heard the whole story. I said if she quits, I'll recast it."

I said, "Seriously?"

He said, "Oh, absolutely."

Mike was like a good bitchy girlfriend if you were in a bad spot.

So I went on the set, hung out with Matthew and Carrie, Mike, and the rest of the guys. Penny wasn't scheduled to work, but she did have to come to base camp for a costume fitting, and the whole cast and crew were obviously working hard to make sure that she and I did not cross paths.

Reader, I *know*. I know what you're thinking, and I know how oblivious and naive I must seem. Yes, you are clearly much wiser, more capable, and more willing at this moment to fully grasp what I was not able to take in back then. I super-duper didn't want to see what I didn't want to see. So, I didn't.

They were shooting a scene with Chris Walken, as the sergeant, where he's delivering a big speech to his platoon. I was in heaven watching from behind the camera maybe the greatest director of all time, Mike Nichols, directing one of my favorite actors. After a few takes, Mike moseyed over to me and, under his breath, asked if I wouldn't mind leaving, because Chris was struggling to remember his lines and had blamed my short shorts for distracting him.

I might have been flattered if not for the growing sense that I was widely unwelcome on this set.

My return flight to New York was very delayed, and I ended up in the airport bar with Chris Walken, who was booked on the same flight. We got along like ketchup and fries. He turned me on to Wild Turkey and we spent what seemed like hours there. I'd never been happier to be delayed, stuck in an airport bar, hearing Chris talk about his early days as a dancer and laughing our asses off. Getting drunk with this mysterious and complex actor I had been so in awe of, finding such an instant and easy connection with him definitely took the edge off the fraught trip to visit my boyfriend. It almost made me forget how much pain I was in.

• • •

Matthew's mother, Patsy Broderick, was a playwright and painter. She had no tolerance for Hollywood bullshit or anything else she didn't consider to be high art or culture. She had an air of superiority, hated polite conversation, and cared not a whit about anyone's opinion of her. She couldn't help but speak her truth. She was offended by lies.

She was what was then considered to be an older mother, having given birth to her third child and only son, Matthew, when she was thirty-seven. She'd been widowed just a few years earlier, in 1982, when Matthew's dad, James Broderick, the beloved father from the TV series *Family*, died of cancer. Patsy herself had been in ill health from before I'd come on the scene, having survived lung cancer and triple bypass surgery, and was often in the throes of some legitimate and potentially life-threatening health crisis. When Matthew stayed over at my place, it wasn't uncommon for his mother to call, wheezing, unable to breathe, just as we'd fallen off to sleep. Her son, of course, would throw on his clothes and rush to her side.

One evening, from a pay phone on the street, I called their apartment looking for Matthew. When Patsy answered, I could barely make out what she was saying, except that she was alone and obviously in some kind of agony. Hearing the distress in her voice, I ran over there like some dopey Florence Nightingale.

I found her writhing in her sickbed. From her bloodless complexion to her tangle of hair chopped into a bob, she was a study in gray. Her palette was like a faded black-and-white photograph that had been ever so subtly hand-tinted to approximate a color print. She was on top of the bed sheets, wearing only a worn nightgown, her legs thrashing to and fro. I couldn't tell if she was on medication or just out of her mind in pain. I was trying to assess if I needed to call a doctor or an ambulance. I didn't know where Matthew was, but hoped he was about to walk in the door, or at least call.

I might have been there for an hour or maybe less, when—perhaps her meds kicked in? or she was just so relieved that someone had heard her cries for help?—she seemed to settle down enough to be able to engage in a little conversation. She and I had never been alone together. She asked how my mom was doing on her own. She began talking about how she and her deceased husband, "Jimmy," and my parents had all started out together as struggling actors coming up in the theater around the same time.

Next thing I remember, she snapped, "Well, your dad's a *fag*."

I kind of laughed it off and corrected her. "No. Um. He's not." I was more taken aback by her aggressive tone than by what she was saying.

"He's *gay*," she said, leaning into my face.

"He actually isn't." I tried to humor her out of it. I wrote it off as her being in pain or on painkillers.

But then her frustration seemed to focus her. "How can you not know your dad's a fag? He's always been. Everyone knows but you. And your mom. But it's not her fault."

It was like a sniper attack.

This wasn't the first time I had been confronted about my dad's sexual orientation. Apparently there's no end to people's fascination with outing closeted celebrities. And while what goes on behind closed doors isn't necessarily anyone's business, I'd never shied away from setting the record straight, though I found it a bit tedious. I was accustomed to chalking up these queries to a lack of showbiz sophistication or just to bored people being gossipy idiots. My dad's uncanny portrayal of the Emcee in *Cabaret*—his stylized makeup and his ability, in full drag, to do the kick line alongside the ladies—was only evidence of his brilliance as an artist, not of a fluid sexuality. Some people just didn't get it.

But Patsy? She was deeply savvy about the theater and show folk.

My dad had always been demonstrative, romantic, and very physically affectionate with my mother. I had never questioned his deep and abiding love for her. To this day, as I write this, my dad still maintains that my mother was the love of his life. And because my dad and I had always been extremely close, I felt certain I pretty much knew everything about him, and I trusted him completely. I had no question about who my father was.

I was sure Patsy was just trying to get rid of me. Maybe if she was awful enough I'd leave her son alone.

I walked home shaking and crying. As soon as I got home, I called my mom. She called my dad. I don't know what went down between the two of them during that conversation, except that afterward my dad said that we needed to get together with my brother to have a talk. It was maybe a week later when Jimmy, Nellie, and I met at my dad's apartment at the Des Artistes. Jimmy came down from upstate New York, where he was enrolled at The Culinary Institute, becoming a chef. I can't recall the conversation at all, but when I asked Nellie about that conversation recently, she remembered that my brother had taken the news especially hard. To this day, every time I try to drill down and get some sort of definitive understanding from my parents about their marriage, they give me a slightly different story from the one they gave me before.

My dad's sexual preference, or anyone's for that matter, is not for me to understand or define. Humans are complicated, and sexuality is shrouded in mystery for many of us. My dad was and is the exact same loving father and extraordinary man I had always known. But Patsy's outburst disrupted my narrative, the only story of my dad, of my parents' marriage, and of our family that I had ever considered. At the time, this new information rattled me to my core. Not for any judgment of my dad's sexuality, but because I had never trusted anybody in my young life more than I had trusted my dad, and for going on twenty-six years I had been under the impression that he was straight. (From where I sit now, it seems pretty harsh and unsophisticated, dehumanizing, and unloving to consider that any one of us should be bound to so reductive a label, so simplistic an identity.) Unconsciously, I'm sure I'd been taking in plenty of what was unspoken, but never in a way that made this information any less jarring. Many years later, by penning a memoir, *Master of Ceremonies,* my dad came out at the age of eighty-two. From that book, I learned that after confessing a homosexual relationship to his parents at the age of sixteen, his mother turned on him and said, "You disgust me." From his point of view, being an openly gay man in the fifties would have rendered his desires to have a family of his own and become a successful actor impossibilities.

The fact that my dad had to hide from the people closest to him one of the most integral parts of his being for most of his life was a heartache I took much longer to process.

15

Rough Cut

In the spring of 1987, the *Dirty Dancing* producers and Vestron set up a private screening for me to see an early cut of the movie. The sole purpose being to get me to sign off on footage in one of the love scenes where I was more naked than I'd contractually negotiated to be.

When you shoot a love scene, it can be a mood killer and distracting if you're frantically trying to cover your bits and pieces. So that's where your contract comes in. When you're making your deal, if the script suggests there might be possible nakedness down the road, one of the deal points establishes boundaries and guidelines that must be adhered to, so no matter what they shoot on the day, you can feel protected about what will end up in the final cut. In my *Dirty Dancing* contract, I had negotiated "no nipples," "no ass crack." I don't know how I came up with those particulars. I guess I figured, it's not a boob without the nipple or an ass without a crack, and of course, bush was also out (because in those days, bush was not even up for grabs). So I had an ironclad no-nipple-ass-crack-bush clause.

To assess which of my bits the producers now wanted permission to show, I had invited Susan Smith, the owner of the boutique talent agency that repped me, to the viewing. I'd had little to no prior interactions with Susan, as most of her attention was devoted to the care and feeding of Brian Dennehy's career. She and I sat alone in a sea of empty red velvet seats in the Magno screening room, the same venue where I'd had my first peek at *The Cotton Club*. I was hopeful that involving Susan in this "important" decision, about whether or not to allow the world to see my nipple/ass crack/bush (like it cared!) might prove me and my career to be worthy of her attention.

We sat in the pitch black as the unfinished cut of the movie began. I could barely breathe as I tried to acclimate to the surreal experience of seeing my face on the screen, as big as a brownstone. I had no idea if what I was looking at was good or bad—the movie, my performance, any of it. All I could tell was there was an awful lot of me. Much more than I was used to seeing or comfortable with. Throughout this disorienting experience, I became aware of a mysterious intermittent ticking sound, like a metronome. A drunk metronome. Eventually, I discovered the source. It was my agent. Punctuating each moment I was on camera, which was pretty much from the beginning of the movie to the end, with a weary "tsk" of distaste. If an exhalation could convey disgust, that was the sound.

When the film ended, we sat for a moment in silence. We thanked the projectionist, and as we walked out, the mood was grim. "Nobody is *ever* going to see this movie. So you don't have to worry," Susan said. "You're just going to have to get something else in the can as soon as possible." She straightened her wig. "And the nudity? Let 'em have it. It's the only scene in the movie that works."

I somehow found my way back home, and once inside my apartment I grabbed the frosty vodka bottle out of the freezer, made a beeline for my bed, and crawled under the covers with all my clothes on, even though it was only late afternoon.

For months after that screening, I had lower-than-low expectations for my first starring vehicle, as did Vestron, which had originally planned a very limited theatrical release (I think it was one weekend), the bare minimum necessary to support their home video sales. But in the end, in order to get the PG-13 rating they wanted, the producers cut all nudity out of the film anyway.

Then I attended a cast and crew, friends and family screening, where I thought, "Ya know, this isn't that awful." Was this new edit so much better than the one Susan and I had seen? Had the rough cut been just *too* rough for me to see what the movie could eventually be? Or had my opinion and experience of that early cut been too colored by my agent's intensely negative reaction?

As the date for the movie's opening drew closer, there began to be rumblings suggesting that *Dirty Dancing* might not be a total disaster. Whether it was through the work of the film's editor, Peter Frank, or just the way this particular story intersected with the zeitgeist of that particular year, 1987, the fate of this little movie seemed *maybe* to be turning around.

16

Ireland

The day before had been a dreamy one. The farmer who lived next door had enlisted our help in making hay, and afterward we had lain atop the giant haystacks in the golden late-afternoon light. Before bed, we'd taken a walk under the dark and starry sky, one of those night skies visible only in the most remote of places, where the black is so deep, the stars so plentiful. I'd never seen anything like it except at the planetarium. The inverse ratio of darkness to stars favored the stars.

Matthew said, "Oooh, didya see that? Shooting star."

I said, "Uch! I missed it. I think I might be the only living person who's never seen one."

He said, "C'mon. That's not possible. Oh—there's another one."

No sooner did I gaze up with the set intention of finally catching a star in action than I saw one, and no sooner did I see one than I saw another, then another. The sky broke out in flashes of shooting streaks of light. A meteor shower.

When Matthew was eight years old, his parents had bought a modest cottage in Ireland on the bluffs overlooking the deep periwinkle ocean in Kilcar, a town in County Donegal. It had been his family's vacation home, a retreat from Hollywood and New York City life. He grew up spending Christmases there. And when he spoke about this special land, where his father's ashes were buried, I thought it was maybe the place he felt the presence of his father the most.

The weather was super romantic. Foggy and dreamlike most days. Every day a variation on rain. And where there is rain, there is green. What Donegal always was, was green. When the sun came out, although it almost never happened, the low ceiling of clouds lifted to reveal a high blue heaven.

It was a very quiet and simple kind of vacation. Matthew and I fished off the dock just down at the bottom of the hillside. We asked the local butcher how to make traditional corned beef, cabbage, and potatoes. We took day trips to hike Slieve League's glorious ancient trails along the craggy cliffs with picnic lunches of homemade brown bread, Irish cheese, and chutney.

There wasn't much to do when it was raining, which was often, but it was cozy by the peat fire. I was finally reading *Anna Karenina,* and loving it, lying on the carpeted, sparsely furnished living room floor with a pillow under my head. After dinner, sometimes we'd walk down the pitch-dark road to the lively pub for a pint with the locals. It seemed that everyone in the tiny town knew Matthew growing up, from before he was an actor, and was always so happy to see him.

A few days before Matthew and I were scheduled to leave on this trip, I was with my roommate, Meg, at our neighborhood hang, the White Horse Tavern, eating knockwurst platters with sauerkraut and mustard, drinking frosty mugs of black-and-tan beer on one of the picnic tables out front. One beer in, I began sharing with her my growing panic about the faraway romantic vacation. I had this dread I was trying to make sense of. I knew I didn't want to go, but I couldn't see how to get out of it, because, as I told Meg, "I can't cancel now. We leave the day after tomorrow."

Matthew and I had been together for going on two years, and we were now living together, in the apartment I shared with Meg. What was right about Matthew and me together was undeniably right. There were a lot of laughs, and I just felt we were alike in so many ways, lucky to have found each other. But there were definitely problems. There were periodic spikes of tension and drama. It was never smooth sailing.

I didn't know if my misgivings about our impending trip were just me being neurotic, because I've always experienced a certain level of anxiety right before traveling, particularly to new places, especially faraway ones. I was trying to discern if what I was feeling was my irrational fear, which I needed to quell and push through, or if it was my wise mind, my deepest intuition, the small voice that can be hard to discern because the tumult in my brain can be so noisy, signaling that relationships should be easier than this. In spite of my misgivings, I chose the path of least resistance, and went ahead with the trip.

One of the topics Matthew and I had heated discussions about while lying around reading in the cottage was the upcoming premiere for *Dirty Dancing*. He really didn't want to go with me. He said he didn't like premieres, and after the cast and crew screening, had said, "I won't ever sit through that again. Do you know how hard that was for me to see you up there with Patrick like that?" But Matthew was a seasoned professional, a movie star, he of all people should have understood that a love scene was just part of the job. Right?

It wasn't that I thought the movie was going to be a big deal or anything. As far as I knew it might even be a tad embarrassing, but it was my first lead in a film, and he *was* my boyfriend. I was confounded and hurt by his steadfast refusal to accommodate something so important to me.

When we'd get into these circular arguments, the isolation of the remote Irish countryside and being unable to get some distance or call a girlfriend for a reality check seemed to render me more vulnerable to feeling confused, questioning the validity of my point of view. Was the movie opening as inconsequential as he insisted it was? Or was it possible that my boyfriend was not supportive of my career? He would've vehemently denied that assumption as preposterous and offensive. And it was impossible for me to fathom that someone who loved me, which he certainly seemed to, wouldn't be my biggest cheerleader and supporter.

About ten days into our vacation, the old house phone that never rang, rang, startling us both. It was Matthew's mother, announcing that it had been a while since she'd been to Donegal and that she had booked herself on a flight to join us for an impromptu visit. There was no way I was staying for that. That Matthew was allowing it, on top of the stress I was feeling about my movie opening in two weeks, made something in me just snap. I said, "If she's coming, I'm leaving." I thought, "I've had enough. This is too fucked up. I'll just hold it together, get myself home, and when he comes back, I absolutely have to break up with this guy."

Matthew and I had flown into Shannon, but because his mother would be flying into the Dublin airport, we changed my ticket to leave from there. We were going to drive to Dublin, which I'd never seen, stay the night in this nice old hotel, and I'd leave for the States the following morning.

The day after the baling of the hay and the night of the shooting stars, it was your typical Irish morning in the countryside: misty, overcast, roads wet from the light rain that had been falling. I was feeling pangs of sadness welling up in me about the impending likely end of the relationship and the seductive pull of what could still be. Before we left, I picked a few of whatever wildflowers were growing scattered around the property, tied them with some scrap of ribbon, and placed them on the spot where the family had buried Matthew's father's ashes.

As we were heading out, we stopped in to say goodbye to the neighbor we had commissioned to knit a sweater for me. The cable-knit cardigan was beautiful, made of scratchy tobacco-colored wool with leather buttons. I loved it and had worn it for most of our time in Donegal. The neighbor served us brown bread, still warm from the oven, with her homemade jam and the creamiest butter, along with a farewell pot of tea in front of the fragrant peat burning in the hearth.

When we'd first landed at the Shannon airport, the car rental office had given us our choice of vehicles. Being a thrifty sort, Matthew had opted for the least expensive one, but I'd intervened, urging him to spring for the BMW, reminding him of the explicit instructions of his good friend and father figure, Jason Robards: "Always drive a BMW if possible." Because Jason had credited the BMW for saving his life in a near-fatal accident.

In Ireland, Matthew was always the driver, because he was very accustomed to driving on the left side of the road, and I was not. And he was a good driver. I was happy to be the copilot in charge of the music and maps. Our bag of cassettes was on the floor by my feet. We'd listen to the whole tape, both sides, and when it would pop out of the cassette player, I'd grab another tape out of the bag, look to see which side was ready to play, and push it in. We'd been listening to U2's *The Joshua Tree* on a loop. We, along with pretty much everyone else on the planet, were obsessed with that album that summer. I thought it was synchronistic that Matthew and I were Americans having an Irish experience, while listening to the Irish band's first album about their American experience—"With or Without You," "I Still Haven't Found What I'm Looking For." The country roads we were navigating were not well marked, so when "Where the Streets Have No Name" came on, it was like they were singing to us.

We got lost, and as it was raining really hard, we stopped for gas, to get directions, and to wait out the downpour. While Matthew was putting gas in the car, he asked an off-duty policeman for directions. I remember noticing the wide-wale, olive-colored corduroy pants Matthew was wearing, and thinking those pants looked so good on him he should get more like that.

It was afternoon. There were few cars on the road.

We had been listening to *Joshua Tree* so much I wanted to switch things up a little. I took the *Sounds of Soweto* cassette out of its hinged plastic case and was sliding it into the tape deck when I heard Matthew scream. As I jerked my head up, I saw something completely filling the windshield, and there it was, like a sledgehammer. The sudden and stunning force of impact.

Then eerie silence.

My forehead stung. My head must have been whipped into the dashboard. There was a searing sensation on my chest where, I later learned, the seat belt had burned off the top layers of flesh below my neck.

Time was in slow motion and compacted, as if time were on mushrooms.

I spit out a mouthful of what I thought were my broken teeth. And, glancing down, was relieved to see on my sweater instead a spray of translucent, perfectly formed cubes of safety glass, the size of baby teeth. The windshield had exploded.

I looked over at Matthew, unconscious, his bloodied face slumped forward onto the steering wheel, his chin split open like a Pez dispenser.

South African music started to play. *Sounds of Soweto.*

I struggled, punching at the buttons to silence the bizarre soundtrack of this nightmare. I was alive. But this was bad. The smell of acrid burning metal, like bumper cars, and the temperature, so hot, like we were in an incinerator. So much smoke, I thought we were about to burst into flames. I knew I had to get Matthew out. I opened my door, ran out to his side to pull him out of the wreck, but couldn't open his door. There was no longer anything that resembled a door to be opened. What was once a door was a blackened crush of metal wrapped around his frame.

I looked up and down the deserted country road for any sign of a car, but there was nobody. Nothing. No people. Only mist, and a road in both directions, as far as the eye could see. Green and peaceful. And quiet. Except for a faint keening of maybe an animal that was hit? I couldn't place what this sound was, or where it was coming from.

Finally, I saw a car in the distance, coming toward us, and, waving my arms and screaming, flagged it down. The driver pulled over up the road and came running toward me, looking terrified and holding a plaid wool blanket.

He handed me the blanket and ran back to his car to go for help, and I thought, "Oh no, please don't leave! You can't—"

I got back into the car on my side. All I could think of was that I had to somehow pull Matthew's body out through my side of the car. I lifted his head off the steering wheel, kissing and stroking the side of his forehead, talking to him, trying to get him to regain consciousness. From his jawline hung a bleeding open wound, a surreal shock of color against his white, white skin. "Hey, honey. Can you help me? Let's get you out of here. I'm going to undo your seat belt." As I started climbing over him to unbuckle his seat belt, he opened his eyes, completely dazed.

I heard distant sirens—a blessed sound when you are waiting for help—then two ambulances arrived and the medics descended. Asking me to step away, they moved in. They swarmed Matthew, taking his vitals and assessing his injuries. It was then that I noticed one of his legs was making no sense. Instead of his thighbone going directly from his hip to his knee, his pants, those same corduroy pants I'd just been admiring, bent at a very sharp and confusing angle, midthigh. The next thing I knew, the medics were putting away their equipment and heading back to the ambulance. I called out, "What's going on? Where are you going?"

"We can't get him out." They were hurrying back to the ambulance while they were talking to me. "We have to send someone with the equipment to cut the car open. We're coming back."

"But you can't leave him."

And they were gone. I couldn't figure out what was going on. I didn't see another car. When I think back on it now, knowing that it was a head-on collision, I would have to assume the other car had gone off the road. But at the time, that sort of deductive reasoning was beyond my ken.

After what felt like an eternity, a fire truck arrived, cleared the area. It could have taken fifteen minutes or the better part of an hour.

Once they'd removed Matthew's side of the car, they had to lift him out of the wreckage and get him onto a gurney, into the ambulance, which had returned. Imagine having to move someone whose femur is at a perfect right angle. I can't remember exactly—memory at times may be a merciful editor—but I'm pretty sure he was screaming like a motherfucker.

I got into the ambulance alongside him. I was kissing his head, reassuring him that everything was going to be okay. They took us—with the sirens wailing and lights flashing—to the local hospital in the small town of Enniskillen.

Once Matthew had regained consciousness, whenever I was asked to step aside, he would grow agitated until I was back in his field of vision. Then, flooded with relief, he'd say, "Oh god! I thought you were dead." Initially this seemed to me like the most romantic thing in the world, but when it happened over and over again, I understood that it was really just a symptom of receiving a violent blow to the head.

I ran alongside as they wheeled Matthew's gurney into the "casualty ward." I noticed out of the corner of my eye a body lying on the gurney next to us. It was a nude body of an older woman, with white-gray hair and skin, a different hue of white than any I'd ever seen, slightly mottled gray and white, like marble. As I reflexively looked away, a nurse whipped the flimsy privacy curtain between us, the clatter of metal moving through the aluminum track like a reprimand.

As the small team of ER doctors descended upon Matthew, I retreated to the outer perimeter of his curtained cubby, my antennae way the fuck up to try and grasp what the damage was, as someone's scissors hastily cut the corduroy pants off him. Everything felt unreal, like a dream or a movie, a medical drama I was watching play out, randomly interrupted by flashes, snapshots taken by my mind right before and after the crash, like unwanted commercials. I was unsure if any of this was even actually happening, or was perhaps imagined, suspecting that at any moment my life would snap back to something I'd recognize. The next thing I knew his gurney was on the move, to what the doctors there called "the operating theatre." The irony. It seemed only fitting for the level of drama.

This was a small-town hospital, built in the sixties, but where it was lacking in state-of-the-art medical amenities, it more than surpassed expectations in the quality of care, kindness, and humanity of the hospital staff.

They asked me if I was injured, and I knew for certain that

something bad had happened to my body, but I couldn't for the life of me determine or express what that was. They took me over to radiology for X-rays to see if I had broken any bones. I remember the technician asking if there was any chance that I might be pregnant. I told him I didn't think I was but couldn't be sure. I think they did some kind of basic X-ray and determined that I was not injured.

Matthew was still in surgery.

The next memory I have is of me walking the halls until I found an administrator's office, where I asked if I could use her phone to call my family in the States. I remember saying, "Don't worry, I'll call collect." I had to reach my parents or Matthew's manager, at least one person who could alert the others, because no one back at home knew what had happened. But I couldn't remember my parents' numbers. I couldn't remember Matthew's manager's number. I couldn't remember any numbers. I kept apologizing to the woman who was kind enough to let me use her phone. She stood patiently alongside her desk as I tried over and over.

I guess eventually I came up with someone's number, but I distinctly remember being supremely freaked out by my inability to retrieve information that I knew like the back of my hand, because my brain was *not right*.

A young doctor approached me while I was wandering the hospital corridors to let me know what Matthew's status was. He informed me that Matthew was still in the operating room, that he had fractured his femur (the largest and strongest bone in the body), and that the impact must have been very severe to have broken that bone in half. In addition, one of Matthew's lungs had collapsed, punctured by the force of the steering wheel. The injury to his jaw was not a big deal and only required stitches. The doctor said the team was discussing moving Matthew to the Royal Victoria Hospital in Belfast, where they had a state-of-the-art trauma ward. I was in my hyper-efficient mode, or so I thought, matter-of-factly asking all the right questions, when the doctor said, "You're in shock. We're going to get you something that'll help."

"I'm in shock? I don't think so." I was shocked at his assessment of me.

He said, with a slight smile, "Yeah. You are."

He flagged down a nurse, who promptly handed me two tiny paper cups, one with a yellow pill in it and one with water.

Sometime later, I was alone, curled up on a hard vinyl couch in the hospital waiting area, which had grown quiet except for the television set, its volume low. The local news was on, and I was half listening, half watching, but my ears pricked up when I heard the anchor say something about a tragic car accident in which two local women were killed. It struck me as surreal, like a bad dream, to be hearing a news story about a terrible accident when I'd just been in one.

I got the attention of the first nurse I could find, and said, "Excuse me. I just saw something on the news about two women who died in a car crash today. Did they have anything to do with our accident?"

And, as if I'd asked the most ludicrous question, she assured me, "Auck, no, dearie. The people from the other car? They left already. They went home."

17

The Premiere

ACT I **BELFAST**

Once the ER doctors in Enniskillen had stabilized Matthew, they transferred him to the Royal Victoria Hospital in Belfast. The Royal had a renowned major trauma ward for treating the thousands of victims of violence from the Irish conflict.

In Enniskillen, the doctors had stitched up the gash under Matthew's chin, reset and splinted his broken finger, placed a chest tube into his collapsed lung, and set his fractured leg. Once at the Royal, the orthopedic surgeon inserted a metal rod inside the length of his thighbone. Matthew must've also incurred some sort of head injury, because he'd initially been unconscious and suffered amnesia about the accident. He had no recall of the crash, the events leading up to it, or even our vacation. I asked him what he could remember, if anything, about the morning before we set off on the road to Dublin, and he remembered nothing.

While Matthew was still in surgery, Patsy arrived. I was surprised at how overjoyed I was to see her. Grateful for a familiar face, for the presence of someone I knew, someone with whom I could share the responsibilities in this dire situation. Once Matthew was out of surgery and in his hospital bed for the night, Patsy and I got a hotel room nearby, with twin beds. It was the first time in at least forty-eight hours I'd laid down my head.

The next morning, I was awoken by a searing pain that overwhelmed every inch of me, hurting in a way that I hadn't known was even possible. I literally could not move. At first, I couldn't remember where I was or what had happened to me. I wanted to turn my head to see where I was, but I couldn't move. Then I began to remember. My body felt like it was trapped in a cast of sharp pain, from the base of my skull to the bottom of my feet. Like someone had put me into a dryer wet, and now there was no longer room for me.

I tried to stay completely still—afraid I might cry, frightened of using any muscle. I couldn't get out of bed. At first, I couldn't even talk. Tears tumbled out of the corners of my eyes, pooling in my ears, and then I whimpered, "I want my mommy."

From the other twin bed, Patsy barked, "How's that supposed to make me feel?" Which made me want to cry harder. The pain shot up another notch.

The X-ray taken in Enniskillen had shown that no bones were broken. But it turned out, predictably, that I was injured in ways they couldn't assess at the time. I had soft tissue damage throughout my body. I'd suffered severe whiplash, which happens when the head is violently forced in one direction and then is whipped in the opposite direction, while the upper body is forcibly held in place by the seat belt. The soft tissue that attaches my head to my body—those muscles, tendons, the ligaments in my back—got thrashed: overstretched, strained, and torn. Though I wouldn't know it for another twenty-two years, a thrashed ligament capsule would eventually cause my head to fall forward, and basically be hanging off my spine. But in 1987, the only evidence of injury visible to the eye was the small patch of skin on my chest, just below my neck, that had been burned off by the friction of the seat belt.

I eventually, slowly, painfully got myself up. I'd gone to bed a twenty-seven-year-old and when I woke the next morning, I was 103.

The ride from the hotel to the hospital was a short distance in a taxi, but being a passenger in a car was suddenly terrifying. I was freaking out and embarrassed, taken aback by my overreaction. But my terror overrode the embarrassment. That brief ride was like a very bad psychedelic trip, like being on a roller-coaster ride and then hung from a bungee cord over a great chasm. It was untenable to feel so unsafe.

I'd been trying to quit smoking on and off for years. I'd successfully quit for some time before the accident, but after the accident I immediately began chain-smoking, as if I had to make up for all the cigarettes I'd missed. I was unable to eat. By day, I'd keep Matthew company in his hospital room. In the evenings, or for lunch, I'd cross the street to the Crown Liquor Saloon, Belfast's most famous bar, as well as its most bombed by the IRA. I drank and smoked, picked at the pub food. I started taking Valium before bed to try to get some sleep. One of my first nights in Belfast, I had an extremely vivid nightmare in which I was visited by the Grim Reaper. He looked just like you'd imagine, scythe toting, dressed in a billowing black robe. He was coming for me, and I told him to fuck off.

On nights when I'd stayed late with Matthew in the hospital, as I was walking the eerily quiet and darkened halls to leave, there would be lines of soldiers, in all black, full riot gear. They wore gas masks and helmets, their machine guns poised at the ready across their chests, legs marching in rhythmic syncopation like the guards outside the castle of the Wicked Witch in *The Wizard of Oz*. We were in Northern Ireland in the thick of the Troubles. (Three months later, in November 1987, the IRA's Remembrance Day bombing in Enniskillen would kill a dozen people and wound more than sixty others.)

There was a war on, and one couldn't not be cognizant of the death grip the conflict had on Ireland, but I wasn't able to fully take all of that in. I don't remember exactly when or how I learned the truth about what had happened to the passengers in the other car, but the nurse in Enniskillen had lied to me (perhaps because I was already in shock?). Two local women, a woman in her sixties and her adult daughter, had died. Matthew was not only seriously injured, but there was an investigation under way about his possible culpability. And since the head-on collision had occurred on a deserted country road and Matthew had amnesia, I was the sole surviving witness.

On a bench outside the hospital, a pleasant man with a pocket-sized memo pad sat down alongside me. I'd been told he wanted to ask me some questions about what had happened, and he began to ask probing questions, trying to extricate clues from the events leading up to the accident. He did a good job of behaving like someone who just wanted to have a friendly conversation. I didn't have anything to hide and was trying to be as cooperative as possible. I could sense his growing frustration, although I was being as forthcoming as humanly possible. He kept repeating the same questions over and over, as if that might somehow loosen a kernel of previously hidden information that would yield the story he was looking for.

"You're Americans. You're used to driving on the other side of the road. Did Matthew ever get confused and drive on the wrong side?"

"No. Never. He was very accustomed to driving in Ireland."

"Is it possible he just naturally had drifted to the other side of the road?"

"I have no idea. I wasn't looking up. I had been looking at the cassette deck."

"Had you guys maybe had anything to drink?"

"No. Nothing."

I wanted to remember something new or different. I wanted to come up with a choice nugget for the nice gentleman. If I tried harder, if I could get my head straight, perhaps I would be able to recount something meaningful. Preferably something that might exonerate my boyfriend. But I could only recall inserting the *Sounds of Soweto* cassette.

Then Matthew's guttural scream.

Our seat belts had saved our lives. The mother and daughter in the Volvo had not been wearing theirs.

ACT II THE CONCORDE

Dirty Dancing had been shown to distributors at the Cannes Film Festival in May. And by late summer, when Matthew and I left for Ireland, there were premieres scheduled in New York and LA with a respectable press rollout.

I knew *Dirty Dancing* wasn't an art film. It was hard for me to understand what it could be, but I had started hearing the word "sleeper." And the New York opening had been moved to one of the biggest, most prestigious movie theaters, the Ziegfeld, where *Cabaret* had opened.

Before the accident, I'd still hoped that Matthew would come with me to at least one of the premieres, but he'd stuck to his idea that premieres weren't important, and that press wasn't something "really good" actors needed to do. If you were really good, you didn't need to do any of that bullshit. An opinion that probably originally stemmed from his mother, who made no secret about her disdain of Hollywood and its trappings.

And then the accident happened.

My mother arrived in Belfast a day or two after Patsy, and we all took shifts being with Matthew at the hospital.

My mother was wonderful with Matthew. But when we were alone, I could tell she was concerned about my fervent allegiance to him. She seemed to see then what I can see now: that I was struggling to maintain any sense of my life separate from his. Once it became clear that he was going to be recovering for the next month in the Belfast hospital, my mother was insistent that I return to the States for the premiere.

I *was* really curious to see if this movie I was the lead in was maybe not *horrible*, yet I felt extremely guilty for even thinking about going. And Matthew began to make an even stronger case than before about me not doing press. The gist was, *You don't have to go. A premiere isn't going to make any difference to whether people hire you or not. And if you do go, you're going to have to do press. And all any interviewer is going to want to talk to you about is the accident.* I felt like I had been paddling around in the shallows with my surfboard for a decade, waiting for a decent wave, and at last, a big, beautiful wave was coming. I'd never seen a wave that big up close. And Matthew was telling me I had to get out of the water.

Matthew's big-time entertainment lawyer had flown in from Los Angeles, and he quite plainly was in agreement with Matthew. They explained that it would not only be in bad taste for me to fly back to the US at this time, but it would ultimately be better for my career, for my dignity as an actress, and for Matthew's very serious situation if I did not show up at my premiere.

I know what some of you dear readers might be thinking. "Why were you listening to him? You wanted to break up with him, you should have broken up with him. He was being a jerk." But it wasn't that simple. In the days leading up to the accident, there had been enough magical moments to justify putting off the inevitable, the breakup. And after the accident, something else happened, something profound. In the first days after, as I've already described, anytime we were separated for even a few minutes, Matthew would "forget" that he'd just seen me alive. The terror caused by my absence and the subsequent relief that washed over him when he saw me were beyond startling. The way he looked at me in those moments of relief was like an X-ray of how he felt about me. He was so beautiful. All I saw in his face was love. Reduced to his essence, there was no asshole left in him, he was just love.

And I loved him in a different way than I'd ever loved him before. No matter how much I might have wanted to get out of this relationship, seeing him bloodied, unconscious, his head slumped on the steering wheel, unresponsive, immediately renewed my commitment. Because nothing says "I love you" like "Oh my god, he's dead."

And the two women in the other car had actually died. Over and over, I kept asking myself, "Why am I still here? Why are those women gone? Why am I still alive?"

I was experiencing a dark night of the soul, but I couldn't figure out how to rescue myself except to keep functioning. I wasn't taking stock of the severity of any of the situations I was in. I was injured and acting like I wasn't. I was in a toxic relationship and pretending I could make it right. I was in a serious accident in which people had died and I should have been dead, but I was behaving as if none of that had happened. I was on automatic pilot, unaware that my nervous system was fully shot, like a charred cartoon character after an explosion. It wasn't that I couldn't cope; it was ridiculous how much I was coping.

I've always been pretty fierce when fighting on behalf of others, but less so for myself. I was designed to be that girl. And what could be more enticing to this personality kink of mine than someone who was injured, had nearly died, and was facing an uncertain future?

I had no internalized fight for myself. I was punch-drunk and vulnerable, exhausted, and traumatized. My mom was that coach for me that no one ever was for her. She showed up for me big-time. She said, "There's nothing more you can do for Matthew at this point. The producers are flying you back on the Concorde. This is too important. This is about your career. You have to go." I told her everything Matthew, his mother, and his lawyer were saying, and she said, "Jen, I understand this is hard for you, but you need to go. Matthew will be fine. You can come right back, but you cannot miss this."

I tried to assure Matthew that I would not discuss the accident once I was back in the States and that there was nothing more for me to actually do for him in Ireland. He was now stable, out of danger, and just needed time to recover. I promised to jump right back on a plane and return to him in Belfast four days after I'd left. Still, he begged me not to go. There were a lot of tears.

Ten days after the accident, two days before the premiere, I was flown to New York on the Concorde with my mom. The producers had sent us the tickets for the supersonic aircraft whose tagline was "Arrive Before You Leave" for its ability to fly its passengers across the Atlantic Ocean in about three hours. I cried the whole way to the airport. I cried and smoked all the way across the Atlantic, at "an altitude right at the edge of space." I arrived at JFK in a fucked-up haze of nicotine, alcohol, and jet lag. Flying home for the premiere of my first big movie meant only one thing: that I was not a good person.

My mother and I were greeted at the gate by the movie's young publicist, Mark Pogachefsky, who was very happy to see us, welcoming me with an armful of press clippings. He told us there was "a lot of growing excitement around the movie." And he pointed to one newspaper in particular, an advance copy of the "Arts & Leisure" section of the Sunday *New York Times*. "This is going to be out tomorrow," he said.

The entire top half of the front page of the paper was a giant close-up of Patrick and me from the film. Was I dreaming? Everything that was happening was so bizarre.

ACT III NO RED LIPSTICK

The premiere of *Dirty Dancing* was one of the more baffling occasions of my life.

The first morning back in my apartment after flying home from Ireland, from my bed, in my half-asleep stupor, I could vaguely make out the sound of the outgoing message on the telephone answering machine in the other room. "Hi, we're not home right now. But leave a message after the beep." Followed by the high-pitched screech of a car careening out of control, a loud bang, and then the sounds of women screaming.

Confused and scared, I got up and played back the recording. I couldn't believe anyone would be this awful. Who would go to the trouble of finding our home number and leaving such a menacing message, terrorizing us?

The next morning, I was awakened by another incoming message. "Good morning! This is So-and-So from the Blah-Blah Driving School. We would like to offer, free of charge, driving lessons for Matthew Broderick."

I didn't know this at the time, but I later learned that these "prank" calls were made live on *The Howard Stern Show*. The radio shock jock, in his second year on the air (long before his dramatic evolution into the Howard I now revere), called our home a few mornings in a row, hoping to get someone on the line.

Matthew was right. We couldn't underestimate the human capacity to exploit tragedy for entertainment.

I didn't have my own publicist, but I made it clear to Mark that I was game to do whatever press he set up as long as he understood any questions regarding the accident were strictly off-limits.

Mark said, "Great news. We got you on the *Today* show."

I said, "That's exciting. But you told them, right? They can't talk about the accident. Like, at all."

Cut to Bryant Gumbel: "I'm here with Jennifer Grey who's coming out in her first starring role in the movie *Dirty Dancing*. That must be exciting for you! Tell us, what's this movie about, and what is 'dirty dancing'?" On the heels of me stringing a few words together about the hormonal explosion of a young girl's coming of age and trying to act and sound like it wasn't my first time doing a morning show opposite a television anchor I'd been watching for years, Gumbel's affect abruptly changed. "Two weeks ago, you were in a tragic car accident in Ireland with Matthew Broderick where two local women were killed. What happened?"

I felt like someone had pulled a trapdoor under me and I was free-falling. Why had I assumed that my explicit requests, as conveyed by my newcomer publicist, would be honored? "You know, uh, Bryant . . . I . . . I can't talk about that."

The *Today* show went to commercial, and as the sound guy was unclipping my mic, Bryant, looking only a little sheepish, said, "Sorry 'bout that. It's been in the news. I couldn't not ask you about it."

———

Of course, I'd known for a while that I'd need to get something to wear to the premiere. Two premieres actually! I also knew I didn't have the cash to go all out. I just figured I'd find something. I'd assumed I'd have more than one day to come up with an outfit. But that was before.

With no time to waste, I went to my go-to, reasonably priced Norma Kamali store on 56th Street and picked up a slinky, off-the-shoulder stretch jersey sheath in cherry red, springing for the signature eighties wide, elastic black belt. I'd worn the long, more formal version of the dress in teal to the Oscars with Matthew five months before, so I knew it was a safe bet.

My mom was with me at my apartment while I was supposed to be getting ready to go to the Ziegfeld, but I found myself stuck on one of those awful phone calls with Matthew in Ireland. I pulled the phone into my bedroom to get some privacy. I was crying my head off. Matthew was continuing to give me a hard time about going to the premiere.

Because of the phone cord, the door wouldn't fully close, and my mom stuck her head in, mouthing to me emphatically, "Hang. Up. The. Phone." Her eyes were huge. She was incensed. "This is your big night. This is crazy. You need to get off the phone!"

I hung up, but at the last minute, I almost switched from the Kamali to a far-too-casual-for-the-occasion skirt and top. My mom said, "Oh. You cannot wear that." I switched back into the Kamali. The limo driver buzzed from downstairs. And before Mom and I headed out to get into the car, I splashed my face with cold water, reapplied the mascara I'd cried off, scrunched some extra mousse in my hair, and put a little gloss on my lips.

My dad and Nellie were waiting for us in the back of the stretch limo. Nellie, poised as always, was vibrating with love and pride.

In front of the Ziegfeld, it was a mob scene. The strobing cameras of onrushing paparazzi were like a lightning storm. I was swallowed up, buffeted in the melee, until some handler took me by the arm and ushered me through the maze of invited press. In the center of the action, Patrick and I saw each other for the first time since the movie wrapped. He was decked out in Texas finery, a suit and bolo tie, his hair greased into a bit of a pompadour. There was a feeling between us of shared wonderment at being part of this little movie making surprisingly big waves. The pandemonium of the premiere night was nerve-racking, but I had been living in such a state of high anxiety and fear in Ireland that this media blitz was child's play by comparison. And it was such a relief to be back home in New York, with my parents and Nellie.

I have very little recollection of this premiere, or of any of the very good stuff that happened in the wake of the horrifically bad stuff. Is it possible that my nervous system had already shorted out to survive?

I know that eventually we settled into our row of roped-off seats, my mom and dad on either side of me, Nellie a seat away, with the eleven hundred other audience members around and behind us.

As the lights dimmed, I felt my heart in my throat. The theater went pitch-black and silent. And out of the darkness came this startling drumbeat. Like a giant hook that slid under my sternum and grabbed me.

Boom boom-boom psh! Boom boom-boom psh!

Its bass reverb so rumbly our seats vibrated. The snare drum, crackle of castanets, throbbing guitars, a full string section, the signature layering of instruments of Phil Spector's "wall of sound." Then a pure, yearning vocal solo sailed in over the lavish instrumentals— "The night we met I knew I needed you so"—and the girl-group harmonies chimed in, "Be my, be my baby."

As Ronnie Spector's singular voice and the backup harmonies of the Ronettes melded into each other, across the enormous Ziegfeld screen emerged the vintage black-and-white, slo-mo counterpoint to the urging beat: lusty dance partners' hips grinding, limbs rising and crashing, undulating, as if underwater.

This song so distinctly of a time, the emotional grab so involuntary, penetrated every inch of me, flooding my mind, my body, taking me. And I needed that. To be taken into the moment. A title sequence so powerful that it wiped out, for a minute, everything I had just been through.

And then I saw my name. Scribbled longhand in the hot pink that screamed eighties, against the blurred dancers in their rapture. I heard the pop of cheers from each of our respective posses as our names appeared briefly up on the screen.

The stylized grainy black-and-white of the opening credits gave way to the saturated, golden Technicolor hue of an idealized memory: the interior of a family car en route to a summer vacation at a Catskills resort. It was the summer of '63, the last gasp of innocence for the country. And for Baby Houseman. Beyond her sexual awakening, her worldview would be forever changed. She was not going to drive out of that resort the same way she drove in. And sitting in that movie theater, I didn't know what I can plainly see now, which is that I, too, had suffered a radical shift in my perception of the world.

I don't remember much of anything else after the title sequence, except that there was a lot of me up on that enormous screen. I'd never seen so much of me, and I found it uncomfortable to watch.

Pretty much the only thing I remember about that night is that after the movie, my mom, my dad, Nellie, and I got into the limo to go to the party at the Roseland Ballroom a few blocks away. Once we were in the car, driving in the dark intermittently lit by the flash of streetlights, I could tell my dad was crying. I could hear him, and I could see him wiping his eyes.

I said, "Are you okay?"

Nellie, Mom, and I were looking at him.

"Dad, what's going on?"

It was a little confusing. He could barely speak he was so over-come with emotion, and muttered something like, "It's just . . . a lot," and gathered himself as we approached the venue. Then we got out of the car and walked into the party. I never knew what exactly my

father was feeling that was causing him to blubber like that, but it's one of the things I remember most from that night.

I wish I could tell you anything about the LA premiere, the flight there, or watching the movie. I might not even have actually sat through it again. Sadly, it's almost like this second premiere never happened. The only reason I know it did is because I still have a stack of Polaroids. Some were of me in my hotel room before I left for the premiere, posing adoringly next to oversized images of Matthew in army garb, dog tags, etc., from *Biloxi Blues*. A red lipstick kiss on his cheek. Probably for an upcoming ad campaign for his movie that maybe his manager had brought over for me to bring back to Matthew in Ireland?

Then at the party after, held at the fifties-style diner Ed Debevic's, I remember my dad's longtime publicist, Richard Grant, who happened to be there, though not as my publicist, swooping in just as someone was asking me to pose for a shot, and Richard taking the glass of whatever I was drinking out of my hand. After the photo was taken, as Richard handed me back my drink, he leaned in close and said in a very serious and conspiratorial tone, "Never take a photo with a glass in your hand."

Oh, and I remember that Cher was there, and she said something nice to me.

I have Polaroids taken at the party of me and Lea Thompson looking a little wasted, drinking good champagne straight out of a bottle. And there's one of me at the party, head tilted back, my hands crossed over my chest, my eyes closed, maybe sleeping, maybe passed out? In the same red Kamali dress I'd worn for the New York premiere two days before.

I'd been put up at the Sunset Marquis hotel, and the day following the premiere, interviews were scheduled for me at a table poolside. My agent, Susan Smith, stopped by for a bit, having, like the rest of the world, suddenly taken more of an interest in me, and I remember her saying, "Don't wear the red lipstick."

So I got out a tissue and wiped off the red lipstick.

ACT IV Good Girl Redux

The following day I flew back to Belfast. I left my own party right when it was in full swing. Mark Pogachefsky had put together a press package, a folder of reviews and press, which I took with me. I was getting an insane amount of coverage and really great reviews.

Back in Matthew's hospital room, I pulled out my clippings folder and was skimming through the reams of material when I came across a review from *Newsweek* that said some pretty nice things about me. I thought *Newsweek* was legit. Even Matthew would have to agree, *Newsweek* was no slouch. I got kind of excited and wanted to share the review with him. I said, "Oh wow! Can I read you something?" I started reading aloud to him, and after a bit he stopped me and said, "I really don't want to hear this."

I immediately regretted sharing my excitement the moment he said that. I felt called out, ashamed for being so boastful, or giving any value or import to a review. I knew better.

18

Mrs. Broderdepp

As Matthew and I had met on a film set, there was a built-in understanding from the start that, going forward, our relationship was not going to follow anything resembling a typical courtship trajectory. Matthew already had a full slate of work, films scheduled well into the future. It was a given that our time together would be regularly interrupted by one or both of us going away for months at a time to work on location.

I knew from childhood that periods of separation from loved ones were the "price of doing business" for a working actor, that the rules of engagement and lifestyle were different from those of civilians, but well worth it. My father was often away for work, sometimes for months on end, shooting in another country, performing his club act in Vegas, or doing the national tour of a show. The feeling of missing my dearest person was familiar to me. And scarcity adds a value of sorts. The honeymoon stage of the relationship can

have an extended shelf life when one person or another is always leaving.

When we could, Matthew and I would find windows for a vacation in between gigs. One time, we stole away to the British Virgin Islands for a romantic holiday at Little Dix Bay on Virgin Gorda. One of those perfect, old-school, private Caribbean resorts with no cars. Individual huts with thatched roofs lined the crescent shoreline, a beach of powder white sand.

There was the most magical barrier reef. We'd put on our snorkels and fins and hold hands as we swam along through a mind-blowing profusion of tropical fish. Big clouds of silvery synchronized swimmers enveloped us, then in perfect unison parted, just long enough to let us pass. We'd turn to each other, eyes wide framed by our masks, every time we'd see something thrilling. As we glided through the crystalline waters, nerding out at the spectacle being put on in the peaceful silence, our exclamations of delight were unintelligible, muffled by our snorkels' bulky mouthpieces. Back in our hut late in the afternoon, our skin warm and glowing from the sun, the room would sometimes go all wobbly, like we were still bobbing underwater. We pored over a fish directory, identifying each species we'd spotted that day in the mysterious aquatic parade. There were no televisions, computers, or iPhones. There may have been no phones at all. We were off the grid, secluded, and perfect.

When Matthew and I were good together, we were very, very good. And when we weren't good, we were awful.

In New York, we regularly went to the theater, just as my parents always had, and after we'd go to Orso for a late supper with a bottle of wine. We would be seated on full display, at one of the prime tables in the small, well-lit restaurant, and since we were regulars, we knew all the waiters, and often many of the theater folk at the surrounding tables. It was awkward when I'd find myself in tears about I don't know what, trying to hide my face as Matthew quickly got the check. After we'd broken up, one of the waiters confessed to me that he was so sick of seeing me with tears running down my cheeks he'd wanted to punch Matthew out. Strange as it may seem, if that waiter hadn't made a point of expressing his distress on my behalf, I would not even have registered how commonplace those crying scenes had become. While I can't recall what had precipitated my tears, I'm pretty sure that the bottle of wine consumed probably didn't help matters.

Our cycle of painful-to-loving feelings and back seemed inevitable. Things would get terrible, but afterward, I would double down, recommitting myself, like an amnesiac, to the notion that we would be good again. There was this point of deep connection between Matthew and me that no one else could touch: the lingua franca of our inner Borscht Belt comedians.

Our relationship went on like this for a few years, until we returned from Ireland, changed. Bonded in a new way. By trauma. Once we got home after the accident, my resolve to break it off vanished. We were living together in my apartment, along with my roommate, Meg. Matthew was gaunt, still on crutches, at the start of months of physical therapy to rehabilitate his leg. I couldn't help but fall into a deeply ingrained mindset. I loved him. Whatever Matthew's needs were, especially if they posed a serious threat to his health or work, they would have to take precedence. His grave injuries, the sudden question mark that loomed over his career, the public flaying that ensued, and the fallout that continued to swirl around him—all of this rendered my needs, my life, my injuries, my career, inconsequential to me.

As the international release of *Dirty Dancing* rolled out across Europe, Matthew, his lawyer, everyone in his camp, were adamant that putting me in front of the European press on the heels of the accident was not only a bad idea but one that could possibly be injurious to Matthew's case (despite me not being in possession of any damning evidence). The European press is famously savage in its blatant exploitation of personal tragedy. I stood by my man and stayed in New York. Patrick did the European tour solo.

I was jealous that Patrick seemed to be emerging from *Dirty Dancing* with all the heat. I was in almost every frame of the movie, the story was told through the eyes of my character, yet he had emerged as the star. I was "the girl in the Patrick Swayze movie." I'd become famous but felt somehow cast aside. But I couldn't tell which had come first, the chicken or the egg. Was I to blame for not claiming the moment I'd been waiting for all my life? Was I destined to follow in the footsteps of my mother and grandmother, who'd abandoned their dreams?

I'd been paid that fifty-thousand-dollar low-budget movie paycheck for *Dirty Dancing* and was receiving no financial compensation from its runaway success. I'd worked as a waitress, doing catering gigs to make rent right up until the movie was released. I hadn't worked as an actress since, and had now become far too fucking famous to wait tables. I was broke. I'd been raised in the business but hadn't a clue as to how to take care of myself from a financial standpoint. I couldn't afford to hire my own publicist, while Patrick was never without Annett Wolf, the renowned press agent who'd been by his side since the beginning of his career.

I finally decided to leave my agent, Susan Smith. Matthew's agent, Todd Smith (no relation to Susan) at CAA, wanted to sign me, but Matthew did not like the idea of us having the same agent. My dad's longtime and recently former agent Sam Cohn at ICM was also trying to sign me, so I went with Sam. My dad was extremely hurt and upset by my decision. He couldn't understand how, in good conscience, I could sign with someone who'd stopped answering his calls. (Sam, the celebrated überagent to the biggies—Streep, Fosse, Nichols, Redgrave, everyone—was legendary for failing to return his clients' calls, yet somehow my dad thought he should have been the exception.)

After love-bombing me until I signed with him, Sam swiftly passed me on to the day-to-day care of an up-and-coming agent in the ICM LA office named Tracey Jacobs, who began sending me stacks and stacks of scripts. I'd tear through them in my Bethune Street apartment, looking for the just-right follow-up role, the perfect vehicle, relieved to finally have the support of someone so smart, passionate, and fired up about my career's potential. I was teed up, or so I thought, to finally make some serious coin, and more important, to have the opportunity to be able to work with directors who made the kind of first-rate films I had fantasized about doing all my life. I began taking meetings with directors, screen-testing for parts. I tested for *Cocktail* with Tom Cruise, but got a bad case of the giggles during the love scene, so I screwed myself out of that one. I was super excited when my dream director, Mike Nichols, wanted me to come over to his place and informally read for the lead in *Working Girl*, but the night before, Matthew and I got into a fight; he wasn't keen on me working with "his director," and the next morning I arrived at Mike's exhausted and plainly unprepared, hoping it wouldn't matter.

In the months after *Dirty Dancing* came out, it seemed like everyone wanted to see me for their project, but something was off, out of alignment. Even though I was hurting for cash, I was turning down the jobs I was being offered. Out of fear—fear of not being a good enough actress to overcome subpar material. And when I had an exciting audition for something A-list, I either didn't prepare adequately or got super close to getting it, which happened a lot, but for some reason . . . didn't make the cut.

Finally, more than a year after making *Dirty Dancing*, I took a job. I joined the ensemble cast of the movie *Bloodhounds of Broadway* in which Madonna and I sang a duet, and Matt Dillon played my love interest. Everyone was paid scale (see: bubkes).

Madonna was in the midst of a very high-profile split from her husband, Sean Penn (a relationship that made mine look downright jolly), and had escaped to New York to distract herself by taking this job. She was in fragments from the dissolution of her volatile marriage, and I was also in pain, stuck in a relationship, unable to break free and unable to stay. Each of us cracked pretty wide open. Each of us, unaccustomed to asking for help, showed up for the other, with guns blazing. We were joined at the hip—in rehearsal, at the gym, hanging out, sharing books (she read a lot), talking about everything, from the most intimate, deep emotional wounds, to the most mundane things, like fashion and boys. When we first met on the movie, while I really liked some of her early music, I hadn't been a fan of her public persona. But when I got to know her, I was very surprised by the person I found. She was disarming and interesting, powerful and scrappy. We took turns hyping each other up, emboldening the other to get on with it, to live our best lives.

Around that same time, in January, I was nominated for a Golden Globe for Best Actress, one of four nominations *Dirty Dancing* received. My fellow nominees were Holly Hunter, Diane Keaton, Bette Midler, and Cher. The awards ceremony arrived just two weeks after the nominations were announced, and Matthew came with me to LA, where they put us up in a hotel. I can't remember why my boyfriend declined to be my date the first time I was up for a major award. Perhaps he was still maintaining a low profile? Maybe he hadn't walked a red carpet since the accident? So I took my agent, while Matthew went to the Ivy for dinner with his agent.

The event was black tie and I still couldn't afford to buy myself a proper gown. So I went to some random costume house in Hollywood and rented a beaded flapper dress from the twenties. (I don't think, from what I can tell from the photos, that dress was in any way a good choice, or that I even had a professional hair or makeup person for the event.) That night I sat next to Emile at the *Dirty Dancing* table in the ballroom at the Beverly Hilton, with no speech whatsoever prepared, praying hard (and very effectively) that I wouldn't win. The thought of going up on the stage was far more terrifying to me than losing.

If I had to do it over, I would borrow whatever money would have been necessary to hire a publicist. A publicist would have asked designers to dress me for these premieres and award shows. I would've had the kind of guidance that would've enabled me to do whatever press I needed to do, because a seasoned publicist could've run interference around the sensitive topics of Matthew and Ireland.

Looking back, I'm baffled that no one offered to help me navigate this new and very tricky terrain, and that I didn't see how much I needed help. I obviously had enormous ambivalence about going after what I wanted, though I didn't know it at the time. Ambition had a strangely distasteful and negative connotation to me; it smacked of self-involvement, entitlement, soullessness, being cutthroat and driven. I had never been a big fan of competition and was quick to avoid conflicts—with Patrick, with Matthew, with my dad. If there was going to be a tussle over who should stand in the limelight, I was out. Still, it didn't feel good that Matthew wouldn't be next to me, holding my hand at the Globes that January.

Throughout the previous fall, the Bethune Street apartment had begun to feel a little too close for comfort. Matthew had started looking to buy a place of his own. Sometimes we looked together, trying to envision what we might look like going forward. But he ended up buying a place in Soho for himself, and sometime in February or early March we broke up, which was really hard because, in spite of everything I knew, I still loved him.

Madonna was extremely supportive of me joining her in her single ladydom. She was my most fervent cheerleader. At the end of March, she threw me a birthday party at the Canal Bar. She said it was going to be a "slut party." Everyone was instructed to come alone, whether they were in a relationship or not, and the only beverage served would be martinis.

My problem was I couldn't think of any guys to invite. Madonna was incredulous. "Oh, c'mon, you don't even have a *crush* on anyone?" When pressed, the only person I could think of was maybe this actor I'd seen a few weeks before in the play *Serious Money*. Madonna told me to just invite my girlfriends and she'd take care of the rest.

After procuring this actor's phone number from her agent, she called him up, "Hey, Alec. It's Madonna," to which he quipped, "Sure you are, and I'm the fucking queen of England." Still suspecting that the invite was possibly a prank, he showed up at the Canal Bar with one of his younger brothers as wingman. Nothing says "good friend" like someone hand-delivering the sexy-as-fuck thirty-year-old Alec Baldwin as your surprise birthday present. A generous act, second only to ordering up a male stripper, dressed (briefly) as a waiter, to present the chocolate "slut cake" decorated with hilarious squirts of white icing.

After that night, I started dating my crush's brother, the even more yummy Baldwin, Billy. And when I was invited to the Academy Awards at the last minute to present the Oscar for Best Cinematography with Patrick, I brought Billy as my date.

Sex and love addiction, call it what you will. When the pain of mourning the loss of a deep romantic bond becomes too much to bear, as quickly as humanly possible replace it with a new shiny object of desire. Presto! No more heartbreak. (Also known as switching deck chairs on the *Titanic*.) When it comes to this particular "fix," I have two speeds: off and high. And if I've learned one thing, it's this: my body cannot metabolize the excitement I crave.

I'd been drinking and smoking—cigarettes and weed—pretty much on the regular for more than a decade. I also found it necessary to pop a Xanax or Valium whenever anxiety threatened to flood my system—and around this particular time there was some pretty serious flooding going on. It had never ever occurred to me that these coping mechanisms might be having a deleterious effect on my life. I had come to rely on them as helpful and necessary, to rescue me from "feeling too much." I couldn't see that while these habits were effectively turning down the volume on my overloaded nervous system, they were also muting the intuitive voices that were trying to save me from myself. Silencing the voices saying, "Get out! Get the fuck out! What is wrong with you? Stop the madness!"

One morning at the end of June, I was in my apartment getting ready to go out when I got a call from Matthew, who had just gotten off a red-eye from LA. He said he had to see me. I told him I was heading out to go to my shrink. (While I knew I was in real need of some kind of therapeutic intervention, whatever was going on there was not doing the job.)

After my fifty-minute session, as I was leaving my therapist's building, there was Matthew. He got down on one knee in front of me on the sidewalk, opened a jewelry box, and said, "Will you marry me?

Let's spend the rest of our miserable lives together. Have miserable children in our likenesses. Whaddya say?" I burst into tears and laughter. He had driven straight to Tiffany from the airport, waited for the store to open, and bought me a diamond solitaire engagement ring. It was weirdly romantic. While also being completely fucked up.

Time became even more elastic than usual in the days that followed while I tried to grapple with what I really wanted and needed to do. I couldn't differentiate between the voices that were stridently vying for my attention, bullying me hither and yon. Was this love or the dance of death? Was he my guy or my worst nightmare? The voices of my family history, the voice of cozy habit, the voice of fear of letting go were chattering away inside me. I couldn't decipher whether the pull on me was love or addiction. I had to tell Billy that I needed to take a beat, that I still had feelings for Matthew. I didn't wear the ring in public, but tried it on when I was alone, or when Matthew asked me to. I was agonizing over what to do. But at that point, I didn't have the sense God gave a chicken.

By the second week of July, I couldn't take it anymore. I said yes to Matthew. And he and I escaped the heat of the city to enjoy our new status privately in the bucolic Connecticut summer, spending a few dreamy days at Mike Nichols and Diane Sawyer's house—riding Mike's horses, playing with their litter of puppies, swimming, cooking swordfish and eating on the screened-in porch, lolling in the haze of newly engaged bliss. Not only was the relief from the searing pain of being broken up enormous, but now being engaged had the added boon of realizing my hopes and dreams.

I wanted to believe that what had been so painful about our relationship could be wiped out by Matthew's declaration of undying love and the sparkly diamond perched on my fourth finger. Based on how good we felt together in Connecticut, I knew I had made the right choice.

When we returned to the city, me to my apartment and Matthew to his, we had a day apart, which also felt great. I felt peace for the first time in a long while.

The next night, Matthew was going to hang out with the playwright Kenny Lonergan, his best friend since childhood, and I went to a birthday dinner Madonna was throwing for her assistant, Mel, at Sfuzzi. The party was a bunch of girls, mostly Madonna's entourage. One of the guests at the long table mentioned in passing that our pal in common, Helen Hunt, was in town. It felt good to get out, back in the city, buoyed by my secret and newfound faith that everything was going to be okay. A refreshing little dip in Lake Me after a week of Us in Connecticut.

I stayed out late with the girls, got home around one in the morning, and called Matthew to say goodnight. Got his machine, so I left a message. Called again, every half hour after that until seven in the morning, then at seven thirty, I went to his apartment. He didn't answer his doorbell. I pounded on the door. I was shaking from adrenaline and lack of sleep, and eventually his neighbor let me into her place. She didn't have keys to Matthew's, but from her apartment, I called Richard, Matthew's houseman. Richard came over at eight thirty to let me in.

Matthew's bed hadn't been slept in. I called his mother, who said, "Why should I know where he is?" and hung up on me. I called Kenny, who said he had not been out with Matthew the night before. While I sat at Matthew's desk trying to think of who else I could call, I opened the drawer, and was greeted by an 8×10 headshot of our friend Helen Hunt, penned with some personal inside-jokey inscription.

And suddenly, I knew. I saw the Matrix.

Helen.

Penny.

The old family friend.

Nobody's ever been slower to get it, right? Nobody's ever been dumber? But I was just that invested in believing what I wanted to be true. Until that moment when my denial wore so thin that I had to see through it.

I closed Matthew's desk drawer, went home, took a Valium, and tried to sleep.

———

At noon, Matthew called, told me he'd been out to breakfast with his sister Janet. I said, "Oh really? That must have been a pretty earrrrly breakfast, because I was at your apartment at seven thirty this morning and you weren't there."

He said, "Let me come over and tell you what happened."

I said, "Tell me on the phone. I don't want to see you."

He said, "I want to explain in person."

I said, "Let me guess. Helen Hunt?"

He said, "Yes. But it's not what you think."

I said, "Oh, okay. Sure. Let's hear it."

We went on like that. Back and forth.

He said, "I swear to you on my father's grave that we didn't even kiss."

I said, "You're a liar. You blew it. I never want to see you again."

And that was it for me.

The next order of business was to call Helen. She picked up.

"Hi, Helen?"

"Yes?"

"It's Jennifer Grey. He's all yours." Click.

Within minutes, Matthew showed up on my front stoop, just below my bedroom, and rang the buzzer incessantly, but I didn't respond. He called up to my window from the street. He went to the corner pay phone to call me. While he was down the street calling, I hurried out and into a cab. Within an hour, I was checking in at the airport. I'd reserved a seat on a flight to LA on MGM Grand Air (*the* airline of choice at the time, with first-class cabins that looked like Liberace's living room).

I was going home to mother. In style.

The other passenger in my cabin was Peter Allen, Liza Minnelli's sexy, Aussie ex-husband, the first gay man who'd lit me up. The most perfect person in the world to be my crushed-velvet seatmate. The interior of the aircraft looked like the Orient Express if the Orient Express were a Vegas brothel. A lot of burgundy and gilt, with satin curtains you could draw for privacy, which of course we did. By the time I had fastened my seat belt and was slugging back my mimosas, I had monkeys flying out of my hair. In this Ken Russell movie, my character was a tear-stained, smoking, drinking mess, delivering my tale of woe faster than a Gilbert and Sullivan patter song. If I ever had any doubt there was a god, finding Peter Allen plopped there to unconditionally love me up with every twist and turn of my woeful opera was all the proof I needed.

I landed in LA emptied. I settled into my mom's condo, sleeping on the daybed in her home office. I checked my New York answering machine; there were multiple messages from some florist trying to make a delivery to my apartment. Meanwhile, Madonna sent flowers to me at my mom's, with a card that read, "Happiness is the best revenge."

It's one week after fleeing the scene of the crime and I'm recovering at my mother's place. She's left town for the weekend. I hear the buzzer, press the intercom, and announce that I'll be right down. I take the elevator, head down the pebbled concrete steps, and as I swing open the heavy security gate, there, under the streetlight, standing in front of a nondescript old sedan, is the most beautiful man-boy I've maybe ever seen. His cheekbones, nose, lips, eyebrows, dark eyes, every minute detail, set off an electrical storm in my brain. Then there's the smile. There is a lot of story incoming on a rush of dopamine. What exactly am I looking at? A swoosh of brown hair over one eye. Some kind of art on those arms? Oh, I get it. It's a tattoo of a Cherokee chief in a full feathered headdress. And on the other arm? A red heart with a banner. *Who's "Betty Sue"?*

He's wearing old motorcycle boots, worn Levi's, a T-shirt. And tied around his waist, a flannel shirt that looks so soft it could be a transitional object for a baby. The perfect fade, the perfect plaid. The shirt you hope to god he forgets at your house. This guy's adorned—mismatched tiny hoop earrings, a few silver chains around his neck, and a leather wrist cuff. Every inch of him says, "I just woke up like this." He's like an apparition. An angel. If a mirage could have been a person in the summer of 1988, that mirage would have been Johnny Depp.

My agent, Tracey, had set me up on a blind date with this guy. He'd told her he had a massive crush on me after seeing *Dirty Dancing,* and she was desperate to sign him. Having just had my most serious relationship to date go up like a flaming ball of shit, I was in no shape to go out with anyone. Sitting over lunch at the Ivy, while I picked at my grilled vegetable salad, she implored me to just go out with him once and assured me that I wouldn't be sorry. I didn't know who this kid was. Never heard of him. She told me he was on this TV series *21 Jump Street* and had a rabid preteen following. Nothing about that description even somewhat intrigued me.

Tracey couldn't ask for the check fast enough and drove us straight to a Thrifty drugstore, dragging me over to the rack where the mecca of *Tiger Beat*–type fanzines were on display. There, on every one of these magazine covers designed to drive a thirteen-year-old wild with desire, was a little cut-out face, bobbing in a sea of other teen heartthrobs, of this actor she was pimping. I had no interest in dating a teen idol.

Tracey said, "I'm telling you, this kid is one of the kindest, sweetest human beings I've ever met." She just wouldn't shut up about how great he was. She was like a pit bull. She'd locked on. So, I said, "Okaaay."

He asked if I liked soul food, and I said yes. A bumper sticker on the back of the beater he was driving read Happiness Is Being a Grandparent. "It's my stepfather, Bumpa's, car," he explained.

We headed over to Maurice's Snack 'n Chat on Pico east of Fairfax. As soon as we got into the car, he grabbed his box of Marlboro reds off the dash, and said, "You want one?" Yeah, I did. Marlboro reds were my brand.

Maurice's didn't serve alcohol, so first we popped into the corner liquor store for a flask-sized bottle of Jack. Johnny was a regular at the restaurant, and Maurice, aka "Mama," lit up when she saw us like we were her kids home for the holidays. We ate on the makeshift patio out back, drinking our Jack out of plastic cups. He ordered everything. Meat loaf, candied yams, black-eyed peas, and Mama's signature southern fried chicken. We took our time over the incredible home-cooked meal. We ate, talked, drank, laughed our asses off, took cigarette breaks midcourse. I found out who Betty Sue was. His mom.

He liked the booze I liked. He liked the cigarettes I liked. He liked the food I liked. And he looked like every girl's wet dream. He packed his Marlboros, rhythmically pounding the pack against the heel of one hand until the cigs were half an inch shorter. This boy was so ridiculously beautiful. And surprisingly open, funny, quirky, and sweet. (Note to self: send flowers to Tracey.)

After Maurice's, we headed over to Tower Records on Sunset and bought a bunch of music we'd been talking about. We sat in the parked car, with the light from the store spilling in, taking turns playing our favorite songs for each other. We started making out to Bobby Darin's "Beyond the Sea," Freda Payne's "Band of Gold," Al Green's "Let's Stay Together," the Isley Brothers' "For the Love of You."

He drove me back to my mom's and parked out front. The darkness of the residential street lent itself to an even more intense make-out session. I invited him up, and he slept over with me on the daybed in my mom's office.

Within two weeks Johnny'd asked me to marry him, and within the month he had signed with Tracey. We went to Tiffany in Beverly Hills and picked out a small, emerald-cut diamond with two little emerald baguettes on either side of it.

On August 12, I wrote in my journal, "I'm in love, pretty sure for the first time in my life. . . . He's kind, funny, smart, moral, thoughtful, respectful."

After flying the coop, I didn't return to New York for months. Johnny and I rented Carrie Fisher's log cabin in Laurel Canyon. I was saved.

We played house, fixing up our one-room rustic love nest with French country pieces we found at the antique store downstairs from ICM on Beverly Boulevard. We hung these old floral rayon curtains from the forties we'd scored at the Rose Bowl flea market. We were into Native American anything and bought these vintage blankets from a store on La Brea. Somehow, it all went together.

All we did was talk about how much we both wanted to start a family and how lucky we were to have found each other. On the way to some flea market in the Sherman Oaks Galleria we passed a pet store, and behind the glass piled with shredded paper we saw the most ridiculously adorable, tiny puppy. She didn't even look real. They said she was a Peekapoo—a Pekingese-poodle mix. We named her Lulu. She was our practice baby, and someone to keep me company when Johnny was out of town.

In the fall, when his *21 Jump Street* hiatus was over, he'd be shooting in Vancouver. And since we couldn't bear the idea of being apart, we decided that I would go live up there with him. We briefly tried that out, but the loneliness, the interminable days sitting around in his empty rental apartment, waiting for him to come home in a city where I knew no one, wasn't working for me. We decided it would be better if he'd just come back to LA whenever he wasn't shooting.

At Christmastime, we went on the meet-my-fiancée tour. Johnny took me and our furry love child to Florida to meet Betty Sue, his sisters, and brother. On Christmas morning, Johnny gave me a diamond eternity band from Tiffany. Our next stop was Boston, where I introduced him to my father, who was doing a show there. Johnny bought all three of us matching TAG Heuer watches. Next stop, New York City, where we threw a small New Year's gathering in my apartment, and Johnny and I, as host and hostess, instigated a "dorky dance contest" to see who could, one at a time, out-dork the other, sending up the most embarrassing dance moves we could come up with. When it was your turn to show off your killer moves and grooves, you did so with dead seriousness. The competition was fierce.

All my pals who met Johnny gushed, "Oh my god, he's the sweetest! You so deserve this. And are you kidding me? He's so beautiful."

We'd started twinning. Or at least I did. He'd given me his perfectly broken-in motorcycle jacket. He bought me a pair of black leather engineer boots. I wore his faded plaid flannel shirts.

I went with him to some stadium event for *21 Jump Street* fans. He hated it. As his growing heartthrob status accelerated, he felt exploited and trapped in this teen idol machine, dogged by paparazzi and crazed fans. He was desperate to get out of his TV contract so he could be free to work in movies. I could see all of what he could be, much better and more comfortably than I was ever able to do for myself. I had no doubt about Johnny's potential, his talent, and the kind of career he should be having. The way I believed in him? I've never had that unwavering kind of vision for myself. Instead, I focused my energy on him, advising him, encouraging him to see the limitless opportunities and to swing for the fences.

Meanwhile, there was still a significant amount of activity and noise around my career. There was pressure on Tracey to come up with a gig for me as a new client, and I felt a lot of pressure to make the right choice. I was reading scripts, taking meetings, and development deals were being set up, but the more time passed after *Dirty Dancing,* the more pressured I felt to make my next role the perfect next thing. No strong contenders were being offered, but the vibe was that any day this career of mine was going to hit its stride. I remember Jeff Berg, the chairman of ICM, saying, "We've just got to get you out of the Catskills."

Johnny was commuting every week back and forth from Vancouver but had begun to more and more regularly be getting into trouble, fights in bars, skirmishes with cops. He'd started missing his flights home to LA, having overslept, or when he did come home, he'd be crazy jealous and paranoid about what I'd been up to while he was gone. I attributed his ill temper and unhappiness to his feeling miserable and powerless to get off *Jump Street* when all he wanted was to be in movies. He became moodier and less and less present. I kept wondering how or if I was ever going to get that easygoing, funny, devoted, adoring guy back.

Tracey was on a mission. She had to find him something to do over his hiatus, so when *Cry-Baby* came in, it was the perfect next move for him. Everything about it seemed tailor-made. It was a musical spoof on the 1950s teen rebel genre. It was camp, the perfect vehicle to lampoon Johnny's pinup image. He was still under contract for *Jump Street,* but now he had the lead in a movie—along with a big paycheck.

We'd decided to give up the log cabin and spend more time in my apartment in New York, but now that Johnny's career had begun to pop, we had started looking at houses to buy in the Hollywood Hills. As time went on, it seemed that more and more when Tracey called and I'd answer, she wasn't calling for me. I'd pass the phone to Johnny.

I still wasn't seeing the perfect next part for me. And I was broke. Really broke.

One night early that spring, in 1989, I was in LA having dinner with my mother in one of those curved booths at the Imperial

Gardens, and with an all-too-familiar, knowing look she said, "You should really just do your nose. It's too competitive out there. It's much harder to photograph you than a Michelle Pfeiffer. It just is. You want a career, make it easier for them."

The worn business card with the surgeons' numbers from a few years back began to beckon me from the inside pocket of my Filofax. All the arrows were pointing to this as a possible solution. I took what quickly diminishing funds I had, and like some desperate Vegas craps player in their last-gasp attempt at believing they could win it all back, I spun the wheel and played my hand. I called and made an appointment for the day after my twenty-ninth birthday.

A few days before my birthday, Johnny was flown in from Vancouver and put up at the Four Seasons in West Hollywood by the studio so he could take a meeting with a director who was interested in casting him. I flew in from New York to be with him for a few days for my birthday, and then I was going to stay on in LA with my mom for my scheduled surgery.

Johnny left our hotel room in the morning for his meeting, planning to be back in a few hours. I waited. And waited. No phone calls. Nothing.

Where was Johnny?

Fuck Johnny. Where was Jenny?

At a certain point early that evening I left a note on the bed saying I was done.

The day before my twenty-ninth birthday, I cut the cord from Tracey Jacobs. It had all gotten too toxic and confusing. I left ICM, I signed with Madonna's agent, Jane Berliner, at CAA. And I broke off my engagement with Johnny nine months after we'd met.

19

Heeeere's Jenny!

The Tonight Show Starring Johnny Carson ran for thirty years, from 1962 to 1992, and it seemed like all of America religiously tuned in to NBC at 11:30 P.M. to watch Johnny from under the covers, a grown-up bedtime story, told by a legendary host and his carousel of famous guests.

A year after *Dirty Dancing* took the world by storm, I at last hired a part-time publicist of my own. She set up an interview for me with one of *The Tonight Show*'s producers at the NBC Studios in Burbank, where I was asked all of the questions I'd grown accustomed to fielding: What was it like growing up the daughter of my famous father? How did I feel about my "overnight success"? What was it like to be the envy of every hot-blooded woman, crazy for Swayze? Any funny stories about the making of the movie?

I tried to come up with something fresh to say that wasn't just premasticated goo. The interview was basically an audition to assess if I was "Carson ready," which apparently I was not. No specific reason was given other than, "They didn't think you were ready," according to the publicist.

It seemed like everyone who was anyone, many of whom I knew personally, including my costar Patrick, had taken their seat on Johnny's couch. Patrick, goofy but charming, delighted the host and the audience with his endless deadpan recounting knee surgeries, graphic descriptions of injuries sustained while calf roping, and other good ol' boy death-defying pastimes on his ranch. He wasn't trying to be funny, he was just being Patrick, his kooky thrill-seeking hobbies and lifestyle setting up Johnny beautifully to do his shtick. Growing up, I'd watched my dad on *The Tonight Show*, where he never looked anything but relaxed. My dad and Johnny had a chummy rapport, you know, that effortless thing show people do so . . . effortlessly.

I was flummoxed by the show's flat-out rejection of me, so my inner critic leapt at the opportunity to fill in the blanks and provide more than enough data to support what I was lacking. Maybe I was just not as funny or interesting as I thought I was, but I was too mired in self-doubt to talk back to this inner bully.

That initial Carson rejection stung, but eventually I brushed it off. Who really even gives a shit? (Okay, I did.) To shore myself up, in the back of my mind I plotted my revenge. Someday I would be ready, and then I would slay. I would blow the fucking roof off the place. "Who's ready now, motherfuckah?"

That first time, I'd had no clue how entirely scripted those talk shows were. To the general public, including me, the spirited, fun-filled, easy-breezy repartee between Johnny and his guests seemed to be the most natural, impromptu thing in the world. Which was not the case at all. Instead, guests trotted out bite-sized, compelling (shocking, embarrassing, or hilarious) anecdotes that had been passed on to the show's writers ahead of time so they could craft Johnny's setups, comebacks, and punch lines in advance.

Later that same year, when I got another crack at *The Tonight*

Show, I understood that "preinterview" was code for "show us your prepared bits." So I sifted through the grade-A nuts I'd squirreled away to use if I was ever asked to interview for Carson again. I decided to bring my sassiest, most ribald game, walking that razor's edge of shock and awe, a femme fatale who'd make Johnny sweat and break out his signature shtick of bugging his eyes to the camera as he loosened his collar. Well, a girl can dream, right?

This time the preinterview warranted only a phone call with the same producer from before. The reason for this appearance was so I could plug the television movie *Murder in Mississippi,* a chilling drama based on the true story of three civil rights workers murdered by the Ku Klux Klan. Obviously, the subject matter didn't exactly send up comedy flares, so it would be up to me to lighten the mood after Johnny showed the clip.

Though I hadn't planned on it, and before I could stop myself, I proceeded to shower the producer with a slew of juicy tidbits about my well-publicized engagement and subsequent broken engagement to Johnny Depp a few months earlier. I spouted off about things more appropriate for a drunken tête-à-tête with a girlfriend, determined to prove how fucking funny and exciting I could be when I wanted to.

Neither my ex nor I ever spoke publicly about our private travails, so part of me just watched in shock as I sold myself down the river, while the other part hissed back, "Can you shut up and let me do this? You're the one who got us into this mess with your 'taking the high road' bullshit. If I left it up to you, we'd never get on this show." Fuck discretion, I was on a roll and was going to spill all there was to spill about being engaged then unengaged to the teen idol. But why stop there? I explained I had been engaged to marry both Matthew Broderick and Johnny Depp within the same month, like it was a legit thing to boast about.

Perhaps the success of *Dirty Dancing* had made me too popular to ignore, or a previously scheduled guest had suddenly dropped out. Whatever the reason, I was now considered officially "Carson ready."

I'm sure oversharing in my interview didn't hurt my allure to ensure my seat on the couch.

Upon hearing the news, the feeling I had was not one of triumph as I'd expected, but one of dread. Any time I expressed my mounting apprehension and real nervousness to anyone who knew me, their pat response in an attempt to assuage my terror ran along the lines of, "Are you kidding me? Just be yourself, you're so funny!" and, "Get yourself a smokin' hot dress and flirt with Johnny. He's gonna totally looove you!"

Johnny was known for regularly pushing the envelope of sexual innuendo with visiting starlets. There was a famous, yet apocryphal, story about the time Zsa Zsa Gabor brought her cat on the show and provocatively cooed in her heavy Hungarian accent, "Vould you like to pet pussy?" Johnny's fabled reply was: "I'd love to, but you'll have to move the damn cat."

Johnny felt so familiar. I'd watched him every night since I'd been old enough to stay up until eleven thirty. I bought into his public persona 100 percent. He was beyond charming, funny, paternal, and always so in control, like he could save you from anything bad ever happening to you on his couch. What could be easier than hangin' out with Johnny and letting the conversation roll?

As soon as I figured out what to wear, I'd be good to go. (Again, this was in an era well before stylists and freebies from designers were considered a constitutional right for celebrities.) Chez Gallay on Sunset Plaza was *the* destination where everyone would go to procure the best edit of pieces from top designers like Alaïa, Romeo Gigli, Dolce & Gabbana, but if I'd learned anything from premieres past, I needed to invest in the dress. This was no time to be frugal, I was gonna be on Carson.

I briefed the impossibly chic salesgirl about the mission I was on. She returned with a Giorgio di Sant'Angelo, which in her arms looked like a green shapeless pile until the stretchy jade mesh was wound around my body like a colorful cocoon, a sexy mummy. The salesgirl circled me, demonstrating the myriad ways I could crisscross, tie, and wrap my little body in its matcha latte embrace. This dress was the silver bullet I was looking for if ever there was one. It was all I needed to turn myself into a Va-va-voom bombshell, eliciting that jackpot reaction, "Why, Miss Jones!" I couldn't help but feel confident in this dress. It was all about curves and held me like a good lover: all over me but allowing me the freedom to move however I pleased.

I couldn't find the right shoes to go with such a, well, tropical color. I'd always been very nervous (see: guilty) about spending money, but finally decided on a pair of Manolos, one of my biggest "What the hell was I thinking?" purchases. They were sling-backs, but the front of the shoe was . . . printed pony skin, white with irregular Dalmatian dots. Well, it was the eighties. These special kicks, bought expressly for said limeade extravaganza, were the shoes that Cinderella would be wearing to the ball. This odd choice, a minor misfire, would turn out to be the least of my problems, yet it was indicative of the tsunami of missteps I was making, unbeknownst to me. As far as I was concerned, this outfit was all I needed to kill. I was locked and loaded.

Personal publicists, at least the good ones, charge a pretty hefty monthly fee, but for most big stars, and the more business-savvy newcomers like Patrick, they're a permanent fixture on the team. I had hired a publicist, but only on an as-needed basis, which meant a few months lead time up to and just after an opening of a movie. Or in this case, the week before the scheduled airing of a television movie.

Publicity has always been an integral part of the Hollywood myth machine, a way to manipulate an actor's identity, to rebrand them or show another side to them. In the best-case scenario, it's a well-orchestrated plot to win hearts and minds, to introduce you, or reintroduce you, to an audience that thinks they know you from previous work, and make them fall in love with *you,* the person. Publicity whets the public's appetite to crave a bit more of you. I'd always heard it talked about as an essential professional tool, rather than a luxury, that should pay for itself, because the right kind of exposure can create a buzz that should, in theory, translate into more work, drive up your salary, maybe even help garner trophies if an Oscar campaign is launched.

I had all sorts of regret from having missed out on the *Dirty Dancing* press opportunities. I was trying my best to make a new start, to be more ambitious, more focused on my own career, on my own life, determined to course correct, having learned the hard way from mistakes made in the past.

As soon as I'd signed with CAA, I'd booked *Murder in Mississippi*, made my first bit of cash ever, and decided it was time to get my ducks in a row. The publicist I hired, who's still considered one of the best in the business, worked at the same PR firm as Patrick's long-standing person, and I'd envied how tight she and Patrick were. She took such great care of him, and I longed to feel taken care of in that way. I was in very professional hands, though we didn't really know each other, having just met. She had booked hair and makeup people who would arrive at my apartment the morning before the late-afternoon taping, and the show would air later that night.

I'd moved back to the West Coast a few months before and rented a one-bedroom apartment in a building that was like the set of a movie about young, aspiring actresses. The building itself was typical of the area: old Hollywood, 1920s Spanish style, wood floors, arched doorways, with black, wrought iron door pulls, but there must've been some crazy, electric force field of ambition, desire, and aspiration. Jodie Foster was renting the front apartment down the hall but was always away on location, and Winona Ryder, only seventeen or eighteen at the time, had moved into the apartment next door to mine. Our bedrooms shared a wall, making us a twisted version of bunkmates.

Winona felt very much like a baby sister whom I needed to look after, which is saying a lot, since I was one sandwich shy of a picnic myself. I remember her knocking on my door in her pajamas one night, feeling unwell and looking for cold medicine. She seemed pretty out of it, and when I asked her if she was okay, she said she'd taken a

Valium. I tried to impress upon her that was probably not the recom-mended treatment for a cold (though that had never stopped me).

Winona would confide in me about her various crushes, and one time when she sought my counsel, I'd passionately tried to dissuade her from getting involved with Sean Penn, where she was clearly out of her depth. It was like watching a mean boy slowly pull the wings off a butterfly. This all took place during my Madonna years, so when Winona happened to drop by while I was on the phone with the Material Girl, Sean's ex-wife tried to warn our young friend that she was playing with fire. Like a dumbass, I actually thought this sweet innocent would heed two grizzled ol' broads' sage advice, but of course she just parroted everything we'd said back to Sean. Soon after, I received a threatening anonymous message on my answering machine in a barely discernable growl: "Why don't you mind your own fucking business. You'll keep your fuckin' mouth shut—if you know what's good for you." And after a long silence, "If you see me on the street . . . you cross to the other side." When I replayed the message for M, she confirmed that it was indeed her ex. "Yep. That's Sean." Hindsight being twenty-twenty, I gotta say, Sean wasn't wrong. My own business could've used some minding.

I had been trying my best to manage the emotional fallout from my breakup with Johnny and had begun regularly attending meetings for people who were struggling in relationships, often, though not always, with alcoholics. The day after I left Johnny, on my twenty-ninth birthday, the day before I did my nose, a casting director friend who had recently broken up with her husband, seeing the pain I was in, had suggested I come with her to a meeting. The concepts being discussed couldn't have been more foreign to me. I didn't relate at all to the idea of my life being affected by alcoholism (which sounded so dark and extreme), but when the people in the meeting talked about "needing to put the focus on themselves instead of on the alcoholic" and "admitting that they were powerless over people, places, and things and that their lives had become unmanageable," I was like *ding-ding-ding-ding.* And there, in Malibu, my old neighborhood from elementary school days, a handful of complete strangers sitting in a circle of metal folding chairs in an empty auditorium would change the course of my life.

This breakup with Johnny was just the inciting incident that set the whole next sequence of events in motion. A backlog of accumulated, excruciating grief I'd been collecting, hoarding, since the dramatic Matthew breakup (and before), which I thought I'd cleverly done away with by being swept up in the Depp of it all, was now ablaze like an emotional dumpster fire.

Breaking up with Johnny, firing our shared agent, "fixing" my nose—this self-imposed streak of impulsive, destructive decision-making had knocked the wind right outta me. Admitting that I was powerless over people, places, and things was strangely liberating. I had this fledgling relationship with a higher power and was almost grateful for my newfound surrender. My new life seemed almost to be going great.

That is, until I learned that my darling neighbor was banging my ex—the classic nightmare of feeling replaced, like you'd never happened, but on steroids. A bizarre, virtually seamless changing of the guards but with the added fun of the blow-by-blow press coverage of what would become one of the most beloved celebrity couplings of the nineties, so I couldn't help but see and hear every little way my ex had moved on with someone else. Not only was Winona photographed donning Johnny's motorcycle jacket, still warm from my nine-month stint in it ("Look who's wearing the Dreamcoat now?") but he'd wanted us to get tattoos of our names and now his arm read Winona Forever. It would've perhaps been more practical if Johnny had inked: Your Name Here, but there's really no such thing as a practical tattoo. And if ever I found myself sliding down that slippery slope of romanticizing or misremembering our engagement and love affair as being better than it actually was, I could be mercifully jerked back into reality by a crop of bumper stickers at the time that read, "Honk if you *haven't* been engaged to Johnny Depp."

The timing of their fateful meeting practically dovetailed with our split. It felt like it nullified our previous nine months together. While I was experiencing this quite overwhelming grief, though much of it really had little to do with Mr. Depp (he was just the face of grief at the time), the photos plastered everywhere of the two beautiful young lovers passionately entwined, conjuring a kind of love none of us mortals would ever know, didn't feel awesome.

I never saw Winona in our building again. (I did, however, many years later while looking at homes to buy, recognize the furniture Johnny and I had bought for our cabin in Laurel Canyon, and when I asked whose house it was . . .)

How great would this *Hollywood Squares* soap opera of my sweet li'l neighbor running off with my ex play on Carson? Of course, this bit would have been the kind of high-wire act only a precious few could have pulled off. So I figured I'd stick to the original plan from my preinterview and go with the simpler version.

The morning of my Carson debut, I sat in a straight-backed chair set up in the middle of my modest living room, naked under my robe, ruminating about what exactly I had divulged on my call with the producer, feeling slightly sickened and ashamed that I'd written a check I probably couldn't cash.

Flanked by a hairstylist and a makeup artist having their way with every square inch of my head, I tried to act like everything was cool. But my armpits weren't fooled by my outward attempts at savoir faire and swagger, so I kept my arms clamped down tightly to my sides, their telltale slipperiness my well-guarded secret. When I'm nervous, my stomach goes into a stress-induced lockdown, and that morning I hadn't been able to eat so much as a Triscuit.

As the harsh midday sun streamed in, I tried to siphon off some of Neneh Cherry's resolute girl power in "Buffalo Stance," playing on my portable CD player. Tried to feel the sexy comfort of the Fine Young Cannibals. But not even the crooning Cowboy Junkies could shake the unfamiliar darkness that threatened to envelop me.

Eventually, we were joined by my publicist as she busied herself on the sofa with business calls, while I tried to make small talk with the glam team. I didn't actually know any of the people surrounding me that day, which heightened my feeling of being strangely alone, with a dread that felt more ominous than jittery butterflies. All I could think was, "If I'm this nervous now, I'm only going to be more nervous the closer we get to taping the interview. How the hell am I gonna be even remotely funny or cool?" Waves of queasiness moved through me, alongside the other charming symptom of an unhappy gut. I was walking an emotional gangplank. Dead chick walking. I kept trying to pretend it wasn't anything, pressuring myself to snap out of it, but in case you haven't tried that approach, let me share some advice: It doesn't work any more than when someone tells you, "Just *relax*." Because, according to Carl Jung, "What you resist not only persists, but will grow in size." And to add insult to injury, I felt a lot of shame for feeling anxious, as if it were proof that something was wrong with me.

The makeup and hair team finally announced their work was done. It was time to put on my dress. But after sitting for so long, when I tried to stand, I could barely feel my legs. Like a wobbly new colt trying out her limbs for the first time, I made my way into the bathroom to painstakingly rebrush my teeth without messing up my makeup, as my mouth felt like a little corner of the Sahara, and with a washcloth and a bar of soap, to freshen up in earnest my now profusely sweating armpits before donning my knockout-punch dress.

By the time the limo came to pick me up, I had fully retreated into an isolated terror. There was no way in hell I could talk about my breakup on air! What was I thinking? I couldn't speak on a late-night talk show the way I confided to my closest friends. It wasn't in me to exploit a still-tender breakup from someone I had really cared for. I made the game-time decision: I would find a way to just commiserate with Johnny about our shared fate of failed marriages, or in my case, engagements. I figured that ought to be a close enough cousin to what I'd offered up in my preinterview, right?

At the NBC studios, my publicist and I were ushered to a

dressing room door with a big gold star that had my name printed on it. Inside the small room, below the vanity lights and mirror, an unripe banana leaned against an almost grossly oversized Red Delicious apple and a tired bunch of grapes, and cheese slices fanned out alongside individually wrapped saltines.

At that moment, I noticed the sickening hollow feeling in my stomach, and it occurred to me I hadn't eaten anything that whole day and should probably mouth a triangle of the vinyl, orange cheese or at least attempt a benign cracker. I then noticed a screw-top bottle of white wine relaxing in a bucket of ice, next to an assortment of soda cans and four red plastic cups stacked upside down beside it.

I caught a glance of myself in the makeup mirror, but in the state of mind I was in I knew enough not to linger in that dangerous neighborhood. The lights were aggressively bright and there was no way I was going to like what I saw.

My eyes started to blur, and I could feel the panic start to rise in me. Panic about my ability—or lack of it—to walk onto the stage. I couldn't feel myself. As if I was suspended out of my body, or somehow not real, like in a nightmare when you can't get home no matter how hard you try. I didn't have the slightest clue what was happening and thought, "Oh, this is a problem. I can't go out there." My mind was blank. Nothing made sense. I couldn't see how I was going to even live through this because I was definitely not right in the head. I was not myself, had no idea where I'd gone or when I might be expected to return. I unscrewed the bottle of wine and poured myself a generous cup, downed it, looking for the effect that might turn down the terror and turn up my usual, default joie de vivre, the confidence, the chill. No such luck.

The sharp knock on my door startled me. The sound guy announced he had come in to wire me, which meant the bullets were getting closer. A new onset of bone-deep frostiness filled my being. I was fucking freezing, but also clammy, as my armpits didn't get the memo and were working overtime.

The sound guy's concentrating face was so close to mine that I had to avert my gaze while he futzed around inside my already plunging neckline, skirting my nipples to secure the tiny microphone out of view. This was business as usual when taping anything involving dialogue, but I leapt at the awkwardness as an opportunity to sharpen my comedy claws, so as not to go on stage cold and to reassure myself of my brazenness and fortitude. I playfully assumed a jaded, wisecracking persona, intending to come off as cool, but somehow came off like a poor Mae West imitation. After the sound guy had miked me and left, I decided my last hope was to forcibly loosen up with a bit more wine, because there's nothing funny about an actress having an anxiety attack on late-night television. I chugged what I could of the awful-tasting stuff.

A young woman wearing a headset knocked, poked her face in, and announced it was go time. "Okay, you ready?" I threw back the remains of the nasty swill and said, with as much conviction as I could muster, "Let's do this!" I looked to my publicist on the couch for some kind of last-minute intervention or magic, as I managed to eke out a manic singsong cry for help, more of a yodel come to think of it. "Ohhhhh, I am sooo nervous!" She looked slightly uncomfortable but forced a smile and said, "Aww, just go out there and—have fun!"

Because my publicist was, and is, a formidable, seasoned professional, it's very possible there was more conversation or engagement than I'm remembering, and maybe because I was locked in my own private hell I just can't recall what all was said. I do remember how loaded this moment had become in my head. I had far too much riding on it. It was meant to somehow retroactively catch me up on all the opportunities I'd missed out on due to my own self-sabotage.

I followed the assistant stage manager down the long hall leading to the entrance to the soundstage as she mumbled into her walkie-talkie that I was "on the move." The air-conditioning backstage was so hard-core you could hang meat in there. I was shivering as I was ushered into the darkened shadows just offstage where I was delivered to the stage manager. And officially into the belly of the beast.

The stage manager, with the requisite headset, whispered a warm welcome, and from our hiding place I peeked around to see bits of the audience out there. Their shiny faces were brimming with joy, thrilled to be so close to a legend and to be part of a show they'd experienced thousands of times on their television sets at home.

The stage manager leaned down to whisper the plan in my ear. "Okay, so when you go out, you're going to bear right and then you'll see Johnny. He'll take it from there. You'll be great!"

Wait! My entire panic became about making sure I retained, or heard correctly, his instructions. I silently mouthed along with the hand gesture to ensure I wouldn't walk in the wrong direction. "Wait, what did he say again? I'm going to bear left. No, I'm bearing . . . right, and I'll see Johnny on my . . . left?" Then under my breath, I repeated my mantra, "Right. I'm gonna turn right. Right, right, right. Go the right way . . ."

The stage manager's hand gently rested on my shoulder. *Why can't I just stay here with him?* His other hand, raised like at the start of a race, his eyes heavenward, listening for my cue. Next thing I know, I'm hearing that voice I knew so well, saying my name, introducing me, and the stage manager whispers with an intensity meant to propel me like a top out onto the brightly lit stage, "Aaaannnnd . . . GO!" The music plays me in (I'd have to assume it was most likely the band's rendition of "The Time of My Life") but I can't make out what it is, all I know is it's intense, all around me and extraordinarily loud.

I'm jettisoned down an enormous slide, the momentum taking me. I can feel myself careening down the hot, shiny silver metal slide in Central Park, so slippery I can't slow myself by pushing the rubbery edge of my Keds into the side of the slide. The velocity would just tear my tiny feet off. So I surrender to the speed. Instantly, my head flies out of my body and is floating above me.

I guess I survived the entrance because I was suddenly doing the handshake, but not the kiss! I think Johnny had leaned in for the kiss so maybe that was my first mistake. Maybe I was doomed right then and there because I'd shoved my arm out and rebuffed the kiss? Why

did I not lean in for the kiss? So "off-brand" for me. This was no time
to suddenly channel Sigourney Weaver.

Johnny's previous guest for the evening, the comedian Carl
Reiner, was already on the couch. Carl Reiner, of the brilliant *2000
Year Old Man* routine with Mel Brooks, that favorite piece of comedy
Matthew had turned me on to. What were the chances of Carl being
the other guest? He was one of the kindest humans *and* friends with
my parents. He leaned in and kissed me on the cheek. Beside him
was Ed McMahon, Johnny's sidekick, the giant Irishman with the
booming voice. Again, I shoved my hand out, and Ed and I shook.

I guess Johnny was speaking, and I was for the most part respond-
ing as if I were any normal celebrity sitting on a talk show couch, but
I couldn't feel myself, I couldn't land in my body. These body parts
felt like they were just on loan and what was I supposed to do with a
foot or a hand? Like I'd never been encumbered with such useless
appendages before.

The next thing I knew, I leaned forward and put my hand directly
on Johnny's flat, hard chest. It was a bold move and not a smart one.
I said something about my pounding heart and asked him if his heart
was also pounding. He barely responded. Fuuuuuck, fuck, abort,
abort, abort. I retracted my hand. And smiled.

Some kind of conversation continued, although I was no longer
conscious or in any way present, or aware of what was being said. I
kept reaching desperately for a life raft of some sexy something to
save me. I smiled, I stroked my neck, and I'm not a neck stroker by
nature. I tried sending Johnny Carson Morse code with my eyes darting in secret patterns of SOS, begging him to see I was a dying woman,
bleeding out, hoping to appeal to his chivalry, that this superhero of
late-night talk would swoop me up and carry me safely back to land.

When I searched those familiar, usually twinkling, smiling eyes
for salvation, there was an odd coldness to them, almost reptilian,
devoid of empathy. I felt like I could see very clearly into his brain,
and the subtext under his blah-blah was: "What the fuck do you think
you're doing on my show?" I felt like Johnny hated me even more

than I hated myself at that moment. To someone just watching the show, it might've just appeared to be an awkward, uncomfortable segment, but I was certain that he wished me dead. I had unilaterally decided to bail on the preapproved subject matter of my recently failed romance, ignoring Johnny's prompts. Choosing to go rogue, I had broken the rules by leaving my host hung out to dry. This was unacceptable to the king of late night.

I tried gracelessly, on the fly, to create some kind of rapport and camaraderie by lumping us together as members of the same club, bouncing from one failed relationship to another. Of course, this fell flat. I was dying up there, not killing it as had been my plan. I was cruising on adrenaline, cheap wine, and fear of death. Public death. On the most watched show on television.

When they mercifully cut to the commercial, tears instantly started streaming down my cheeks. Johnny refused to look at me and instead busied himself going over the notes on this desk. Carl Reiner was engaged in conversation with Ed McMahon. I was alone, surrounded by people—an entire audience even—and still dying. There was no disputing the fact that I had bombed. And not because I was bombed, because I wasn't really. This was not a Norman Maine in *A Star Is Born* moment (trust me, *really* not worth googling). But I knew, in no uncertain terms, that I was officially in the doghouse, and after the commercial break I was going to have to finish what I had started in the presence of someone who I felt hated my guts. Perhaps Johnny was merely annoyed or just couldn't be bothered, but this was my first time being in the crosshairs of that kind of banked white-hot rage. Johnny's reputation as being mean as a snake hadn't yet surfaced, and wouldn't for years to come, so I was sure I was alone in my capacity for inciting this easygoing man's wrath. I must've been pretty despicable to make him look at me like he wished there was a trapdoor that I would just disappear through. Or maybe everything I was experiencing was wildly distorted, flooded with enough fight, flight, or freeze chemicals to outrun a bear.

We came back on the air, and I got through the rest of the

interview, though I'm not sure how. My lips and tongue knew, when I didn't, how to answer the question, how to look like any other actress sitting on Johnny Carson's couch.

At the close of every show, as the end credits rolled, the guests and Johnny would stand, hug, shake hands, throw their heads back in laughter, or whisper in each other's ear like they're at the best cocktail party that you, the viewer, were only invited to observe from a distance. A party for just the cool kids, a party I had been expressly asked not to attend, and my ride hadn't come yet.

When it was over Johnny refused to acknowledge me. No one looked at me. I was actively crying at this point. I didn't even try to hide it because at that point it no longer mattered. My publicist had been hanging back, just off to the side of the stage, and as soon as the cameras stopped rolling, she stepped up onto the stage, her mouth pursed, took my hand, and led me back to the dressing room where the tears just kept coming.

I don't remember her saying much, but I remember her not even pretending it had gone better than I thought. She was probably quite embarrassed for me and possibly for herself, but because my lid was officially flipped, if she said anything, I couldn't hear it.

She helped me gather my things, and as I was on my way out, I circled back. I grabbed the crap bottle of wine from the ice bucket and slunk out to my waiting limo. Settled into the back seat of the stretch, I took a long pull of the awful-tasting wine straight from the bottle and cried with relief to be safe again in the plush dark of the leather seats. My hero, the faceless limo driver mercifully taking me away from everything bad.

When I awoke the next day with my eyes encrusted with mascara, I couldn't help but replay the disaster from the night before, in utter disbelief that it had actually turned out worse than I had imagined. I called my sponsor.

Beth G. had been working a solid program in two different fellowships for years. The one that dealt with the sometimes more subtle yet insidious insanity that can arise from feelings of powerlessness over problem people, places, and things, and another one that dealt with putting down the drink and drugs. (Her dual membership status was referred to as being a "double winner," though I used to wonder if that label was slightly facetious.) I'd ask Beth to be my sponsor in the people struggling with relationships group (aka, the "people who don't mind their own business" posse). Beth was from Georgia, her accent was still thick as grits, and she never was not working as a character actress. She asked, like a mother asks her kid after their first day of school, "Sooo? How was it?" which sounded like she added about nine extra syllables in her most cheerful singsong lilt.

"Oh, Beth," I groaned. "It was so bad. It was reeeally bad . . . like my worst nightmare. What's that phrase I hear in meetings, when you're publicly shamed, humiliated beyond anything you can imagine, and you just wish you could die?"

"Oh, you mean 'ego deflating at depth'?" She recited the phrase so cheerfully, as if she were delivering the best news in the world.

I started crying. "Yes. That's it. I swear, Beth, it could not possibly have gone worse! Everyone saw me make a total fool of myself. I don't want to talk to anyone or see anyone. I—I can't stop replaying the whole thing over and over in my mind. I can't even explain how badly it went. I mean, everyone knew, like they didn't even try to pretend. I am so fucking embarrassed, I just hate myself. And I'm hungover, I feel so gross. But I'm not exaggerating, I couldn't believe how mean and cold Johnny was. He hated my guts!"

There was silence for a moment. "You said you're hungover?"

"Well . . . yeah. I'm telling you it was bad."

"Why are you hungover?"

"I totally tanked on Carson! Then I went and got drunk after. I wanted to die, I was so . . ."

(Note: At the time, it *hadn't* dawned on me that I had something to drink *before* the show. I didn't feel drunk, per se, so it never occurred to me, until months later. But I did cop to getting pretty wasted on red wine afterward and making out with some guy at Chianti Ristorante.)

"Well, I'm just curious . . . do you do that often?"

"Do I do what?"

"Drink, when you're upset?"

"Well, yeah! Of course I do. Trust me, if you saw how—"

Beth's voice slowed to an even more serious southern drawl. She was choosing her words very carefully. "Well . . . I would be remiss if I did not tell you that was a red flag."

"What? Oh nooo! Hah! Oh honey, I've been going to my meetings, I know alcoholics, and I'm definitely not one. I wish I was."

"Well . . . Would you be willing to not drink for thirty days and go to some meetin's?"

She had my attention now. This had never even crossed my mind. I'd always been taking Xanax or Valium as needed, smoking pot, and drinking every day, even before and after my meetings. It had never occurred to me to stop drinking. Even for a day. Even for a meal.

"Well, yeah . . . I guess so. I mean, sure. It shouldn't be a problem. As long as my parents don't die in the next thirty days." I could maybe conceive of not drinking, as long as nothing really horrific happened.

So on that day, after what felt like the most devastating, publicly humiliating event of my life, I stopped everything. I stopped drinking, stopped smoking pot for the first time in fifteen years, stopped taking Valium. But I held on to my cigarettes.

I eventually changed my sobriety date to a month later, after my birthday in late March, because I took NyQuil on my thirtieth birthday. (Woo-hooo!) I was legit sick with a bad cold in a hotel room on location for an HBO movie, and then drunk dialed a bunch of my exes. (I'd had fond memories of getting super wasted on that noxious green swill years earlier and was very much looking forward to a freebie.)

At that point I was still unsure if I was indeed in need of such a radical approach, but I started to go to these more fun and lively meetings for alcoholics, which I preferred to the ones for people who loved alcoholics. I actually looked forward to them.

I started counting days from my last drink. Initially, I felt like a fraud for even being there. I liked it. Fuck, I loved it. And even though it made no sense to me, I just felt better. I got all the jokes, and I cried in all the right places. Once I got sober, I weirdly couldn't *stop* crying in meetings, and people just put their arms around me and nodded.

I didn't know if it was my sobriety or my newly acquired aquiline profile that had afforded the sudden upgrade in my life, but since I'd never really made money before I'd stopped drinking, and now all of a sudden I was, I thought, just in case there was a connection between the two, why risk losing everything over a *beverage*? I was told in the meetings for alcoholics that if my life got better when I stopped drinking, I might want to stick around, and my life definitely did get better, so I stuck.

Ten years passed before I would find the courage to sit on the couch of another talk show. Twenty years passed before I would dance in front of an audience again. But I did. I stopped drinking. I sat on couches. I danced.

PART THREE

20

Baby Love

From adolescence and through the highs and lows of the first ten years of my career, from fresh out of the Neighborhood Playhouse through *Dirty Dancing,* and even the first year after that first nose job (the one that kept my nose front and center, but with a tip), I'd taken a certain pride in being an original, not looking like every other actress. I wasn't *so* insecure that I was going to succumb to the knife to adhere to some cookie-cutter standard of beauty and eradicate what made me *me*.

Then my beloved doctor "went in" to smooth the teensy bump protruding from the tip he'd made for me. And what? He fiddled with it, fine-tuned it? Or perhaps "reset" it a little higher up on my nose? I can only speculate, after spending far too much time trying to figure out what the hell happened. His tinkering left me unrecognizable and stopped my career in its tracks just as it was pulling out of the station. It was a freaky thing that happened, worthy of a *Twilight Zone* episode, like a disfiguring accident in which I became "prettier."

The general public and *Dirty Dancing* fans seemed to react to my amended profile as a kind of personal affront. Perhaps because they had identified with my realness, my humanness, because I was relatable, more like them than the typical leading ladies, the impossibly perfect goddesses they had grown accustomed to seeing up on the screen. Perhaps their connection to me as an actress or as Baby, was inextricably linked to my physical imperfection, to my ability to "pass" for beautiful. I'm a big fan of *wabi-sabi,* the Japanese concept of the perfection of imperfection. But is there no statute of limitations on how long people think they are entitled to ownership of my face? Entitled to not only have a personal preference about my nose, but feel obligated to declare their allegiance to it, to write about it, and to assume I should be pilloried for allegedly not loving myself enough?

And overnight, I was basically reduced to a punch line. It seemed people would rather believe that I hated my God-given Jewish nose than believe that something had gone seriously awry. I would've thought the same if I hadn't been there. But to this day, I'm flummoxed by the legs the story of my nose has had. I can't go near Google without getting an eyeful of vicious headlines: "What Ever Happened to Jennifer Grey?"

What can I say? Schadenfreude sells.

Meanwhile, work dried up. As if I'd been ghosted by all of showbiz. The feedback my agents received from casting people was that I did a great audition and they "loved" me, but felt it was too "confusing" or "distracting" to hire me because I just didn't look like myself.

"I *am* me," I'd say.

"But you don't *look* like you."

I'd been raised to believe that if you study with the best, work your ass off, and stay true to yourself, when you get that big break, and you eventually will, because you're talented and hardworking, you'll have the career you've always wanted, the life you've always wanted. I'd never considered being anything other than an actor. I had that singleness of focus. I'd closed off all the exits, had no backup plan. And to be the female lead in a movie as big as *Dirty Dancing* and never to get a seriously good gig after that? It felt like I'd been dumped on my head by a business I had entrusted to be the arbiter of my value. It was the value system I was raised with, among people who worked hard and then, as nature intended it seemed, went on to win Oscars and Tonys.

I felt very alone. There was no one I could call to ask, "How did you get through this?" because I couldn't think of a single person this had happened to.

Emotionally, it was just shy of unbearable. Newly sober, I was feeling all my feelings pretty much for the first time since I was fifteen, which, by the way, is not for the faint of heart. I was learning that my feelings wouldn't kill me, and that each feeling had a beginning, middle, and end. But every day the grief, shame, and confusion of being judged and misunderstood by millions of people crashed over me. I found it excruciating to be as sensitive and vulnerable as I was. In my twelve-step meetings, I was told that my vulnerability was my strength. *WTF?* I discovered that I could settle myself by dropping into the moment, into the *now* of now. That no matter how bad I was feeling, if I could interrupt whatever madness I was caught in long enough to ask myself, "But right now—how am I *right now*?" the answer was usually, if not always, "Oh, uh, I guess—right now? *Right now*, I'm fine." As long as I was in the moment, it was manageable. That's how basic I had to keep it. Today, those fundamental skills are still what ground me in moments of overwhelm. *Where are my feet? Oh. Right here. Okay.*

There is also something beautiful about being stripped bare.

Surrendered. How do you ever know your true value if people are always telling you you're the greatest? The less input I got from the outside world, or the more negative the input, the more I was left on my own to determine who and what I was. I'd been so consumed by feeling abandoned that I hadn't seen all the ways I had abandoned myself. I was forced to show up for myself. It wasn't pretty. I had to claw and scrape, and it was gnarly and bloody and gross. But there was a certain grace in that mess.

There I was, skinned alive, stripped of sex, drugs, and showbiz, the things I'd used all my life in an effort to feel good, and everything I had been avoiding feeling was just waiting for me. Including genuine tragedy. Trauma-lama-ding-dong. But there's plenty of evidence that good things can arise out of the muck. Perhaps even glorious things. I felt these tiny, wispy, little shreds of . . . what was this? Peace.

Trying out these new rules to live by afforded me a brief intermission from my personal hell. I heard, "You can't do anything to make yourself happy, but you can stop doing the things that make you unhappy." And I was beginning to identify the things that made me unhappy.

But, uh, how was I supposed to make a living? Prior to Schnozageddon, I'd really only had one good year financially. Yet I'd always managed to support myself somehow. Time and again, whenever I was feeling lost and scared about the future, I'd figured out how to survive, how to get by with less, and still make a cozy nest for myself. I'd always have enough food to eat, a roof over my head, and friends I could call on.

I believed in my ability to bounce back. I've always been eager to learn whatever was required to move forward. I trusted that whatever breadcrumbs I could find would lead me where I needed to go.

I started working with an inspiring acting coach who reminded me why I wanted to be an actor in the first place, and I took every workshop she offered. I took acting jobs that were not great, one after another, and applied what I'd been working on in class to make each experience more meaningful for me. Even so, staying in the ring when I felt so porous, looking for work in a business that seemed to be over me, made about as much sense as a hemophiliac who juggled knives for a living. But I had no other recourse. I focused on my sobriety. I tried to get behind the initially preposterous notion that *I was not my job.* And that *what other people thought of me was none of my business.* At first these concepts made no sense to me. But I was told, "Fake it till you make it," so that's what I did. And whenever I was in the grips of self-centered fear over losing what I had or not getting what I wanted, I tried to help someone else. And just hung in there.

I had to sell my house and my car, put all my stuff in storage, and move to a tiny apartment in New York. I got hired to do an HBO show, but I was replaced after the pilot. Soon after that, my agents at CAA "let me go." So much for sobriety making my life better. Except that my life *was* better, just not in the old ways I would've defined as better before everything went haywire. I started to feel less crazy, less like I was at the mercy of outside forces. Like I had choices. I could redesign my life in a way that served me and pleased me. I could decide how I wanted to spend my energy and with whom I wanted to spend my time. I couldn't afford to care too much about what others thought of me, and how I felt about myself was much more up to me than I had realized. I could change my attitude. I could be in this moment instead of being mired in the past or panicked about the future. My life had become more fluid and interesting as opposed to fixed and narrow.

Back in New York, humbled, my wings singed, still smoking from having flown too close to the sun, I used Valentine's Day as an excuse to visit my new and long-distance boyfriend, who lived in LA. I told my new agents I was coming to town, and they sent me a script for a little independent movie titled *Fate* and set up a meeting with the writer and first-time director Clark Gregg at the restaurant at Shutters, a posh hotel on the beach in Santa Monica.

Clark Gregg and I had been orbiting each other for more than a decade. When I'd auditioned for the David Mamet play *Speed-the-*

Plow in 1988, Clark had been hired to read with the auditioning actresses. A few years later, I was introduced to him in passing at
Sundance by John Slattery; the next day I ran into him boarding the
plane back to New York. A month later we met to discuss *Fate*.

At Shutters, we sat at a table outside discussing his script, a love
story about two emotionally unavailable people. I made sure to
impress upon him that I had plenty of firsthand experience to know
my way around just such a part. I spoke of the wonderful boyfriend I
was in LA visiting, who was fifteen years my junior, and Clark talked
about his wonderful girlfriend, who was also fifteen years younger. As
my mouth was busy extolling the virtues of my current flame, I could
hear clear as day the voice in my head, like the "honesty subtitles" in
Annie Hall, saying: "Why am I not with a guy like him? He is who I
should be with." The meeting went swimmingly, but nothing ever
came of the movie.

A month later, back in my modest one-bedroom rental above the
Oscar Wilde Memorial Bookshop on Christopher Street, I was chat-
ting on the phone with my friend Peter Mehlman, who'd been one of
the writers and producers on *Seinfeld,* and he was telling me about a
pilot he was developing. It was a sitcom about weird LA life called *It's
Like, You Know . . .* , and one of the characters in the ensemble was
an actress who would play herself. I said, "Like who were you thinking? How 'bout me?" I pitched myself to play myself—and it turned
out I was perfect for the part. I sent him some of the first writing I'd
ever done, about how the *mishigas* with my nose had turned my life
into a fucking freak show. Mehlman used that material as a jumping-
off point for my character. I thought *for sure* this bullshit about my
nose would lose some of its mojo if I confronted it publicly, head-on,
like a boss. No such luck. It lost no mojo. But doing a few seasons on
the show did boomerang me right back to LA. It was around that time
when that Clark Gregg showed up again; I'd see him periodically at
game-night parties hosted by his old Atlantic Theater Company pals.

The next thing I knew, I was forty years old.

And that's when I realized, "I don't have time to wait for this curse to be lifted; I have to have a fucking baby." My priorities suddenly and completely shifted. And you can never, ever win against that kind of deep, primitive programming.

Until this clarion call, I'd been fooling around almost exclusively with guys who were, for any number of reasons, not baby daddy material. I'd been basically romantically oriented to just pursue pleasure, like a dude. But because I now wanted a baby more than anything in the world (and because I had become a fan of Dr. Pat Allen, author of *Getting to "I Do": The Secret to Doing Relationships Right!*), I finally understood that my "dating style" was one of the reasons married life and motherhood had eluded me. I had been going about it completely backward.

Around that time, I ran into that Clark Gregg at yet another party. And then again at another party. We started dating, and one night after making out for far too long for two people so long in the tooth, he said, "And *why* can't we have sex?"

I said, "Because I know myself, and if I have sex with you, I will bond to you, and because I'm forty, I can't afford to bond to one more guy unless he wants what I want, which is to have a baby."

"Um. Wow. But how can I know if I would *want* to have a baby with you if we haven't even had sex yet?" to which I responded straight up, "I *know. It's crazy, right?*"

On the morning of my forty-first birthday, when Clark came to pick me up to take me to Palm Springs for the weekend, I said, "So here's the thing. You've given me a present I can't return."

He said, "What? That camisole? I know the lady at Barneys, you can totally return that."

"No," I said. "You've. Given. Me. A present. I can't. Return."

He said, "I don't understand what you're talking about."

I kept repeating it over and over until the coin dropped.

"Oh. How do you know?"

I showed him the stick.

"Well, those things can be wrong. We should get another one."

The test wasn't wrong.

Within weeks, he decided we should get a place together. And then get married—"If we're having a baby, we should get married." I said, "Okay." And then he wanted a wedding. I said, "You want a *wedding*? I'm four months pregnant."

I was just at the end of that first trimester, and I wasn't so much sick as I was tired. Really, really tired. But I was marrying someone very funny, very smart, who had come up in a theater company and knew a thing or two about producing. He took over, and in three weeks he'd organized our wedding—on Martha's Vineyard at the height of the summer season.

My belly was growing so fast that every time I went for a fitting for my off-the-rack Vera Wang wedding dress, the seamstress would say, "Oh boy, you better hurry up. I don't know how this is going to fit at the rate you're growing." But it did fit (albeit snugly). And the wedding came together. Our parents met one another for the first time the night before the rehearsal dinner. Nellie was my maid of honor. Tracy had married the actor Michael J. Fox and—along with one of Maggie's daughters—their young twins were our flower girls. Our baby was very much in evidence, shrink-wrapped in taut white satin, as I walked down the aisle, outside on a bluff up-island in Aquinnah. Clark's dad, an Episcopalian minister who spoke Hebrew, married us. The vows we wrote together were dope. Maggie sang an a capella rendition of the Stevie Wonder song "You and I." There wasn't a dry eye on the bluff. We had a raw bar and served lobster and corn. We had the greatest band and everybody danced. The toasts were moving and funny, about how "busy" we both had been before finally settling down. Clark's Atlantic Theater Company family had a long history of roasting each other with brilliant limericks. There were lots of tears and laughs.

I'd had a taste of being pretty famous, and for me, it wasn't so hot. I'd also made money in fits and starts, and that didn't do it for me, either. I'd gotten jobs that I liked, and jobs that I loved. As an actor, if you're really lucky, once in a blue moon you get a gig that's pure happiness— collaboration and process, creating something exciting with other gifted people, mixing it up with kindred spirits—but that's pretty rare, like lightning in a bottle. Or that's just been my experience. So far. Crappy acting jobs are definitely better than real crap jobs, but most aren't of the thrilling variety. The real torture is not having any control over being able to work. To be 100 percent dependent on someone to give you a job in order to do your thing, to be able to practice the craft that makes your soul take flight. All the while living with the very real possibility that that chance might never come. Or ever come again. But I grew up with the utter certainty that my dad, the parent with the big career, got the sweeter deal than my mom, who had to stay home with us kids. I knew I wanted to follow in my dad's footsteps, not my mom's. He seemed to hold all the cards, and to me, mother-hood looked like a bum deal. I assumed that being a mother meant forfeiting your dreams.

It turns out that being a mother was actually my dream job. I loved it more than anything. From the moment I became pregnant,

I had no ambivalence whatsoever. For once, there was nowhere else I wanted to be, no one's life I envied, no acting job I should have been getting. There was no question that what I was doing was something that mattered. Becoming a mother was, for me, the greatest thing on earth.

I planned on giving birth at Cedars-Sinai. (I'd been born at Cedars of Lebanon, back when the hospital was downtown.) I had a midwife with my OB/GYN standing by as the backup plan. After laboring for going on twelve hours, I gave in and got an epidural, which instantly slowed everything down, so they gave me Pitocin to ramp it back up. Then, when they could see her head, it was time to push.

I pushed, full-on, for three and a half hours. When my doctor said, "Listen, Jennifer, you're going to have to *really* push now," Clark almost bit his head off. "You think she's *not* pushing? Have you ever met my wife?"

The next thing I knew, my hospital room was swarming with a team wheeling in all kinds of equipment—suction machines, forceps—trying to get my baby out, because she was not budging. The plan changed. I was being prepped for an emergency C-section. All I knew was that I wanted this baby safely out of me in one piece, and if they needed to slice me from stem to stern, that was fine.

By the time my doctor lifted this baby girl out of me, I could see Stella had a head of thick, black, stick-straight hair. Not what I was picturing at all. *This* is my baby? I couldn't hold her because I couldn't feel my arms (thanks to the generous spinal block), but my doctor brought her squinched-up little alien face next to mine so I could tenderly kiss her sweet cheek and whisper my unintelligible undying love as they whisked me away so they could put me back together. When I recovered the use of my limbs, Stella and I were reunited. Our pediatrician, Jay Gordon, placed her on my boob, and my eyes rolled back into my head. That was it for me. I was floating in a bliss field I hadn't known existed. An embodied disembodiment. This ecstasy was not of this world. That we humans have the capacity for such a sudden and completely revelatory experience blew my mind.

It was almost absurd to me that something so commonplace could feel so earth-shattering. But it did.

Having a baby annihilated any competition for my attention. It was a love more powerful than any passion or ambition I'd ever known. I was a changed person. Being a mother interrupted patterns that were desperately in need of interrupting. I didn't think about what I looked like. I didn't think about work. I didn't care what people thought of me. I certainly didn't think about my nose. Nothing interested me but her. I was more than happy to get up in the middle of the night. An overenthusiastic older mother who'd gotten in just under the wire. Sensing the faintest of movements from inside her bassinet, I would be jolted awake, because I was never actually asleep. What I *was* doing was nothing I ever would have previously defined as "sleep." It was more like highly vigilant resting. I happily nursed her on demand. I needed nothing more than to gaze into her eyes, wipe her bum, hold her soft little feet. Her tiny perfect fingers wrapped around my finger with indescribable tenderness. Biological imperative blotted out any other choice or preference. It was a welcome and profound relief to know exactly where I was supposed to be and what I was supposed to be doing. For the first time, I felt that what I was doing was actually meaningful. There is a sound reason for this primordial hardwiring: to keep your baby alive. This myopia was instantaneous, and nonnegotiable from the moment she was born. I liked my world being small. My concerns were limited to making enough milk, interpreting what she was trying to communicate with me by her cries and red face. Gas? Poop? Wet diaper? Hunger? Or just an indictment of me? "Lady, you don't know what the fuck you're doing!"

Having this baby made me reconsider my story. If my career had gone the way I'd wanted it to, I might never have stopped to have a baby. And if I had read Pat Allen's book years earlier, I wouldn't have been with Clark. And if I hadn't been with Clark, I never would have had this exact child. The only thing I knew for certain was that there was no other child for me.

I remember thinking a lot about how so many women in the world don't have the luxury of a partner they can pass the baton to, who is willing and able to go out and slay the dragons the way Clark did. He made my dream a reality, made it possible for me to stop working so I could devote myself to the care of our newborn. His first produced screenplay, *What Lies Beneath,* starring Harrison Ford and Michelle Pfeiffer (not too shabby), came out when we were newly together, and after that, he started getting hired more and more as a screenwriter. Clark, having lived the lone wolf life of a bachelor, had never been responsible for anyone other than himself before, and he took on the role of provider with as much gusto as I took on the role of full-time mom. I'd never been with a guy who showed up for me like that.

My job, meanwhile, was to keep Stella safe. Around 4:30 P.M. I'd begin the bedtime ritual, which always started with her nightly bath. I'd set up the little plastic basin on our round kitchen table, and holding her head at the perfect angle, I used my hand to shield her eyes as I poured the just-right temperature water gently over her head with a cup. And God forbid the suds from the baby shampoo should run into her eyes. She did not like it.

When we eventually moved her into a crib in her own room (I can only laugh at myself now at what felt like such a huge deal at the time), she was not the kind of baby who babbled adorably to herself upon waking. We could tell she was awake from the bloodcurdling scream that rattled the baby monitor. We knew pretty early on that she had to be our baby, because she seemed to have only two speeds: joyful goo-goo gaga and full-out Medea.

And when they say, "The days are long, the years are short," they're not kidding. Every day was like climbing a mountain. There was so much to do. It was relentless with no end in sight. Getting her sleep schedule in order took what felt like Herculean effort. When mothering was good, it was really good. And when it was challenging, I thought I was maybe gonna die.

Before I became pregnant with Stella, I always thought I was going to die of one thing or another (heartbreaks, crushing career disappointments), but from the moment her skin touched mine, I recognized a different timbre of threat, a different feeling of "if this all goes wrong . . ." Everything I'd previously suffered over became insignificant in comparison. Babies are resilient, but try telling that to a first-time, older mother. And if this was "last call" for your fertility, then even the pregnancy has a particular fragility and intensity to it.

You can kid yourself that there are more coming, but realistically? Check your FSH (follicle-stimulating hormone) before you count them chickens.

When I was nine and a half weeks pregnant, Clark came with me to my scheduled CVS (chorionic villus sampling), a prenatal test used to detect chromosomal abnormalities and other genetic problems. It's recommended for knocked-up broads on the older side, which it turns out is thirty-five and up. The doctor extracts a small amount of tissue from the placenta and also examines your little peanut with an ultrasound.

Once they had the tissue sample and the technician had taken all the initial measurements, the doctor, who'd done more of these procedures than anyone else, arrived in the little exam room to talk to me and Clark. He was extremely professional and soft-spoken, but the atmosphere changed soon after he entered.

At first I didn't know what was going on, and then the doc said, "See this area between the back of the neck and the bottom of the skull? It's called the nuchal translucency, or nuchal fold. In addition to the CVS, we also do a nuchal translucency screening to identify risk factors for chromosomal abnormalities. This here—" He moved the mouse on his computer to draw our attention to the black-and-white image projected up on the screen. "When there is more fluid here than usual, it's called 'increased nuchal translucency.' The measurement here is—it's probably—double the size we like to see at this point."

Whatever language he was speaking, I couldn't understand it. I stopped really hearing.

"It's always difficult when we find things like this. But it happens. Unfortunately, it's more common with women your age. I'm sure your doctor can talk to you more about this."

Crazy as it sounds, I had never considered that any of the old-lady risks and statistics might apply to me. I didn't have any trouble getting pregnant. I was ageless, right?

Within minutes the CVS doc was on the phone with my OB. As

soon as we got back to my place, Clark and I got on the phone with my OB, too. I had met with several doctors before deciding who I wanted to deliver my baby, and as I was only nine weeks pregnant, I'd only met with this doctor once or twice so far. She said, "Jennifer, you have to trust me, you don't want this. You're only nine weeks. You'll get pregnant again. You don't want *this* pregnancy."

The nuchal translucency screening was clearly spooking the CVS doc as well as my OB. They were concerned about the baby's heart, and other scary stuff I couldn't even take in. My OB said her office could schedule a time for me to come in for a procedure to terminate after the weekend.

"Could we wait and see what the CVS results are?" I asked feebly.

She said, "Well, we could wait. But based on what I'm seeing? No. The final results can take up to two weeks. The sooner you do this, the sooner you can try again." This was a Friday. She scheduled a D&C for the following Tuesday.

For the whole weekend before the scheduled procedure, I wept and wept and wept in my bed. Keening like an animal. I couldn't stop crying.

Clark and I had been dating for maybe seven months when I realized I was pregnant. When we found ourselves faced with this terrifying stressor, we weren't even living together. We hadn't yet worked out anything about what we were going to do going forward. But Clark went on the Internet and started googling and found people online who had similar stories to ours whose babies had turned out fine.

Maggie, who had also moved to California a while back and was the mother of two young girls, was a huge fan of her OB/GYN, Paul Crane. She urged me to call him. He was the Warren Beatty of Hollywood obstetricians. He wasn't a womanizer, but every woman I knew went to him, and every one of them was in love with him. He was the most unassuming, un-Hollywood guy. I'd met Paul before, but his office felt a little too midwifey for me, a little too crunchy. I wanted the reassurance of a slicker, more Western medicine approach, so I'd gone with a more Beverly Hills practice.

But while I was wailing in agony of the impending loss, Maggie said, "Please, c'mon. Just call Paul. I told him what's going on."

I cried to Paul Crane.

He said, "Why don't you come in tomorrow, we'll do an ultrasound and have a look." On Monday, I lay in the darkened office while Dr. Crane studied the imaging on the screen and measured the nuchal translucency. And as he stared at the monitor he very calmly said, "Let's just wait and see. We don't have to hurry. Let's just keep an eye on it. It could change. Let's wait and watch."

In the weeks that followed, I was out-of-my-mind anxious. I'd call Paul Crane from the street corner weeping. And he'd say, "Just come on in, we'll have a look. Let's see if it's any thinner. If it isn't, we'll deal with that then. But it could get better."

And it did.

I never felt fully out of the woods after that scare. I needed to be routinely examined and scanned by a neonatal cardiologist, who was checking for every possible heart problem throughout the remainder of the pregnancy. Each time she found nothing to worry about I was profoundly grateful, and I realized that the welfare of this being growing inside me had made me forevermore changed.

Stella was better than fine. She was perfect. She was a strange creature, and I loved her immediately. Her straight black hair (birth hair, who knew?) eventually fell out and became wispy, curly, blonder, and she had the pinkest, palest skin like Clark's. She was like him, and she was like me—and she was also very much an entity unto herself.

Her hardwiring was, it turns out, her hardwiring. She came with it. But there was also this malleable, impressionable softscape of her. I knew there was enough that was gonna be on me to oversee, and I really didn't want to fuck that up. I was keenly aware of how much my choices and behavior were imprinting on her, and that it mattered. It mattered too much, and if I could do it over, I believe a healthy dose of benign neglect would have benefitted everyone. They say you should raise your first kid like you raised your third, but I had only the one crack at it. I felt the internalized pressure, like most parents, to not repeat my parents' mistakes.

I noticed that other people's kids were napping for three and four hours a day and mine would nap, at most, forty-five minutes. She'd wake up at five thirty every morning, when other kids were sleeping until seven. At first, the hardest part of being a mother for me was my perfectionism.

I knew that the most effective way to instill in Stella the stuff she would need was not through telling her, but through leading by example, modeling for her. I couldn't teach her things I wasn't practicing. My mantra became, "I must be a living example of what I want to teach her." Even if I have to play catch-up, I have to embody those lessons. If I was being a perfectionist about taking care of Stella, I was teaching her to be a perfectionist, and conversely, the more gentle I could be with myself, the more I could allow myself to be flawed and make mistakes, the more she would develop a hopeful, lifelong learner mindset. A growth mindset.

As the months and early years passed, I was devoted to and present for Stella in a way that I imagined would be the antithesis of my parents' best efforts. The phrase "helicopter parent" was coined during my tenure as a new mom and was so apt a description of my behavior that I felt almost paranoid that someone had been watching me. It was hard for me to separate from her. It became impossible to consider not being with her, to not take her to school, to not pick her up, to not be able to chauffeur her to and from playdates.

The natural order of things requires that a parent be able to downshift, and modulate the intensity of attachment, to titrate the overactive parenting and temper the love affair with one's child, in the best interest of the kid. It's counterintuitive to encourage this natural letting-go process, resulting in their independence. The painful irony: if you do your job well, they will leave you.

I took little gigs here and there, but the quality of the work I was being offered just felt not worth it, especially in comparison to what I would be giving up. I didn't want to miss a minute of my young daughter's becoming, especially in those early years. It felt important that one of us be home with her.

I liked being a mom. Then I realized, I *really* liked it. It was a relief to have checked out of the race, to not be in the chronic heartbreak of my former career. To not be feeling shitty. To not be thrown away. I found it to be safer in the closed system of my new family than in the outside world.

Clark didn't have the same ambivalence about owning his ambition as I did. One day, around the time we bought our first home, when Stella was in preschool, Clark said he was going to audition for the new Julia Louis-Dreyfus sitcom *The New Adventures of Old Christine,* to play Julia's ex-husband, and whatdyaknow? He got the part. And there it was. I was with an actor. Again. His acting career started to really cook. In his forties. There I was, on the red carpet again, not as the girlfriend this time, but as the wife. And I thought, "Oh wow. Didn't see this coming. I've become my mom."

Fame is like clouds. From a distance, it looks like something big, white, and billowy, but once you're up inside it, there's no there there. It's like vapor. It doesn't feel like anything. Becoming a mother felt like everything. It was the most real thing I'd ever experienced.

But . . . where was Jenny?

21

Dancing with the Scars

Every single day, every month, every year, I woke up when Stella woke up. Early. At the very early end of kid circadian rhythms. Made breakfast and the dreaded school lunch, did school drop-off and marketing, then school pickup, snack, homework, dinner, dishes, bath time, and, limping toward the finish line, through that stickiest of wickets, the bedtime ritual. I was in charge of arranging all of Stella's after-school activities—swim class, dance class, art class, playdates—and her dentist and doctor appointments. I did all the driving. (And Stella was not a sleepaway camp girl, so there was no summer break for Mommy.) I looked after our beloved dogs. Of course, whenever Clark's work schedule would allow, he was very hands-on and loved it. I went to Pilates a few times a week after drop-off and before grocery shopping, and I never stopped going to my regular meetings.

From serious *balabusta* stock, I ran our household the only way my being knew how. I have always loved cooking and trying new recipes. It's not home if I haven't placed fresh flowers from the market in every room. I can't go to bed until everything is in its place, counters are spotless, and the kitchen sink wiped clean. I have little tolerance for schmutz or disorganization. I need a clean and orderly workspace, just this side of Joan Crawford.

I couldn't believe how much I loved my kid. And because half measures avail me nothing, I took the job of mothering seriously, which took a bit of energy. I was always in some form of problem-solving mode, aiming to see how I could do better, be more effective.

Clark was, for the most part, working full-time, either writing, or acting, or writing, acting, and directing, which was great, because he was the only one making any money to support our family. When he was off, the three of us would take a vacation, usually with the Foxes on the Vineyard for two weeks every summer.

Clark and I laughed a lot. We loved hanging out at home and being with our kid. We liked the same kinds of movies, theater, and music. We both needed intense physical activity, though he was obsessed with his regular basketball games and jujitsu, and I'd do yoga, hike, and take spin classes.

Anyone who knew me knew that I regularly suffered from chronic neck pain and sometimes from blinding headaches that could last for days. Only Clark knew that I would sometimes wake up unable to feel my hands. I would try to get myself out of pain by seeing a chiropractor, acupuncturist, or body worker, but sometimes I felt worse after treatment. I'd try to come up with "dos and don'ts" to avoid triggering a pain cycle, but never came up with a foolproof system.

Our little family was tight. I knew Clark loved me and I loved him. I wanted the best for him, he wanted the best for me, and nobody wanted the best for their kid more than we did. We were both always striving to be better versions of ourselves for each other and for our daughter.

When Stella was still very little, I tried going back to work. I took a Lifetime Christmas movie, which was going to be shot on location in Canada. They cast Clark as my love interest, and we brought Stella along. A few days into the shoot, I had a full-blown, out-of-my-mind legit panic attack, my first since my Broadway debut in 1993, in *The Twilight of the Golds,* after which I'd sworn off doing live theater. I couldn't tolerate the terrifying distortion of reality, the unable-to-get-back-home feeling of these complete emotional hijackings. This particular Canadian episode of *You Have Lost Your Fucking Mind* manifested in me not being able to sleep a wink for four consecutive days, in the lead role, shooting eight pages of dialogue a day. I had to be prescribed something. I had understood the basic guardrails of sobriety to mean, "We don't drink or use no matter what. We don't take anything that affects us from the neck up." Finding myself in this very scary, disorienting psychological shit storm was a conundrum, because I have always held very dear the gift of sobriety, and try never to take it for granted, but there was no question I needed some kind of medical intervention. A psychopharmacologist (a specialist who prescribes medication to treat mental health or mood disorders) promptly put me on an antidepressant. Having never experienced depression, I hadn't known that antidepressants could also treat anxiety, but as soon as I was on this medicine, I realized that

I'd been suffering from a legit anxiety disorder my entire life. This medication didn't make me feel at all high or even particularly relaxed, I just felt *normal*. Like it put the candy coating on my M&M.

I got a few gigs after that hellfire. I had a stint as a series regular on the HBO drama *John from Cincinnati,* created by David Milch, but the show only lasted one season. I was a guest star on an episode of Clark's show, *The New Adventures of Old Christine,* and on *House.* But when you stop working full-time when your kid is little, and then you try to dip your toe in again, it's like you've become a stranger to yourself. My talent, my drive, my confidence? When I looked for them, I didn't recognize them. These parts of me were wizened, underfed shadows, banished to some dark and dank basement. They hadn't been cultivated or cared for. And I had to be okay with that, because the alternative was to get back in the cage with the tiger I had finally escaped from. I was relieved to have extricated myself from a toxic business and was living a meaningful life beyond my wildest dreams. As an adult, and a sober one, I knew no one had everything, or at least not everything at the same time. I had come to accept and understand that because I wasn't willing to leave my young daughter in the care of a full-time nanny, I was just going to have to set aside the possibility of going back to work. I felt in good company with many of the mothers I'd run into on the schoolyard or in the hallways at pickup and drop-off. But I noticed that the further away I got from being a working actress, a professional person, some- one with a "real job," the further I'd have to swim to get back to that life. After a while, maybe the distance had become too far. Every day that option felt less and less like a realistic possibility. Add to that, I was guilty of committing the cardinal sin of every actress. I was get- ting older.

So I stayed put.

My primary focus was on teaching Stella the essential life skills, as I saw them, and because of this, I began to notice a disconnect between what I was telling her and how I was living my life. I heard myself saying, "It's important to try new things," "It's okay to be a beginner," "How will you know if you can do something if you haven't tried it?" "You're not supposed to be an expert at something you've never done before," and "Not everybody's going to like you." I whole-heartedly believed the words I was saying, but my words were not congruent with my actions. Regardless of whatever wisdom I was attempting to impart, the only thing my daughter was for sure learning was what she saw me *doing*.

I had never watched a reality show. In those years when Stella was little, I wasn't watching much television at all. But twice a year, like clockwork, I'd get the call from my agent with the offer to participate on the increasingly popular dance competition show *Dancing with the Stars* (*DWTS*). I never considered doing it. My automatic response to each offer was one of irritation. Grandiose irritation, fronting for hurt. I took the producers' keen interest in me to mean one thing: "Your legitimate acting career is officially over. The only thing anyone is interested in seeing you do is a humiliating dance competition for people who have no other options and nothing to lose." Let me just confess: I had never seen the damn show. It was just raw fear, pride, and ego. My mom *and* Michael Fox, who both loved me, had on separate occasions repeatedly made a point of telling me how great they thought I'd be on that show. Even their enthusiasm made me feel awful about myself.

Marlee Matlin, whom I'd become friends with in the eighties through Maggie, was the only person I knew who'd been on the show. Marlee is one of those humans that is a force of nature, exceedingly accomplished on many fronts. Not only was she, at the age of twenty-one, the youngest recipient of the Best Actress Oscar for her film debut in *Children of a Lesser God*, but from there she has never stopped doing groundbreaking work as an actor and activist. Plus, she's sexy, gorgeous, funny, and smart. I mentioned to her that *DWTS* had asked me, for the umpteenth time, to join the cast. She went off about how I *had* to do it. The gravity with which she talked about this dance competition shocked me. She said it was incredibly difficult, that I would hardly get to see my daughter, and that it was a job that needed to be taken very seriously. And she said, "It's one of the most powerful experiences I've ever had. It's life-changing." After our conversation, she kept checking in to see if I'd signed on. I couldn't for the life of me understand why Marlee was so hell-bent on this idea, but her insistence piqued my interest.

I hadn't danced at all in more than *twenty years*. I hadn't dared set foot in a class since *Dirty Dancing,* because I wasn't comfortable with people knowing who I was and expecting me to be a better dancer than I was. While I had done all my own dancing in the movie, I knew what it had taken to get me there, far beyond anything that was gonna happen in a class on any given day. But to have a private coach whose job was solely to teach me all different styles of dance was, and still is, my dream. Maybe one of my favorite things on earth. I relish the intimacy and focus of a one-on-one experience, in any realm, as that is my preferred learning style and makes me feel that anything is possible. Knowing that there is something special within me and that I can't unlock it or access it by myself is painful. When I see great dancing, I get this very deep, intense yearning, an almost untenable desire, to be able to do it, too. Not to perform publicly, but to just get good enough to be able to turn off my brain, let my body take over, and be in flow.

In 2009, *DWTS*'s coexecutive producer in charge of talent, Deena Katz (no relation), invited me to a taping of the live show. Weirdly enough, I loved it.

Afterward she wrote me, "You're hooked!" to which I replied, "Oh, I'm fucked."

I had only just barely opened my mind to the possibility of participating, but there was no question that before I went any further, I needed to tackle my crippling stage fright. The antidepressant provided pretty good coverage for everyday generalized anxiety. To address my acute performance anxiety, I decided to try hypnosis. A friend recommended a clinical psychologist and mind-body expert named

Carolyn Conger. Before my first appointment, Carolyn asked me to put together a list of things I did and didn't want. I mostly didn't want to feel paralyzed with anxiety, so I could do the show.

During our recorded session, Carolyn put me effortlessly in an alpha state, guiding me with the repetition of verbal cues. *Anxiety, should it come, or even discomfort, especially before a performance, is energy for the creative moment, is the activation of my body-mind system to go into action and give a beautiful performance that is meaningful to me and inspiring to all. When the activation of my body comes, I will know that it is there to serve me. I'm okay with my feelings and I'm okay with who I am, as I am.*

I was fully aware of everything that was going on the entire session. Afterward, I confessed that I was a bit disappointed in myself, as I was never able to go into the trancelike state. I was just wide awake the whole time. I was concerned that because I wanted it to work so badly that maybe I couldn't let go, and it wouldn't "work." She reassured me that the optimal state for hypnosis was different than I thought. It was more a state of focused attention, heightened suggestibility to vivid fantasies. She told me to listen to the recording of our session twice a day. And I did. Every day. For months. She rewired my brain, my response to panic.

I learned to associate those previously frightening chemical and physiological cues—the heart pounding, breaking into a sweat, feeling disassociated (out of my body), and nausea—with positive rather than negative outcomes, as something I wanted more of, rather than something I had to resist.

Around this same time, as it was looking more and more like I was wending my way toward the ballroom, Clark suggested that I get my neck checked out to make sure it was physically safe for me to do the show. While I didn't really share his concern, I went through the motions and set up a consultation with a neurological spinal surgeon, Dr. Robert Bray, who had just operated on a friend of mine. She said he was *the* guy. Then I happened to see this same Dr. Bray on *DWTS*, treating Buzz Aldrin, the first man on the moon turned ballroom dancer. I had an MRI done before my exam, at the doctor's request, and early one fall morning after drop-off (Stella was in third grade), I drove over to Marina del Rey to D.I.S.C. Sports and Spine, for what I assumed was just a formality.

There was a life-sized flexible model of a spine hanging from a hook in one corner of the exam room, and on the wall hung a chart showing complex and detailed behind-the-scenes maps of the spine and nerves. On a side table, next to a box of Kleenex, sat a flexible, plastic anatomical model of a series of vertebrae with skinny, red rubber tubing protruding as nerves. Like Legos for doctors. I wanted to touch the model, but I was scared the doctor would walk in and catch me playing with his stuff.

I was trying to find a comfortable position, deciding whether it was best to sit up straight or to lie down with my legs dangling over the edge, awkwardly trying not to slip off the papered exam table, when the six-foot-five, bespectacled doctor entered the room, dressed in a white lab coat over scrubs, his name sewn in blue cursive above the breast pocket. I sat up and introduced myself, told him I'd seen him with the famous astronaut on *DWTS* and wanted him to check out my neck just to be sure I was good to do the show.

He sat down on his rolling stool so we were now face-to-face, and said, "I've had a look at your MRI. Tell me, what do *you* think's going on with your neck?"

"Well, I've had problems on and off ever since I was in this car accident a million years ago. It was a head-on collision. People were killed in the other car. I got whiplash. It's gotten worse over time, so I have to go to the chiropractor a lot. I get these neck spasms. Headaches. Sometimes, when I first wake up in the morning, I can't feel my hands. That kind of stuff."

Dr. Bray swiveled around to look at the black-and-white scan on his computer screen. He pointed to a white egg shape alongside what I recognized to be the bones of my neck and skull. "And tell me about this. What's *this*?"

I said, "Oh that. That's just a nodule on my thyroid. I've had it for four years. I have it checked regularly, sometimes every six months. Needle biopsies, bloodwork, ultrasounds. It's gotten bigger, I know it's ugly, but since it's benign I don't really care. I'm not going to have surgery to take it out if it's not cancer." It *had* grown substantially. I'd started to notice it in the mirror and in pictures.

Dr. Bray very cooly said, "Well, it doesn't look right to me. It's probably gotta go. But since thyroid cancer is very slow growing, it can wait."

I didn't say anything, but I was thinking, "Excuse me, I didn't ask your opinion on this. I happen to know this is nothing to worry about because I'm all over this thing. I have *the* guy, the head of thyroid cancer over at Cedars."

"What can't wait," Dr. Bray continued calmly, "is what's going on with your cervical spine. You may have one of the worst necks I've ever seen."

"*Ever?*"

"Pretty much. You see here," and he pointed out the different thicknesses on the illuminated scan. "These levels—C4-C5-C6-C7— see how much thinner and almost nonexistent these discs are here compared to these other ones?" He wheeled himself backward a few feet to grab his handy-dandy model, and rolled back my way, twisting and flexing the segments of squeaky faux spine. "Any other surgeon in town would automatically give you a three-level fusion. I wouldn't do that to you. You wouldn't be able to dance. You wouldn't be able to look at your shoes. You'd hate it. But your head is literally falling forward off your spine. And the spinal canal, which protects the spinal cord, it's usually about one and a half centimeters. Yours is down to a few millimeters. So if you're dancing and you get jolted pretty good, not to mention if you were driving and got rear-ended, you'd be permanently paralyzed from the neck down. You'd be a rag doll."

"So, you're saying . . . I can't do the show?"

"Until that's taken care of? No. You shouldn't even be in a car in my opinion. I would do this yesterday. To get you out of danger I need to fuse levels C4 and C5. Once I've jockeyed back C4, the vertebra that's slipped way forward, I'd stabilize the two levels with a titanium plate and four screws. That alone should alleviate a lot of your pain."

"Oh. Fucking. Hell."

"I performed an emergency microdiscectomy on Karina Smirnoff, who had a severe disc herniation in her neck, just seventeen days prior to the start of the show last season."

"Really? I love Karina."

"Just like I did with her, I'd go in from the front, make the incision through one of the natural wrinkles in your neck." He'd moved in to get a closer look at my neck creases. *My wrinkles?* "We do this procedure as outpatient in the surgery center downstairs. You'd go home twenty-three hours later. You'll feel better right away once those levels are stabilized, and then we'll see if you're still in pain after, we can eventually go back in and clean out the other levels from the back. But at least you'll be out of danger."

"How in the world? Are you serious?"

"The ballistic impact from the whiplash years ago tore the interspinous ligament and facet capsule. This created instability at C4 and C5. And where there's supposed to be a natural curve to the neck"—Dr. Bray started demonstrating with his spine toy—"your neck not only lost the curve and became straight up and down, but over time, has progressed to the point where it's bending in the other direction."

My smiling face collapsed like a Jenga tower. I burst into tears. Dr. Bray wheeled over to the side table and back with the Kleenex box. He waited patiently until I stopped. He'd obviously seen a lot of people cry before.

I left the doctor's office pretty much in shock. I scheduled my surgery a few days later. When Marlee checked back to see what I'd decided to do about the show, I told her I was having neck surgery instead, so I'd have to postpone my "life-changing" experience until I'd recovered.

As Dr. Bray had predicted, as soon as I came out of anesthesia, I felt better. I couldn't believe it. He got me up and walking around my hospital room. He warned me that I might feel a little off-balance initially, because my head was now sitting at a completely different angle than it had been. For years.

I was grateful that I could manage the post-op pain with some pretty hard-core painkillers without triggering my addiction. I had a healthy respect and fear of opiates, and, fortunately, I was able to get off them as soon as possible.

It would take about six months for the neck to fully fuse, but within a few weeks, I felt undeniably better. I told my thyroid doctor that I'd decided to remove the nodule, and he said, "As you know, from everything we've seen so far, there's been no evidence that you *need* to take it out, but if we remove it, we can just take out the one side." The thyroid gland sits at the front of the base of the neck and has two lobes, like a butterfly. "We'll leave the other half, and that way, you won't have to be on medication for the rest of your life."

A week after my overnight stay at Cedars, the pathology report came back: capsular follicular cancer, the kind that's good at evading biopsies and can easily spread to other organs, like lungs or bones. So a few days later I spent Christmas Eve back in the hospital to remove the remaining half of my thyroid.

Within ten days I'd undergone back-to-back surgeries that required tilting my head way back to access my thyroid, and, of course, after that, my neck started to kill me again. Dr. Bray said I still had those two levels (C5-C6 and C6-C7) that had stenosis, a narrowing of the space within the spine, which puts pressure on the nerves. He could go in, this time through the back of my neck, clean out those levels, and then I'd be good to go. I figured since I was already in recovery mode from the fusion and the thyroid business, with my physical activity restricted to short walks for the foreseeable future, I might as well do whatever I needed to get out of pain once and for all. I wanted all of this behind me. I asked Dr. Bray, if I went ahead with this other procedure, could I possibly do *DWTS* by the summer? He considered this for a moment.

"You'd be recovered enough. You could probably last a few weeks."

I said, "A few weeks?" Until that moment, I hadn't considered what might actually happen after I signed on. I had barely been able to picture myself telling Deena I would do it.

"Well, they have professional athletes competing on that show. And most of them are younger than you. By a lot. You'll have just had four surgeries in three months." He explained that the anesthesia alone was enough to fog up a person's brain for a while, but he was confident that I would be able to dance.

Marlee Matlin is a mystic. I hadn't yet agreed to do the show, and it had already changed my life. Fuck, it might even have saved my life.

Dr. Bray cleaned out the stenosis in the back of my neck. The recovery sucked, but having a goal made it manageable. As soon as he gave me the okay, I started strength training in the gym at D.I.S.C. Dr. Bray was, at the time, the US Olympic team doc, so I trained alongside a bunch of Olympic athletes—synchronized swimmers, speed skaters, and one luger. Some were there for strength training, some were rehabbing post-op.

When I officially accepted the offer to do *Dancing with the Stars,* of course my panic flared up big-time. I immediately deeply regretted having said yes. I needed to get out of it. I was sure I had made one of those horrible mistakes. My spiking anxiety wasn't easy on Clark, on top of everything else he'd just been through with me, holding down the fort while I was in the not-so-fun house of scary diagnoses and surgical interventions. I remember walking around the Third Street Promenade in Santa Monica with him, my heart racing, saying, "I can't do this. I have to get out of it." It was obvious that I was already suffering from some severe anxiety right out of the gate. And Clark said, "No. No. You only get one of these in a marriage and I'm using mine right now. *You have to do this.* Because you love dance. And it will be so fun. You *have* to do it."

The hardest thing for me was agreeing to be on the show. By doing so, I was choosing myself, for the first time in . . . since I was forty? Or maybe twenty?

And maybe the next hardest thing was that as soon as I said yes,

I became aware of a sharp, electrical pain on the ball of my right foot, the part that bears all of your weight when in very high heels. "Seriously? I've just gone through fire to get here! Suddenly, with every step, there's a knife in my foot?"

Before my first rehearsal, I was sent to Worldtone Dance in Westwood to get my ballroom and Latin dance shoes. As I was trying on different pairs, I noticed that the suede soles of these specialty shoes were wafer thin, with no cushioning. When the salesman asked how high a heel I was comfortable dancing in, I flashed on Johnny repeatedly correcting Baby, "Don't put your heel down!" The dancing I was about to be doing would almost exclusively be performed on the balls of my feet. (The judges would actually dock points if the woman put a heel down.)

I made the first podiatrist appointment of my life. He told me that I had a Morton's neuroma, basically a trapped nerve on the ball of my foot between my third and fourth toe. I'd been wearing Birkenstocks and flip-flops for the previous eight years. I hadn't really worn high heels for some time, but they were about to be my work shoes. On a good day, it felt like a pebble in my shoe or a fold in my sock that wouldn't unfold. On a bad day, sharp stabbing pain. Rehearsals were beginning the following week, so all I could do was hope that a cortisone shot would help. (Three months after the *DWTS* season ended, Dr. Wang surgically removed my larger-than-average neuroma.)

On *DWTS*, every contestant is assigned a pro. The pro's job is to choreograph each dance, teach it to their partner, and then perform it live the following week. Derek Hough was twenty-five and I was fifty, but based on what little I'd seen while cramming to get the lay of the land, he was the pro for me. He was the right height, and while he was half my age, and not my type, his prowess as a choreographer and dancer had that X factor I found weirdly compelling. Marlee was less sure of him as a match for me because she knew Derek's choreography and style to be riskier and more ambitious. He had that virtuosity I had been trained my whole life to recognize. When I told Deena that Derek was the only partner I could see myself with, she said, "I can't guarantee you'll get him. Sorry. The show doesn't work like that."

I was told that we'd have one day off a week during the three weeks of dance training, but once the show was on the air, there would be no days off. It was up to the individual contestant to determine how much or how little they wanted to rehearse. Some took their pros out on the road with them, treating *DWTS* as a kind of side hustle, but I knew I wasn't going to be able to pick up the choreography quickly, and would need every minute of rehearsal I could get. I rehearsed, on average, seven hours a day. (I was told that to this day, I rehearsed more than any other contestant.) We had to meet every week with the costume designers to come up with the look for that week's dance and then come in for multiple fittings. We had to do interviews to provide content for the show and regularly do interviews with press.

Clark and I hired a nanny for the first time to fill in for me and take care of Stella during the day while Clark was working. And while this dramatic shift in the family system was new and stressful for all three of us, it was also an incredible opportunity for Clark and Stella to bond.

In late August, I drove myself to the rehearsal studios in Hollywood for the reveal of which pro was going to be my partner and was thrilled to see Derek Hough saunter into the room. Of course, cameras were rolling to capture our initial meeting on film, like some prearranged marriage made in BBC heaven (since BBC produces the show; ABC airs it). Each couple was assigned their own skeleton crew of two, to trail their every move. They'd clip a mic pack on us upon our arrival on the premises. There were no private conversations; they filmed every sentence we uttered and every breath we took. Anything and everything was fair game. Every week, the show would mine that video footage from rehearsal and splice together whatever storyline emerged or whatever they decided would make for good TV that week. From the moment I parked my car in the paparazzi-filled lot in the alley behind the studio, to the moment I left at the end of the day, every minute of my time was spent with Derek and our lurking video crew. On Sundays, we would do the camera blocking, and before we went home that evening, the spray-tan crew would set up, put barrier cream on our hands and feet, spray us, and send us home, where we were allowed to shower the following morning.

Once the show was on the air, I never saw my family. Suffice it to say, my dance card was full. I didn't see anyone outside of *DWTS* between August and Thanksgiving.

We arrived on show days at seven thirty in the morning, sat through hours of makeup and hair and a second shellacking of tanner, then ran through our dance on the soundstage for the tempo check with the orchestra, the first time we would be hearing the song played live.

The two-hour show was taped in front of a live studio audience of eight or nine hundred every Monday in the late afternoon. The next night would be the one-hour "results" show, same hair and makeup and dress rehearsal and live studio audience. But on the second night you didn't have to perform, unless you were asked to do the encore dance. If your dance went particularly well on Monday, just as you were getting home, Deena would call and ask you to reprise your dance on the results show. After both shows, we walked the gauntlet of entertainment news interviewers, who were eager to recap the night, looking to scoop any juicy tidbits before we could peel out of our feathered, bejeweled costumes, remove the extra weight of hair extensions, face paint, and the oversized strip lashes that would make a showgirl jealous.

Your pro doesn't teach you how to dance. He teaches you *a particular* dance—a samba, a fox-trot, a cha-cha, quickstep, American tango, Argentine tango—it's your job to figure out how to do it. Initially, it was the greatest thing on earth to spend all day just learning some of the basics of the dances we were most likely to be doing. There was little pressure, and I couldn't have been happier, aside from some foot pain that I was hoping would diminish from the injection I got. Derek was a great teacher; it was like being in dance camp. I'd warned him about my long-standing difficulty learning routines. He didn't believe me at first. Nobody ever believed me, until they were faced with my having retained nothing of everything I'd just been taught.

Each week, neither the contestant nor the pro knows which style of dance they're going to be performing or what music they'll be dancing to until it's assigned to them on Wednesday morning on camera. On the spot, the pro then starts coming up with the choreography. The first week, Derek and I were told we would be doing a Viennese waltz to the Otis Redding classic "These Arms of Mine," which "coincidentally" was also on the *Dirty Dancing* soundtrack. I was stunned by my emotional reaction when I first heard that song in rehearsal, and was enveloped by the undeniable presence of Patrick, who had died almost exactly one year before.

Derek and I worked hard for five long days, and I couldn't remember the dance during the camera blocking at the dress rehearsal. But when Monday night came and we performed live in front of the studio audience and millions of television viewers, I killed it. We won the first week.

On Wednesday morning, we were told that for week two, we'd dance a jive to "Shake It" by Metro Station. Again, I couldn't remember the choreography during the dress rehearsal, and again, the following Monday night, in front of the live audience, we killed it.

I didn't know it then, but the nightmarish adrenaline that I hated and feared, that I wanted to go away because I thought it would cripple me, was like rocket fuel during a performance. I would go into a blackout of terror, and in that blackout, I would slay. My focus had been like a swinging lantern, then suddenly it morphed into a high-powered spotlight. I wouldn't know this for a few more years, but I had undiagnosed ADHD, and the adrenaline rush that hit when I was face-to-face with the real possibility of humiliation was exactly what my brain needed.

Right before we went live for the premiere, I had whispered to one of my favorite castmates, Rick Fox, the super handsome former Laker and stand-up guy, "Are you *scared*? I'm so fucking scared." And he'd said, "Oh. I had to develop a new relationship with my chemicals years ago." His generous admission reminded me that what I was feeling in my body (sweating, nausea, shaking, palpitations) was chemical. I, too, needed a new relationship with my chemicals.

Rick's description corroborated what my hypnosis had been instilling in me. The sensations that arose when I performed actually

Week six, "Rock Week," was even worse. Derek and I were danc-ing a paso doble to "So What" by Pink. The paso is a theatrical dance with explosive, staccato movements, using stomps, striking poses, and flamenco-style footwork to mimic a Spanish bullfight. Derek was the matador, and I was his bull. This was not my dance.

I said, "I don't think I can do this. I think I need to quit."

Derek said, "Well, you'd be the first. No one's ever done it."

Of course, I wasn't going to quit after he said that, but I really wanted to.

I said to Stella, "I really want to quit. I miss being with you, I want to take you to school." She said, "You can't quit. You can always take me to school. You're never going to have this opportunity again." She was eight years old.

When our dance had gone well, I wanted to get out of the show because it could only go down from there. I couldn't possibly do it again. And when a performance went less well, I wanted out because . . . well, for obvious reasons. It was excruciating to get schooled in front of twenty-six million sets of eyeballs. But the paso was my first really bad dance, in a really bad costume, with really bad hair. The judges made a meal out of how awful it was. Carrie Ann said, "You're way out of control. Something is going terribly wrong, and you're going downhill." Bruno said I looked like "a woman at the edge of a nervous breakdown."

Staying in the game depends on an amalgam of the judges' scores and the votes texted in by the television audience. When the judges' critiques feel particularly rough, especially if it seems undeserved, it engages the fans to rally to the rescue of their alter ego.

That season on *DWTS*, one of the fan favorites was the delightful youngest contestant, nineteen-year-old former Disney TV star Kyle Massey. And one of the other contestants getting a boatload of atten-tion was Bristol Palin, Sarah Palin's twenty-year-old daughter, whose teen pregnancy had become public during her mother's run for vice president in 2008. Bristol had no prior dance experience whatsoever, and while just a kid had already been the target of public scrutiny through no fault of her own. She knew that by competing she was making herself vulnerable to criticism because she was the daughter of a controversial political figure, but she chose to do the show anyway. She told her mother, "You know, it doesn't matter what I do, they're going to criticize me, so I might as well dance." I was in a self-imposed media blackout for the run of the show, so I didn't pay much attention to this at the time, but Sarah Palin's extremely organized Tea Party supporters were devoted to keeping Bristol on the show, using the show's large TV audience as a platform to keep Sarah in the public eye, poised to run for office again. Although the judges often gave Bristol low scores, the public voting system kept her in the competition. At the time, I didn't know the half of it, but the Tea Party efforts were impressive. I was too busy just trying not to get the life choked outta me by my inner bully.

And then, after our disastrous paso doble, something truly surprising began to take hold. The machine of the *DWTS* culture—the competition, the eliminations, the ratcheting up of difficult—took over. I stopped feeling satisfied by simply showing up and trying my best. Something unfamiliar and curious, a kind of ambition and competitive spirit, started to rise in me. I began harnessing something new, a strange kind of power. *I gotta finish what I started.* This was interesting, because winning had never been part of my plan. Competing had never occurred to me. I took the job for the pure love of dance and to show Stella that it was important to at least try hard things, but something else caught fire in me. It became too painful to not go for it. The threat of failing without fighting back became too great. I'd already experienced something like that in my career.

I didn't know what this was—was it God? There was a longing in me that I had been dismissing: to take my shape. Something ancient, set in my genetic coding, had made it feel dangerous to be too big, to risk failure by daring to be truly seen. That there were twenty-six million people watching was too abstract a notion to affect me, but I was well aware of the energy in the studio audience at the live performances. At first, their presence had been almost too much for me to handle. (Remember, I'm the girl who didn't like dancing across the room in a class of twenty people.) But I began to acclimate and became able to take in the powerful energy generated by the audience. And I was lifted by it. My performance started to be more for them than for me.

It turns out, I've got some game. That's amazing to know.

And this newfound instinct in me was born not a minute too soon. The show was beginning to feel dystopian, like *The Hunger Games.* In order to survive, someone else was going to have to go, and I didn't like that. But if I had to pick elimination or survival, I picked survival.

The second-to-last night of every season, you get a chance to redeem yourself by taking another shot at your worst dance (the paso doble in my case), and then the highlight of the entire season is the freestyle. The freestyle is the only dance where the strict criteria for competitive ballroom dancing do not apply. This freestyle is choreographed, it's not actually "free," but the pros get very excited about wowing the audience with handsprings, summersaults, flips, and other tricks. They save up every showy move they haven't been allowed to use.

The freestyle was Derek Hough's time to shine. This year, in his mind, his balls-out extravaganza was going to be the final number from *Dirty Dancing.* With, of course, the now-famous lift. I felt the pressure coming from pretty much everyone, but I was never going to do that. It wasn't right. It felt sacrilegious.

On that second-to-last performance, Derek and I wiped the floor with our hot-blooded matador-bull mating dance. And our freestyle (to another song from *Dirty Dancing,* "Do You Love Me" by the Contours) went from me holding a watermelon to Derek ripping open my breakaway dress and leapfrogging over me from a standing position, to flipping me, to the two of us gyrating up on the judges' table. Whatever level of extra the audience was hankering for, we made sure we more than satisfied it. And then, in a never-before-seen move, Derek spun me around from a standing perpendicular position, as my legs flared out behind me. (I might've even been the one to come up with it, like a jackass. That was my only regret from the whole experience.)

My parents were there, Stella and Clark and Jamie were there. The whole night couldn't have gone better.

We did the press line. I was feeling, maybe for the first time, almost victorious. As I was being driven home in the town car we got on show days only, I remember calling Clark. I was lying down in the back seat of the car and said, "Hey, honey, I'm on my way home. Ya know, I don't feel right. I don't know what's going on, but could you please run a hot bath for me and set out a Vicodin? Something feels really weird." I'd never asked him to have a hot bath already drawn for me, and the Vicodin was a very odd request. Actually, a first. I wasn't in pain exactly. But something felt definitely not right. As soon as I got home, I got in the bath, took the Vicodin, and crawled into bed like a wounded animal.

The next morning was the final day of the competition, the day someone would be going home with the mirror-ball trophy. I got up, got in the shower, was shampooing my hair, and was suddenly in unspeakable pain. I got back into my bed, soaking wet, with suds still in my hair. I was moaning. I didn't recognize this bizarre and excruciating sensation deep in my right hip or leg. I was only accustomed to pain from the neck up. I figured I must've pulled a muscle?

Stella found me writhing and crying under the covers and called out for Clark, "Dad! Mom's crying and she's got shampoo in her hair."

I couldn't speak, except to motion for Clark to call Dr. Bray, who said, "Take her to D.I.S.C. I'll meet you there." The car and driver that was waiting to take me to the studio for the big finale followed Clark and me. A few of the nurses scooped me out of the car in a wheelchair and rushed into the MRI, but I couldn't lie still. The voice of the radiology tech came over the speaker in the imaging tube, "You need to try and stay still for just a few seconds." That was not going to be possible.

I wanted someone to take a chainsaw and cut my leg off. Instead, they wheeled me into a room and gave me who knows what or how much pain medication. Dr. Bray had been meeting with the US Olympic Committee upstairs in his conference room. He had to keep excusing himself to check on me.

He said that when he looked at the scan, he saw that I had ruptured my lumbar disc between L-4 and L-5. He could see a big hunk of the disc, which must have shot out of my spine during the freestyle. The reason I hadn't felt horrible pain the night before was that it takes around nine hours for the jellylike substance from inside the disc, which is like battery acid, to eat through the lining of the nerve.

I was out of my tree on whatever meds they were giving me, and while it still hurt like nothing I'd ever felt before, the pain became like a distant something that was happening to somebody else. Dr. Bray gave me a nerve block, injecting steroids into my spine. He offered sedation before he gave me the block, but warned me that it would make me unable to remember choreography. I rejected his offer and took the nerve block au naturel.

It was getting closer and closer to when I was needed on the soundstage for the live show. The nurses wheeled me out to the idling town car, which raced me across town to the studio. Deena and the English producers met me in front of the hair and makeup trailer for a tête-à-tête. They asked if I was going to be able to do the show. I couldn't tell them for sure. I'd been in so much pain, and I was so drugged.

Looking back, it's obvious to me that the scores and the votes from the night before had already been tabulated. They had to have known who the winner was. But I was on automatic pilot. All I knew was that we had done really well and gotten perfect scores. I asked the Brits what the deal was. It wasn't long before we'd be live. If I wasn't able to perform, would Derek and I forfeit our chance of winning? They said that, based on the viewers' votes, if I didn't dance, Bristol Palin would win. Showbiz . . . Ya gotta love it.

In the trailer, the hair and makeup people got me into "the works."

I still had the indentations from the oxygen tubes across my face. Someone helped me into my costume and I did what I had to do. Standing alongside the host, Tom Bergeron, I made an announcement at the top of the show, just in case I was not able to finish, explaining that I'd left a little bit of my spine on the floor the night before when I ruptured a disc. But, "This might be my last two chances to dance on the show with Derek Hough, and so I'd better do it."

Derek and I reprised our first dance, the Viennese waltz. The last hoop we had to jump through was the "instant cha-cha" to music only revealed an hour before.

Meanwhile, Dr. Bray arrived at the TV studio in time for the show and was always in my peripheral vision, following me everywhere I went, as close as any security detail. He knew that at any minute the nerve block he'd given me earlier in the day was going to wear off. He had a steroid-loaded hypodermic needle in the inside pocket of his jacket.

When Tom Bergeron announced that Derek and I had won, I burst into tears. That moment felt like a dream; it was almost too much to process. But the real triumph for me was the joy of the dancing. I met my demons, heard their bullying voices, and danced anyway. I was in a full-contact fight against ancient dragons, and I walked through my own personal fire to beat them.

Kyle and Lacey came in second. Bristol and Mark, third.

After a special, extralong edition of the usual press line, I went into the trailer to change out of my costume, back into street clothes. Dr. Bray came in, I lowered my pants in the back, and he injected a nerve block into my lower lumbar spine. Stella and Clark were waiting for me in the car, which drove us to the *DWTS* chartered jet at the Burbank airport. Along with the other finalists and a few other dancers from the show, we flew to New York, where we boarded a double-decker bus in the predawn dark and rode into Times Square through crowds of screaming fans, to be interviewed and dance on *GMA* and *The View*. I also appeared on my friend Lawrence O'Donnell's show,

The Last Word, where he explained to me the kind of shenanigans the Tea Party had pulled off. They hadn't only rallied behind Bristol, but had taught some of their supporters how to vote for her many times. Some people voted eighty times per show, others three hundred times.

The next day was Thanksgiving.

Seeing the people in my life show up for me in body and spirit was a big deal. To find Jamie in the audience every single week, hooting and hollering and rooting for me, was more than I could have ever hoped for in a friend. My husband, Clark, holding down the fort through my year of living surgically and, on the heels of that madness, insisting that I take on this challenge when my fear had gotten the best of me, was heroic. Seeing him in the audience with Stella, both of them beaming, screaming, clapping madly, so vividly proud, was more rewarding than any mirror ball.

For the very first time, my daughter experienced me as the kind of woman who shows up for herself, fully committed. She saw me struggle, stay the course, and succeed, and never for a second did she question my devotion to her.

I think the challenge of *Dancing with the Stars* requires an inordinate amount of courage for anyone. For me? It took everything I had.

I came for Stella, and stayed for me.

I remembered who I was. I surprised myself. Clark said, "I almost never saw you as happy as when you were doing that show. There was something different about you" (which makes me laugh, because I *think* I was in a kind of hell most of the time). Doing the show rewired me. I had spent so much of my life not advocating for myself, refusing the call.

But taking on this adventure put me in the center of my story. And I became willing to risk that some people might not love me because I'd done this. Joseph Campbell says that to follow your bliss, "You have to recognize your own depth." I hadn't known how deep I went. But I'd gotten a taste.

22

Unbridled

For centuries, little girls have taken to fantasizing about their wedding day, and as they get older, some have been known to even keep a file folder of carefully cut clippings curated from bride magazines. Nowadays, they can use Pinterest to amass a vision board, for manifesting their dream wedding, with images of the gown, floral arrangements, and venue, the whole extravaganza, sitting in readiness for when the time comes, often with no particular person in mind yet to step into the role of groom.

I was never that girl. I was a weird kid, I knew I wasn't typical, and that was how I liked it. I had a secret file, a manila envelope, where I kept a stash of photographs, slyly excised from my mother's *Vogue* magazines. Avedon's black-and-white editorial closeup of a soaking wet form of a woman on the beach (faceless, yet actually Lauren Hutton). Her back arched, head thrown back, in a fully unbuttoned black bodysuit, with one bared breast, *mit* nipple, the sunlight bouncing off her shiny goose bumps. This was the kind of artsy, feminine erotica that fascinated me. I collected images of sexy women not because I wanted to date one or one day marry one, but because I wanted to feel the way they looked. That was what resonated with me.

As a well-trained good girl by day, it appealed to me to be doing something subversive and forbidden, something considered grown-up and somehow naughty, and I took a certain guilty pride in my secret stash of sexy. I'd sequester myself inside a fort I'd fashioned by stretching an Indian print bedspread between my high brass bed and built-in Formica countertop desk. In the light filtered through the colorful pattern, I'd take out my oversized manila envelope, the color of muddy sunshine, from its hiding-in-plain-sight spot inside one of the desk cupboards, and I'd pore over these gorgeous images, appreciating my keen, curatorial eye, like a nerd gazing in wonderment at their glorious stamp collection.

But while I did not daydream about my big day as a bride, I did fantasize endlessly about my future romantic life.

When I was in high school, my best friend, Tracy, and I had a routine we probably started when we were in ninth grade, and even though we might have looked like we were too old for such childish games, we continued it well into adulthood. It was a form of prayer, or wish fulfillment, or perhaps just an escape from the now that we knew, into a then we could hope for. A belief that good things were in store, a homemade antidote to quell the fears of what-ifs, of our dreams not happening, that something beautiful beyond our wildest imaginations was out there waiting for us. A cousin of the magical bedtime stories that can soothe a young child's anxious mind into the comforting sense that the unknown that lies ahead is even more beautiful than what you know to be true here in this moment.

Usually when just hanging around, maybe bored, one of us would instigate with the request, "Fantasize me?" It was a commonplace, very innocent pastime for us, spinning reveries of what our lives would look like down the road. It was like we were reading each other's fortunes, flashing forward. Painting the gorgeous, charmed life that was certainly stretching out before us. Awaiting us in time—when we'd be grown enough to step into it.

Mind you, we weren't designing our own lives. We would each take turns designing a life for the other, incorporating the fine details of each other's secret hopes and dreams as only friends who knew everything there was to know about each other could do. Tracy was the closest thing I had to a sister.

When you're young, you can imagine the best of all possible worlds for each other, really believing that anything is possible, without limitations born of modesty and, of course, without any awareness of the ubiquity of suffering, misfortune, and sorrow, of how hard adult life can be. We were shooting for the highest of what we could conceive of for each other. No walls, no ceilings. Though we weren't thinking one of us would become president, come up with a cure for cancer, or figure out how to create world peace, either. We knew we both wanted to be actors and mothers.

The physical piece that accompanied this fantasizing hobby involved the age-old girls' pastime of arm tickling. The one receiving the fantasy would lie back, after making sure her sleeve was rolled, or pushed up well above the crease of her inner elbow, exposing the soft underside of her inner arm, the skin noticeably thinner there, the delicate network of veins barely visible below the surface, like koi in a pond. She'd close her eyes, completely relax, and submit, as one donates blood.

The other one, all business, settling into a comfortable seated position at her friend's side, would begin tracing the softest possible tracks with her fingertips, maybe a hint of fingernails, rhythmically dragging up and down the tarmac of this most vulnerable of real estate, yet still considered neutral territory, completely innocent in nature.

Tracy and I were able to conjure and make believe far bigger, wilder happily-ever-afters for each other than for ourselves, freed from whatever sensible constraints kept the lid on our own dreams, which were somehow kept in obeyance, more muted, humble, and mindful to never be too outlandish. The highlights of the friend's offering would always involve a very exciting and robust career as an actress, a vision that never failed to quickly, almost immediately shift gears into marriage and family. As if the career section of our lives was something to entertain us, to keep us occupied until we met our husbands. And then the figurative picnic blanket would be laid out, and the real feast could begin: the guy was described—what he looked like, what he did for a living, usually a brilliant director we'd meet and fall in love with while working on a film in some exotic location. There'd follow the farmhouse with horses, somewhere in the European countryside—because he was European—where we'd raise our family. Then the listing of the children—how many boys, how many girls, with their respective, carefully culled names.

It seemed that once we were married off and had begun the business of bearing children, it would be our husbands who would continue with thrilling, artistically rewarding careers. We would be happy and content to have finally found what we were looking for, having landed in frothy and sumptuous domestic bliss. The end.

The recipient would sit up, as if released from a hypnotic state with a command. Enjoying a renewed vigor, she'd roll her sleeve back down, grinning with delight, cooing, "Oh, that was a good one!" and diligently return the favor, making sure she was giving as good as she'd gotten.

How will I ever find him? What if I don't find him? I'd best be ready, in tip-top, top o' my game shape for whenever that blessed moment arrives and he appears. Because I will have spent more time of my young life in fantasy, preparing myself to be deserving, worthy of his affection, devotion, and commitment. The amount of time and money women spend on average—the self-loathing, self-criticism, addiction to perfectionism, incessant advice giving and getting from girlfriends, obsessing over the wrong guy, starving ourselves, working out, preening, improving, body shaming, trying to figure out what men really want, waxing, lasering, exfoliating, and religiously lubricating— as if it was our life's work!

In any era, though, too much time is devoted to the pack mentality of what's considered desirable. Why spend days and nights making yourself into some misshapen idea of what's better for men?

When I was young, I was the rare girl in my little corner of the world who didn't "fix" her nose, dodging what initial pressure existed to alter myself. Still, Tracy and I carried on, as if our moms weren't dedicated feminists, as if Tracy's mom wasn't a groundbreaking magazine columnist, and as if mine didn't work at *Ms.* magazine for Gloria Steinem herself. Why did we imagine the great career he would have instead of considering, "How do I become a force in the world?" Spending so much of a young life toiling in preparation to be deserving of some imaginary man's attention, affection, and commitment is insanity. The idea that we need to do anything to be deserving of love? As if we're supposed to be more than we already are!

Women are born perfect. And powerful. We aren't born with a feeling of lack. Even if women are able to skirt the wedding fantasy and body-mania, or the time spent envisioning our future mate's wondrous career, we may not be able to or want to evade biology. I was "boy crazy," as they called it back in the day. From the moment my brain could figure out how to obsess over some boy, that's exactly what it did. My body was made to be with boy bodies. Nature wanted that for me. Some things never change. And of those of us with ovaries, many have a ticking time bomb within us, and when it goes off, we want to have a baby. I did experience the I've-gotta-procreate imperative, and motherhood did—astonishingly—happen for me. The aftershocks of that are what this episode is about.

I came from a long line of women who became mothers and wives at the expense of the career they'd wanted. The story my mother's mother told was "I didn't get to be a pianist." And my mom knew she didn't want to be like her depressed mother, so she was going to do it all differently, but then gave up her career to be a mother and a wife to my father. There was something imprinted on me by my foremothers that I was resolved to outfox. I thought I'd be able to override the system. I decided I'd be like my dad and not my mom and would somehow not fall prey to her undesirable epigenetics, and yet, there I was. A domestic goddess/mother superior. There'd never been a woman in my family lineage who got out from under that destiny. I didn't know how to get out from under, either, and began to doubt it could be done.

Women have an uncanny ability to adapt to please others, to refrain from privileging themselves out of fear of what might ensue. It takes a certain fortitude to tolerate the risk involved in stressing an established relationship to see if it can handle accommodating some much-needed change. And if in time we become angry or depressed or just feel like we're somehow slowly withering on the vine from adapting so much to the lives of others, we are promptly shamed, either from within or from without. To give voice to our desire to free ourselves from our habituated reflexive overadaptability to others might render us unlovable to our mates or bad mothers, right? That's what we think. So we disappear into servicing and raising our young, muting our dissatisfaction, because it feels shameful to be ungrateful when you're being taken care of. Blurry mothers' faces could be printed on milk cartons, "MISSING—Have you seen me? Last known location: Whole Foods in the organic frozen foods section."

I'm struck by how many married women I know intimately, especially mothers of small children, are right now feeling hopelessly stuck in their lives. They don't dare let themselves consider what they might wish for or what they would want their lives to look like if they could make a change. And there it is! "If they could." Well, of course they could! I'm talking about a kind of paralysis that comes from feeling disconnected from your very own independent life, your own oxygen source, as if your inherent value is now on a kind of sliding scale. As if a woman's value instantly depreciates after motherhood, like a car's sticker price that plummets the moment it's driven off the lot.

Once you've identified that special someone, it's implied, as stated in the vows mutually taken, that you're supposed to stay together until you die. But considering how long we're now living, it's borderline ludicrous to imagine that two separate human beings will grow and change at exactly the same rate in exactly the same directions, like synchronized swimmers or conjoined twin cherries . . . so their compatibility is as robust and true as their desire to be able to hang on to the end. Just because it's a great marriage doesn't mean it's necessarily a great marriage for the rest of your life. It took me a long time, but when I finally surrendered to the nagging feeling that something in me was in fact dying, there was nothing I could do or could even imagine doing to save myself, unless I let it all go.

I never knew to want the profoundly beautiful ritual that was our wedding. Perhaps it was something I hadn't pined for or had girded myself against, for fear of it never happening or of what it would mean to my independence having witnessed my mother's loss of autonomy and self. Marrying Clark gave me the opportunity to experience what it is to start a family of my own. Because of him, I got to become a mother to a child who is now a woman, an experience that has far exceeded my wildest dreams. Clark and I were together for twenty years, married for nineteen, and are partners in raising our incredible daughter. Pretty extraordinary for two people who had been rolling solo for the first thirty-eight and forty years of our lives, respectively.

The good news is our marriage was something we both had needed to let go of. We knew that it had served its purpose. The three of us will always be a family.

And I have become willing to tell the truth in the second half of my life like I never had before. There's an exhilarating relief in my willingness to face my fear of the unknown. I've relinquished the dollhouse as destination, as container of the dream, and it's really all the unknown all the time now. It's the Wild West, baby! With no illusion of "the known, the plan, the way it's supposed to look, or be." And my excitement about the adventure, along with my limitless ability to "fantasize myself," is now officially unbridled.

EPILOGUE

"Nobody puts Baby in a corner"

Urban Dictionary definition: No one is better than you, the world deserves to see you shine, to be heard, loved, see you dance! Never let anyone hide who you are.

The seemingly timeless and universal appeal of Baby Houseman's story in *Dirty Dancing* is perhaps due to the seismic shift she must undergo to discover and claim a more authentic, updated self.

If you're lucky to live long enough, you might get to undergo that reconfiguring again and again. At every age. A continuum. An ongoing coming-of-age story.

I periodically am faced with the same kinds of questions at different junctures. How much am I just going along with, without investigating the validity of what I have been conditioned to think increases my value? What lies about my place in the world have been drilled into me until I finally cry "uncle," and submit to the lowest common denominator, the groupthink?

Am I living my best life? Is this current iteration of who I am the fullest version of myself, or am I tethered unconsciously to my fear of the unknown, to a life or a self that has run its course? Is there a small voice that asks, Is there any call I would regret not heeding if I dared to break out of the familiar? Is there more pleasure, more vibrancy, more truth? More creativity? Might there be more ease and grace on the other side of surrender if I had the faith of someone who knew that life was unfolding for my highest good?

Recommitting to whatever I'm faced with when I look in the mirror today—a softer, wiser, albeit perhaps not quite as sharp, version of myself, due to the natural aging process—can I just hold on to myself, my inherent value, and accept myself even now? Even in the face of these turbulent times, when I feel tossed about, struggling to get my bearings in this changeable landscape, where *change is the only constant*? The inevitable impermanence of everything. Career peaks and valleys, other people's opinions of me, marital status, financial ebbs and flows, body image, aging. With every new chapter, we are faced with fresh challenges to our sense of identity and self. Every phase. As far as I can tell, every age is rife with struggle as well as with incomparable delight, and every end is pregnant with a new beginning.

This memoir is an amalgam of what I've seen and been through, what I've done and whom I've loved and how I've realized who I am and who I want to be. And of the numerous times I've come of age. I'm doing it again now.

Writing this story has been one of the most gratifying things I've ever done. It provided me with an opportunity to be more curious than certain about what I thought I knew, and to look at my life through a lens of compassion, empathy, and, at times, absurdity. I think everyone should do it. I think memoir writing should be taught in school. It helps with life transitions. Write the story of your own life. As you see it today. Slow down and gently unpack what you think went down. What if the story you inherited, or have been telling by rote for years, is not the whole story? Or even a true story? How might your retelling change the way you see your life, yourself, your loved ones? What if the "worst things" ended up being some of the most transformative things, necessary to launch you into your next rendering?

Until then, I offer you these scenes from my life. May your own memories rise up to meet them, and your own life come back to you.

Enjoy. It goes by so fast.

The Ride Home

I've had this theory about why time feels like it's collapsing.

This phenomena of how time is going by, at seeming breakneck speed
  as I get older.

"Wait! It's already summer? But we just had Thanksgiving!

Didn't I just have a mammogram?

How is my daughter looking at colleges?

Just yesterday I was taking her to her first day of preschool.

I've been with my husband for nineteen years?

I'm how old? That's not even humanly possible!"

You know when you take a road trip somewhere for the first time,
  it feels as if it's taking forever.

Are we there yet? How much longer?

And then . . . the ride home feels like a snap,
  as if the mileage couldn't possibly be the same.

Time-warp speed.

Well, I believe the first half of your life can feel painstakingly slow,
  like everything is beyond your reach.

When you're little, you want to be big,
  you want to be older, be cooler.

You want to be doing all of the fun stuff everyone else seems to be doing,
  and when is it ever going to happen for me?

If ever . . .

The road ahead is unknown, everything is a big, open-ended question,
  there's anxiety, so much that is beyond your capacity to even imagine,
  no less control, as you try to have some agency over getting your life
  in order.

From where I sit,

I got to be an actress,

I got to be a part of big, hit movies that impacted generations of audiences.

I got to date hot guys. I got to finally make money, however fleeting that chapter was, it happened. I got to be famous (the capital of fleeting).

I finally found my person (once I was already forty).

We got married and built a beautiful life together.

I got to have the baby I always wanted, a daughter beyond my wildest dreams.

I came to understand what matters most to me, and what was a bogus circus.

So . . . to me, the midpoint in life (that is, if we live to be a fucking hundred), is the point in which time travel shifts into the overdrive of the ride home.

Slow it down, it's going too fast.

But one can't slow it down, any more than one could make the unbearable slowness of the first half speed up.

I don't want this to end, it's just now getting to the good part.

This is my favorite bit.

Slow yer fuckin' roll!

So . . . I guess this is the ride home.

The End

ACKNOWLEDGMENTS

I want to thank my family. My darling daughter, for teaching me about everything important. For being so encouraging and humoring me when I asked if I could read her a paragraph, then always read more, thinking she wouldn't notice, though I'm sure she did and had plenty of things she'd rather have been doing. Clark, for showing up and for the family we built with so much love. My dad, for listening to me read chapters on Facetime all through lockdown, with the added bonus of us getting to fly down those memory chutes together. My mom, for recounting to me her youth, in increasingly layered detail, and for her lifelong, steadfast desire that I "do better" than she did, that the maternal pattern of thwarted dreams stop with her. Nellie Johnson, for being the most constant and unconditionally loving example of what it looks like to live a life of deep and enduring gratitude. My wonderful editor at Ballantine Books, Pamela Cannon, for trusting in my ability as a writer. And Barbara Jones, a freelance editor, who was as close to a miracle as I could ever hope to have in my sidecar for the last stretch of this journey. What I couldn't have anticipated was that after months of exhaustive, intensive Zoom meetings, I would find in Barbara one of the most exquisite collaborators, someone I trusted implicitly, as well as a kindred spirit, a dream doula who patiently (my god, the patience!) and expertly guided me to deliver this baby. And Steve, for keeping her caffeinated, well fed, and heroically rescuing us from near tech disasters. Also Maria, Charlie, and Josephine, even though you're all grown, for allowing me to have so much of your mother's time. My lifelong friendships: Tracy Pollan, for marveling at how weird it was that I was capable of writing a book. Granted, it's weird to know someone so long that you remember how annoying it was to try to do homework with them (guilty as charged). And Mike Fox for reading an early draft and being the smartest, deepest, bestselling author, who's also maybe the funniest person I know, next to his wife. Maggie Wheeler, for finding me outside of Dalton and never straying too far, and for her squeals of recognition when reading my first accounts of our shared history. Jamie Lee Curtis, JLC, for being the person I dared to share my very first chapters with and for your shockingly prompt responses, usually within an hour of receipt, so genuinely encouraging and enthusiastic. It's hard to put into words what your belief in me did for my belief in myself. And when I was in a quandary about the jacket cover, I showed you a photo of me, and you said, "Send that to me." Ten minutes later, you had *designed the cover of this book*. #Whoareyou? And thank you Sally Hershberger, for permitting me to use that image, taken when you were briefly a stunning photographer, a talent eclipsed by your meteoric rise as the queen of hair. Dani Shapiro, who insisted I had a book in me and that I needed to write it myself. Elissa Altman, a gifted writer and teacher of memoir, who gave me such thoughtful notes, and steered me toward her editor, Pamela Cannon, as well as her beloved wife, Susan Turner, the interior designer of this book. Breadcrumbs abound. Lauren Zander, for helping me to see the ways I had *put myself* in corners and therefore could take myself out of

ACKNOWLEDGMENTS   335

them, and to fearlessly dedicate myself to dreaming my biggest dreams. I have no doubt that I've been blessed with the kind of friendships they write books about: Bill Gerber, Scott Cameron, Meg Burnie, David Lewis, Kim Gillingham, Susan Jacobs, Nancy Ellison, Alan Ruck, Cassidy McDonald, Allison Creelman, Pamela Barish, Kate Arnesen, Beth Grant, Bobby Neuwirth, Andy McNicol, Scott Willson, Stephanie Evison Williams, Debra Music, Stephanie Wear, and my friends at Lionsgate Films. Kenny Ortega, you are love, and Dr. Robert Bray, for always having my back. My "continuing education" teachers: Dr. Beverly Berg, Dr. Phillip Bowman, Dr. Robin Berman, Lee Miller, and Erin Lotz. The people in the rooms that perform miracles every day simply with their presence. My agents Pilar Queen and Brandi Bowles. My longtime manager, Jason Weinberg, and Mitch Mason. My hardworking and super supportive team at Penguin Random House: Sara Weiss, for stepping up to the plate with so much heart and muscle, and for my new Sydney, Collins; editorial assistant extraordinaire Sydney Shiffman (a true shero) and the excellent Lexi Batsides before her; publisher Kara Welsh; editor-in-chief Jennifer Hershey; publicist Michelle Jasmine; marketer Kathleen Quinlan; art director Paolo Pepe; production editor Andy Lefkowitz; production manager Maggie Hart; copy editor Faren Bachelis; and proofreaders Stephanie Bay, Michael Clark, and Alison Hagge.

PHOTOGRAPH CREDITS

52 From the author's collection

54 From the author's collection

56 From the author's collection

58 From the author's collection

59 © Nancy Ellison Photography

60 © Nancy Ellison Photography

63 From the author's collection

64 From the author's collection

72 From the author's collection

74 From the author's collection

75 From the author's collection

79 From the author's collection

95 From the author's collection

96 From the author's collection

110 From the author's collection

112 From the author's collection

119 Photo by Klaus Lucka for *Interview*

152 From the author's collection

156 From the author's collection

159 From the author's collection

167 From the author's collection

174 *Dirty Dancing* courtesy of Lionsgate Films Inc.

184 From the author's collection

186 From the author's collection

190 *Dirty Dancing* courtesy of Lionsgate Films Inc.

195 Paul Fortune for Grey family collection

196 Paul Fortune for Grey family collection

208 From the author's collection

210 From the author's collection

231 From the author's collection

232 From the author's collection

235 From the author's collection

236 From the author's collection

241 From the author's collection

250 From the author's collection
275 From the author's collection
282 From the author's collection
285 From the author's collection
287 From the author's collection
292 From the author's collection
295 From the author's collection
306 From the author's collection
310 From the author's collection
322 From the author's collection
332 Bee Gilbert

About the Author

JENNIFER GREY is best known for her iconic portrayal of Baby in the beloved classic *Dirty Dancing*, which earned her a Golden Globe nomination for Best Actress. More recently, she starred in the acclaimed series *Red Oaks* and won season eleven of *Dancing with the Stars*. Her breakout movie role was as Matthew Broderick's sister in John Hughes's *Ferris Bueller's Day Off*. Her numerous film, television, and theater credits span decades. Grey is currently teaming up with Lionsgate on their long-awaited sequel to *Dirty Dancing*, in which she will star and executive produce. She lives in Los Angeles.

About the Type

This book was set in Fairfield, the first typeface from the hand of the distinguished American artist and engraver Rudolph Ruzicka (1883–1978). Ruzicka was born in Bohemia (in the present-day Czech Republic) and came to America in 1894. He set up his own shop, devoted to wood engraving and printing, in New York in 1913 after a varied career working as a wood engraver, in photoengraving and banknote printing plants, and as an art director and freelance artist. He designed and illustrated many books, and was the creator of a considerable list of individual prints— wood engravings, line engravings on copper, and aquatints.